JOURNAL FOR THE STUDY OF THE OLD TESTAMENT
SUPPLEMENT SERIES

413

Editors
Claudia V. Camp, Texas Christian University
and
Andrew Mein, Westcott House, Cambridge

Founding Editors
David J. A. Clines, Philip R. Davies and David M. Gunn

Editorial Board
Richard J. Coggins, Alan Cooper, John Goldingay,
Robert P. Gordon, Norman K. Gottwald, John Jarick,
Andrew D. H. Mayes, Carol Meyers, Patrick D. Miller

From Noah to Israel

Realization of the Primaeval Blessing
After the Flood

Carol M. Kaminski

T&T CLARK INTERNATIONAL
A Continuum imprint
LONDON • NEW YORK

Copyright © 2004 T&T Clark International
A Continuum imprint

Published by T&T Clark International
The Tower Building, 11 York Road, London SE1 7NX
15 East 26th Street, Suite 1703, New York, NY 10010

www.tandtclark.com

British Library Cataloguing-in-Publication Data
A catalogue record for this book is available from the British Library

Library of Congress Cataloging-in-Publication Data
A catalog record for this book is available from the Library of Congress

Typeset by ISB Typesetting, Sheffield
Printed on acid-free paper in Great Britain by Cromwell Press, Trowbridge, Wilts.

ISBN   0-567-08358-6 (hardback)

CONTENTS

PREFACE

My interest in the book of Genesis began many years ago. Doctoral studies at St. Catharine's College, Cambridge, provided me the opportunity to pursue this interest in a way not possible previously. This book is essentially my doctoral dissertation with minor revisions, submitted to Cambridge University in 2002. I am keenly aware that this work would not have come to fruition without the generous support of a number of institutions. I am grateful for the Cambridge Commonwealth Trust Bursary, along with the ORS Scholarship awarded by the Committee of Vice-Chancellors and Principals, which enabled me as an international student to study abroad. The Australian College of Theology kindly granted me a Faculty Research Scholarship while on study leave from the Bible College of Victoria in Australia. Tyndale House in Cambridge provided a welcoming and stimulating context in which to study. Even with the generous support of these institutions, my research would not have been possible without the love and encouragement of friends, family and Bulleen Baptist Church. I am deeply thankful for my husband, Matthew, for his love and commitment to me throughout this project. I also wish to acknowledge Michaela Eyl, for her helpful comments with regard to German translation, and Elizabeth Robar, for her assistance in preparing this manuscript for publication.

I am especially grateful to my doctoral supervisor, Regius Professor of Hebrew, Robert Gordon, whose insightful and critical comments have been invaluable to me. His patience, kindness and encouragement over the years enabled me to press on, especially when the task at hand seemed overwhelming. While any faults in this book are my own responsibility, the careful scrutiny and editing of my dissertation by Professor Gordon have, in no small measure, left an indelible mark throughout the pages of my work.

In recognition that learning takes place in the context of community, I am thankful to a number of scholars who have contributed to my understanding of the biblical text. While I was studying at the Bible College of Victoria, Dr. Rikk Watts, who first introduced me to biblical theology and exegesis, inspired me to do graduate work in biblical studies. Other faculty members at the College, notably Drs. David Price and Ted Woods, provided further encouragement along the way. Subsequent study abroad at Gordon-Conwell Theological Seminary, Massachusetts, contributed significantly to my understanding of the redemptive story in the Old Testament and its fulfilment in the New. I would also like to express my appreciation for conversations with Mary Fisher about how the Bible fits together theologically and its implications for the church. Within the wider academic community, the meticulous research of a number of Old Testament scholars with whom I interact in this book has helped me to clarify and develop my understanding of the theology of Genesis. I have appreciated the dialogue made possible by the quality of their scholarship and their commitment to the study of the first book of the Pentateuch.

Lastly, I am grateful to the God of the Old Testament, YHWH, who has revealed himself to me throughout the pages of Genesis, showing that his redemptive purposes advance in and through sinful humanity. His gracious forbearance leads me to worship and service – with a heart overflowing with thanks.

Carol M. Kaminski

ABBREVIATIONS

AB	Anchor Bible
ABD	David Noel Freedman (ed.), *The Anchor Bible Dictionary* (New York: Doubleday, 1992)
ASV	American Standard Version
AV	Authorized Version
BDB	Francis Brown, S.R. Driver and Charles A. Briggs, *A Hebrew and English Lexicon of the Old Testament* (Oxford: Clarendon Press, 1907)
BHS	*Biblia Hebraica Stuttgartensia*
Bib	*Biblica*
BK	*Bibel und Kirche*
BKAT	Biblischer Kommentar: Altes Testament
BSac	*Bibliotheca Sacra*
CBQ	*Catholic Biblical Quarterly*
ESV	English Standard Version
GKC	*Gesenius' Hebrew Grammar* (ed. E. Kautzsch; revised and trans. A.E. Cowley; Oxford: Clarendon Press, 1910)
IBC	Interpretation Bible Commentary
ICC	International Critical Commentary
Int	*Interpretation*
JB	*Jerusalem Bible*
JBL	*Journal of Biblical Literature*
JETS	*Journal of the Evangelical Theological Society*
Joüon	Joüon, P., *A Grammar of Biblical Hebrew* (2 vols.; trans. and rev. by T. Muraoka; Rome: Subsidia biblica, 1991)
JPS	Jewish Publication Society
JSOT	*Journal for the Study of the Old Testament*
JSOTSup	*Journal for the Study of the Old Testament,* Supplement Series
KB^3	Koehler, L. and W. Baumgartner, *The Hebrew and Aramaic Lexicon of the Old Testament* (5 vols.; revised by W. Baumgartner and J.J. Stamm; trans. under the supervision of M.E.J. Richardson; Leiden: E.J. Brill, 1994–2000)
KD	*Kerygma und Dogma*
KJV	King James Version
LCL	Loeb Classical Library
LXX	Septuagint
MT	Masoretic Text
NAC	New American Commentary
NASB	*New American Standard Bible*
NCBC	New Century Bible Commentary
NEB	*New English Bible*
NIBC	New International Bible Commentary

NICOT	New International Commentary on the Old Testament
NIV	New International Version
NKJV	New King James Version
NLT	New Living Translation
NRSV	New Revised Standard Version
NRT	*La nouvelle revue théologique*
OTM	Old Testament Message
OTS	Old Testament Studies
PTR	*Princeton Theological Review*
REB	Revised English Bible
RSV	Revised Standand Version
RV	Revised Version
SEAsiaJT	*South East Asia Journal of Theology*
SIL	Summer Institute of Linguistics
SJOT	*Scandinavian Journal of the Old Testament*
SNTS	Society for New Testament Studies
TC	Tyndale Commentary
TDOT	G.J. Botterweck and H. Ringgren (eds.), *Theological Dictionary of the Old Testament*
VT	*Vetus Testamentum*
VTSup	*Vetus Testamentum,* Supplements
WBC	Word Biblical Commentary
YNER	Yale Near Eastern Researches
ZAW	*Zeitschrift für die alttestamentliche Wissenschaft*

INTRODUCTION

The primaeval blessing, 'Be fruitful and multiply, and fill the earth', first announced to humankind in Gen. 1.28, is reissued to Noah and his sons in Gen. 9.1 and 9.7. The renewal of the commands after the flood serves as a confirmation that, in spite of the divine judgment against humankind, God's intention for his creation will not be thwarted. Given that the primaeval blessing is renewed in Gen. 9.1, we may well enquire how it proceeds from there. Will it be realized through Noah's three sons, Shem, Ham and Japheth? Scholars maintain that the statement in Gen. 9.19, 'These three were the sons of Noah; and from these the whole earth was peopled' (NRSV), is the first indication that the primaeval blessing is being realized after the flood.[1] This verse is thus understood to be a positive affirmation that God's creational purposes are advancing.

Scholars further note that the verb נפץ, 'scatter, disperse', in Gen. 9.19 introduces the *dispersal* motif which is prominent in the Table of Nations (פרד: Gen. 10.5, 32; פוץ: Gen. 10.18) and the Babel story (פוץ: Gen. 11.4, 8, 9). As with Gen. 9.19, the dispersion in the ensuing Table of Nations (Gen. 10.1-32) is interpreted positively. Scholars argue, in fact, that the primaeval blessing is *fulfilled* in the Table.[2] It is observed that Noah's descendants are not only multiplying, but also *spreading abroad* in accordance with the command to 'fill the earth' (Gen. 9.1).[3]

---

1. B.W. Anderson, 'The Tower of Babel: Unity and Diversity in God's Creation', in *From Creation to New Creation* (Overtures to Biblical Theology; Minneapolis: Fortress Press, 1994; revised version; first appeared in *Currents in Theology and Mission* 5 [1978], pp. 69–81; citations have been taken from the most recent 1994 revision), pp. 165–78 (176); U. Cassuto, *A Commentary on the Book of Genesis*, Vol. 2 (trans. I. Abrahams; Jerusalem: Magnes Press, 1964), p. 149; B. Jacob, *The First Book of the Bible: Genesis* (ed. and trans. E.I. Jacob and W. Jacob; New York: Ktav, 1974), p. 67 (= *Das erste Buch der Tora: Genesis* [Berlin: Schocken Verlag, 1934], p. 259); N.M. Sarna, *Genesis* (JPS Torah Commentary; New York: Schocken Books, 1970), p. 65; L.A. Turner, *Announcements of Plot in Genesis* (JSOTSup, 96; Sheffield: JSOT Press, 1990), p. 29; G.J. Wenham, *Genesis 1–15* (WBC; Waco: Word Books, 1987), p. 198.

2. W. Brueggemann, *Genesis: A Bible Commentary for Teaching and Preaching* (IBC; Atlanta: John Knox Press, 1982), pp. 93–94; Cassuto, *Genesis*, Vol. 2, p. 247; D.J.A. Clines, 'Theme in Genesis 1–11', *CBQ* 38 (1976), pp. 483–507 (494); V.P. Hamilton, *The Book of Genesis: Chapters 1–17* (NICOT; Grand Rapids: Eerdmans, 1990), p. 347; Jacob, *Genesis*, p. 75 (= *Das erste Buch der Tora*, p. 294); G. von Rad, *Genesis: A Commentary* (trans. J.H. Marks; OTL; Philadelphia: Westminster Press, rev. edn, 1973), p. 144 (= *Das erste Buch Mose: Genesis* [9th edn, Göttingen: Vandenhoeck & Ruprecht, 1972], p. 109); A.P. Ross, *Creation and Blessing: A Guide to the Study and Exposition of Genesis* (Grand Rapids: Baker Books, 1988), p. 221; Sarna, *Genesis*, p. 65; G.V. Smith, 'Structure and Purpose in Genesis 1–11', *JETS* 20 (1977), pp. 307–19 (312–13); B. Vawter, *On Genesis: A New Reading* (Garden City: Doubleday, 1977), p. 156.

3. J. Blenkinsopp, *The Pentateuch* (New York: Doubleday, 1992), p. 88; P.J. Harland, 'Vertical

The dispersion of humanity in Gen. 10.1-32 is, therefore, viewed positively since it marks the fulfilment of the primaeval blessing. Accordingly, ethnic diversity is understood to be something that God intended from the beginning. It is the 'fruit of the divine blessing given at creation'.[4]

This positive appraisal of the dispersion in Gen. 10.1-32 raises an interpretative problem, however. According to this view, the dispersion in the Table fulfils the primaeval command to fill the earth (Gen. 1.28; 9.1). But in the Babel story, the dispersion seems to be the result of divine judgment. We might expect, therefore, that YHWH's judgment in Gen. 11.1-9 would have an *adverse* effect on the realization of the blessing. Yet Gen. 10.1-32 seems to indicate that the dispersion actually *fulfils* the blessing. How is one to reconcile these two different assessments of the dispersion – positive in the Table of Nations but negative in the Babel story?

Scholars resolve this problem in one of four ways. First of all, according to source-analysis, differences between the Table of Nations and the Babel story simply represent the views of two different authors. The priestly writer understands that the emergence of nations reflects the richness of the creator, whose divine commands issue in the vast multitude of nations.[5] According to the Jahwist, however, the emergence of nations is not willed by God, but is the result of divine judgment against humankind.[6] The two texts are understood, therefore, to be contradictory and incompatible,[7] although it is acknowledged that this would not prevent the final redactor from placing them next to each other.[8] Von Rad thus concludes that the collector of traditions gave more attention to the theological orientation of the whole than to the harmonization of precise details.[9] Von Rad's solution, however, does not resolve the problem, since these contradictory views are still present in the 'inner theological orientation of the whole'.

Alternative solutions are offered by scholars who interpret these texts according to their final form. One line of interpretation suggests that the Table of Nations has been intentionally placed *before* the Babel story in order that the dispersion

or Horizontal: The Sin of Babel', *VT* 48 (1998), pp. 515–33 (528); J.E. Hartley, *Genesis* (NIBC; Peabody: Hendrickson, 2000), p. 117; Turner, *Announcements of Plot*, p. 29; Vawter, *On Genesis*, p. 156; G.J. Wenham, *Story as Torah: Reading Old Testament Narrative Ethically* (Grand Rapids: Baker Academic, 2004), p. 36.

4.   Anderson, 'The Tower of Babel', pp. 165–78 (176); cf. Cassuto, *Genesis,* Vol. 2, p. 175; K.A. Mathews, *Genesis 1–11.26* (NAC; Nashville: Broadman & Holman, 1996), p. 429.

5.   G. von Rad, *Old Testament Theology: The Theology of Israel's Historical Traditions*, Vol. 1 (trans. D.M. Stalker; New York: Harper & Brothers, 1962), p. 162 (= *Theologie des Alten Testaments*, Bd. I: *Die Theologie der geschichtlichen Überlieferungen Israels* [Munich: Chr. Kaiser Verlag, 1957], p. 176).

6.   Von Rad, *Old Testament Theology*, Vol. I, p. 163 (= *Theologie des Alten Testaments*, Bd. I, p. 176).

7.   S.R. Driver, *The Book of Genesis* (London: Methuen & Co. Ltd, 14th edn, 1943 [1904]), p. 133; J. Skinner, *A Critical and Exegetical Commentary on Genesis* (ICC; 2nd edn, Edinburgh: T&T Clark, 1930), p. 224; von Rad, *Genesis*, p. 152 (= *Das erste Buch Mose*, p. 116).

8.   Skinner, *Genesis*, p. 224; von Rad, *Genesis*, p. 152 (= *Das erste Buch Mose*, p. 116).

9.   Von Rad, *Genesis*, p. 148 (= *Das erste Buch Mose*, p. 113).

not be read from the perspective of divine judgment. According to its placement, therefore, the primaeval commands, 'Be fruitful and multiply, and fill the earth', reissued after the flood in Gen. 9.1, are fulfilled in the ensuing Table of Nations. It is argued that the final author of the primaeval history understands that the dispersal of the nations may be evaluated both positively (as in ch. 10) and negatively (as in ch. 11).[10] This interpretation does preserve the idea of judgment in the Babel story, but maintains that a positive view of the dispersal is also secured through the priority given to the Table of Nations.[11] While this view provides an explanation for the placement of the two texts, it does not resolve the problem of the contradictory views of the dispersal in Gen. 10.1-32 and 11.1-9. The question thus remains whether there is a more coherent theology underlying these chapters.

Other scholars, who similarly interpret the Table of Nations and the Babel story according to their final form, argue that even though YHWH's scattering Noah's descendants is an act of judgment, it is to be interpreted positively since it fulfils God's creative purposes outlined in Gen. 9.1.[12] Scattering, therefore, has a positive *effect* on the realization of the blessing, restoring the order of creation intended from the beginning. YHWH's scattering the Babelites thus provides a fitting conclusion to the primaeval history since it demonstrates that the primaeval blessing is fulfilled. Thus in the final analysis, the dispersion is positive in Gen. 10.1-32 and *ultimately* positive in 11.1-9. This interpretation raises the question, however, whether YHWH's judgment does, indeed, have such a positive effect on the realization of the blessing. Are the primaeval commands fulfilled through 'scattering'?

Finally, a few scholars maintain that YHWH's scattering the Babelites is not to be understood as an act of punishment.[13] It is argued that if the Babel story is read in the context of the primaeval history, then 'scattering' can be understood as a *blessing*[14] or an act of *creation*[15] simply because it fulfils God's intention expressed in Gen. 1.28 and 9.1. Thus the Table of Nations and the Babel story are both unambiguously positive. While this interpretation resolves the problem of the two conflicting views of the dispersion, an examination of the scattering

10. Clines, 'Theme in Genesis 1–11', pp. 483–507 (494); cf. Harland, 'The Sin of Babel', pp. 515–33 (532); E.P. Nacpil, 'Between Promise and Fulfilment', *SEAsiaJT* 10 (1968), pp. 166–81 (169); Wenham, *Story as Torah*, p. 36.

11. Hartley, *Genesis*, p. 126; Hamilton, *Genesis 1–17*, p. 347; B.K. Waltke, *Genesis: A Commentary* (Grand Rapids: Zondervan, 2001), p. 161.

12. Brueggemann, *Genesis*, pp. 98–99; Turner, *Announcements of Plot*, p. 32.

13. K.A. Farmer, 'What Is "This" They Begin to Do?', in F.C. Homgren and H.E. Schaalman (eds.), *Preaching Biblical Texts: Expositions by Jewish and Christian Scholars* (Grand Rapids: Eerdmans, 1995), pp. 17–28 (26); Jacob, *Genesis*, p. 79 (= *Das erste Buch der Tora*, p. 301); I.M. Kikawada, 'The Shape of Genesis 11.1-9', in J. Jackson and M. Kessler (eds.), *Rhetorical Criticism: Essays in Honor of James Muilenburg* (Pittsburgh: Pickwick Press, 1974), pp. 18–32 (32 n. 22); E. van Wolde, *Words Become Worlds: Semantic Studies of Genesis 1–11* (Biblical Interpretation Series, 6; Leiden: E. J. Brill, 1994), pp. 102–103.

14. Kikawada, 'The Shape of Genesis 11.1-9', pp. 18–32 (32 n. 22).

15. Van Wolde, *Words Become Worlds*, p. 102.

motif in the Babel story and its implications for how YHWH's action is to be interpreted is notably absent from the discussions.

It is evident from this brief summary of scholarship that the conflicting views of the dispersion in Gen. 10.1-32 and 11.1-9 are resolved in a variety of ways. These different approaches, however, should not obscure the fact that there is fundamental agreement among scholars on two central yet related points. First, the dispersal in the Table of Nations is commonly interpreted in a *positive* light since it is understood to mark the fulfilment of the primaeval blessing. Secondly, YHWH's scattering Noah's descendants has a positive *effect* on the realization of the command to 'fill the earth'. Scattering is understood to be the means by which the primaeval commands are fulfilled.[16] We may well raise the question, however, whether these two central points are indeed correct. What if it could be shown that the primaeval blessing is *not* fulfilled in the Table of Nations? Would the dispersion in Gen. 10.1-32 still be *positive*? How would the dispersion in the Table relate to the scattering motif in the Babel story?

It is important to note that the two commonly held assumptions, that the primaeval blessing is fulfilled in Gen. 10.1-32 and that YHWH's scattering Noah's descendants has a positive effect on the realization of the blessing, have also influenced how the building activity in the Babel story is interpreted. We read in Gen. 11.4b that the people intend to build a city and a tower, 'otherwise we shall be scattered abroad upon the face of the whole earth' (NRSV). Scholars interpret this to mean that the builders did not want to fill the earth (cf. Gen. 9.1).[17] Thus it is argued that the Babelites are disobeying the primaeval commands.[18] Accordingly, the building of the tower is understood to be contrary to the order of creation. Recalcitrant humans are, therefore, compelled or coerced by God to obey the divine commands.[19] The primaeval history, which concludes with YHWH's

16. Brueggemann, *Genesis*, pp. 98–99; Cassuto, *Genesis*, Vol. 2, pp. 226, 232; Farmer, 'What Is "This" They Begin to Do?', pp. 17–28 (26); T.E. Fretheim, *The Pentateuch* (Nashville: Abingdon Press, 1996), p. 84; D. Garrett, *Rethinking Genesis: The Sources and Authorship of the First Book of the Pentateuch* (Grand Rapids: Baker Book House, 1991), p. 110; Kikawada, 'The Shape of Genesis 11.1-9', pp. 18–32 (32); I.M. Kikawada and A. Quinn, *Before Abraham Was: The Unity of Genesis 1–11* (Nashville: Abingdon Press, 1985), pp. 51, 69; Mathews, *Genesis 1–11.26*, p. 467; Ross, *Creation and Blessing*, p. 247; idem, 'The Dispersion of the Nations in Genesis 11.1-9', *BSac* 138 (1981), pp. 119–38 (119, 133); van Wolde, *Words Become Worlds*, pp. 102–103; Vawter, *On Genesis*, p. 157.

17. H. Alford, *The Book of Genesis and Part of the Book of Exodus* (London: Strathan & Co., 1872), p. 53; Anderson, 'The Tower of Babel', pp. 165–78 (170–71); Cassuto, *Genesis*, Vol. 2, p. 230; R.L. Cohn, 'Narrative Structure and Canonical Perspective in Genesis', *JSOT* 25 (1983), pp. 3–16 (7); A. Dillmann, *Genesis: Critically and Exegetically Expounded*, Vol. 1 (trans. W.M.B. Stevenson; Edinburgh: T&T Clark, 1897 [1892]), p. 202; W. Evans, *The Books of the Pentateuch* (New York: Revell, 1916), p. 41; Harland, 'The Sin of Babel', pp. 515–33 (528); Hartley, *Genesis*, p. 126; Mathews, *Genesis 1–11.26*, p. 474; Ross, *Creation and Blessing*, p. 234; Sarna, *Genesis*, p. 83; Turner, *Announcements of Plot*, p. 30; Vawter, *On Genesis*, p. 156; Waltke, *Genesis*, p. 161; Wenham, *Genesis 1–15*, p. 240.

18. Cassuto, *Genesis*, Vol. 2, p. 243; Harland, 'The Sin of Babel', pp. 515–33 (527); Mathews, *Genesis 1–11.26*, p. 474; Ross, *Creation and Blessing*, p. 234; Sarna, *Genesis*, p. 83; Turner, *Announcements of Plot*, pp. 31–32.

19. Harland, 'The Sin of Babel', pp. 515–33 (531); Kikawada and Quinn, *Before Abraham Was*,

scattering Noah's descendants, affirms that God's creational purposes cannot be thwarted. The universal history of humankind in Genesis 1–11 then provides the context in which the particular history of Israel emerges. This interpretation raises several questions, however. What evidence is there to support the view that the Babelites are disobeying the primaeval commands? Are we to assume that God's creational purposes cannot be thwarted in any way by humankind? We may also enquire whether YHWH's scattering Noah's descendants does, indeed, restore the order intended from the beginning.

These views, which we have articulated albeit in summary form so far, establish parameters for the present discussion. Our focus in this study will be on the realization of the primaeval blessing *after* the flood. It is worth noting at the outset that the blessing in Gen. 1.28 comprises *five* imperatives, which include the subjugation of the earth and dominion of humankind over the created order.[20] Attention will be given in this study, however, to the realization of the first three imperatives, 'Be fruitful and multiply, and fill the earth', which are reissued after the flood in Gen. 9.1.[21] This limitation accords with the aforementioned views, which focus on the first three commands, and in particular, on the realization of the command to 'fill the earth'.

The starting point for our discussion will be an examination of the meaning of the command to 'fill the earth' (Gen. 1.28; 9.1) and whether the statement in Gen. 9.19b, 'and from these the whole earth was peopled', indicates that the command is being carried out by Noah's sons. Is the dispersal in 9.19 to be interpreted positively (ch. 1)? The question will be raised whether scattering is related in any way to the command to fill the earth. The following chapter, then, will focus attention on the statement, 'otherwise we shall be scattered' (NRSV, Gen. 11.4b), considering if Noah's descendants are, indeed, rejecting the command to fill the earth (ch. 2). After examining the relationship between 'scattering' and the primaeval commands, the question whether YHWH's scattering the Babelites fulfils the primaeval blessing will need closer investigation (ch. 3). Having discussed the scattering motif in detail, we will then examine the dispersal theme in the Table of Nations, giving particular attention to the question whether the primaeval blessing is *fulfilled* in Gen. 10.1-32 (ch. 4). This will be followed by an examination of the genealogies of Noah's three sons in the Table. The question will be raised whether there is any indication *within* the segmented genealogy (Gen. 10.1-32) that would indicate how the blessing is being realized.

---

p. 71; H.C. Leupold, *Exposition of Genesis*, Vol. 1 (Grand Rapids: Baker Book House, 1949 [1942]), p. 391; T.W. Mann, ' "All the Families of the Earth": The Theological Unity of Genesis', *Int* 45 (1991), pp. 341–53 (347).

20. The outworking of these two commands has been discussed by several scholars: W. Brueggemann, 'The Kerygma of the Priestly Writers', *ZAW* 84 (1972), pp. 397–414 (407–408); D.J.A. Clines, *What Does Eve Do to Help? and Other Readerly Questions to the Old Testament* (JSOTSup, 94; Sheffield: JSOT Press, 1990), pp. 53–55; Turner, *Announcements of Plot*, pp. 33–41.

21. Turner has rightly noted that the reiteration of the first three commands in Gen. 9.1 indicates that the narrative itself sees these as a self-contained unit (*Announcements of Plot*, p. 33). Hereafter, these three commands will be referred to as the *primaeval blessing*.

Our preliminary conclusions will raise some additional questions regarding the import of Shem's genealogy.

Scholars have focused their attention on the function of the Table of Nations and the Babel story in relation to the primaeval blessing. Yet minimal attention has been given to the function of Shem's genealogy in Gen. 11.10-26, which immediately follows the Babel story and is also located 'after the flood'. The question will be raised, therefore, whether the linear Shemite genealogy in Gen. 11.10-26 has any function with respect to the realization of the primaeval blessing (ch. 5). Conclusions drawn from this chapter will have implications for how the transition from the primaeval history to the particular history of Israel is interpreted. Von Rad has argued that Genesis 1–11 concludes on a note of judgment with no word of grace. This view has gained widespread acceptance among scholars. We will re-examine von Rad's thesis, however, considering whether the primaeval history does indeed end on a note of judgment (ch. 6).

The Shemite genealogy in Gen. 11.10-26 then leads directly to Terah and his three sons, Abram, Nahor and Haran. It is not insignificant that language used in the primaeval blessing reappears in the form of a divine promise to the patriarchs. The question will be asked, therefore, whether the promise of increase to the patriarchs contributes in any way to the realization of the primaeval blessing after the flood (ch. 7). Attention will also be given to Jacob and his descendants, who are the recipients of the promise of increase. The question will be considered whether it is theologically significant that 'primaeval' commands are reissued to Israel in Gen. 35.11 (ch. 8). Finally, language used to describe Israel's increase in Egypt is reminiscent of the primaeval blessing (Exod. 1.7). The presence of creation language in Exod. 1.7 raises the question whether Israel's proliferation in Egypt contributes in any way to the continuation of the primaeval blessing and to the advancement of God's intention for his creation (ch. 9). In short, our discussion concerns the realization of the primaeval blessing after the flood – from Noah to Israel.

1. *Methodology*

According to the aforementioned views, the Table of Nations and the Babel story are interpreted in light of the primaeval blessing, 'Be fruitful and multiply and fill the earth', given to Noah and his sons after the flood (Gen. 9.1). Scholars who examine these texts according to source-analysis note that the Table of Nations is attributed to both J (10.1b, 8-19, 25-30) and P (10.1a, 2-7, 20-24, 31-32), whereas Gen. 9.19 and the Babel story are assigned to J (11.1-9).[22] Given that they assign the primaeval blessing to P (Gen. 9.1, 7; cf. Gen. 1.28) and that P is usually located *after* J,[23] this means that, according to a source-critical approach, the 'priestly' blessing would not have been available to J. Therefore, the statement,

---

22. Anderson, however, argues that Gen. 9.19 should be assigned to P ('The Tower of Babel', pp. 165–78 [176]).

23. G.J. Wenham has more recently argued that P is prior to J ('The Priority of P', *VT* 49 [1999], pp. 240–58). According to his view, the priestly blessing would already be available to J.

'and from these the whole earth was peopled' (NRSV, Gen. 9.19), could not have the 'priestly' blessing of Gen. 9.1 in view. Thus J could not have understood that the blessing was *fulfilled* in Gen. 9.19. Neither could J have in mind that the tower builders were attempting to thwart the divine command to fill the earth. Yet a number of scholars who hold to a source-critical approach argue that Gen. 9.19 and 11.1-9 – texts they attribute to J – are to be interpreted in light of the 'priestly' blessing of 9.1.

It is not surprising to find, therefore, that those who espouse these views are alike in their emphasis on reading the texts in their 'canonical' form. Vawter, for example, notes in his exegesis of Genesis 10–11, that he is using the final form of Genesis. He maintains that the final redactor, whose presentation of the material is similar to that of P, was responsible for combining J and P into the narrative as it now stands.[24] The importance of interpreting these texts according to their present literary form has been noted by other scholars. Harland, for instance, first considers Genesis 10–11 according to J and P sources. He then examines these texts according to their final form and maintains that the 'complete text is more than the sum of its parts'.[25] He proposes, therefore, that the canonical form of the text ought to be examined in addition to analysis of the smaller units according to their sources. Harland has effectively demonstrated how method affects interpretation of a text.[26]

Other scholars have similarly expressed the need for a more holistic view of the biblical text rather than the atomistic approach that has been so prevalent in Old Testament studies.[27] Anderson, for example, has applied this approach to Genesis 10–11. He hopes to show through his study of these texts that 'biblical exegesis ought to move beyond the analysis that has dominated past biblical scholarship toward synthesis – that is, appreciation of how a particular text functions in the larger whole of the biblical narrative in its final formation'.[28] Clines has expressed similar concerns regarding the dominance of what he calls the 'genetic' approach to the Old Testament. His approach to the 'theme' of the Pentateuch (which includes his analysis of Genesis 10–11) is to examine the text according to its final form.[29] He notes at the outset, however, that his view of the unity of the Pentateuch is not a unity in origin, but in its final shape.[30] The point we are underscoring is that the aforementioned scholars are alike in their examination of Gen. 9.1 in its literary context. There is, therefore, a common 'final form'

24. Vawter, *On Genesis*, p. 156.

25. Harland, 'The Sin of Babel', pp. 515–33 (532).

26. For a discussion of Gen. 1.28 according to a source-critical approach, see M. Gilbert, ' "Soyez féconds et multipliez" (Gen 1, 28)', *NRT* 96 (1974), pp. 729–42.

27. Kikawada, 'The Shape of Genesis 11.1-9', pp. 18–32 (30–32); J.M. Sasson, 'The "Tower of Babel" as a Clue to the Redactional Structuring of the Primeval History (Gen. 1–11.9)', in G. Rendsburg, *et al.* (eds.), *The Bible World: Essays in Honor of Cyrus H. Gordon* (New York: Ktav and the Institute of Hebrew Culture and Education of New York University, 1980), pp. 211–19 (213).

28. Anderson, 'The Tower of Babel', pp. 165–78 (166).

29. D.J.A. Clines, *The Theme of the Pentateuch* (JSOTSup, 10; Sheffield: JSOT Press, 1979), pp. 9–10.

30. Clines, *The Theme of the Pentateuch*, p. 5.

of Genesis that can be examined by both source-critics and by other scholars who do not approach the text in this way. The method adopted by the present writer is to examine the primaeval blessing in its literary context according to its final form. Therefore, no particular theology of the 'Jahwist' or the 'priestly' writer will be offered. Rather, one hopes that this study will shed light on the theology of the final author of Genesis and that the coherency of the Genesis narrative will become self-evident. We are now in a position to begin our discussion of the primaeval blessing and its realization after the flood.

2. *The Import of the Primaeval Blessing*

The import of the primaeval blessing has been highlighted by a number of scholars. Brueggemann maintains, for example, that it is the central kerygma of the priestly material and that the five verbs used in Gen. 1.28 'assert God's radical intention to promote well-being and prosperity'[31] amidst the exilic community. He concludes that God's intention for creation cannot be frustrated by any circumstance, not even by the exile itself. Smith similarly argues that the primaeval blessing has an 'overpowering theological emphasis' and that it is the 'key theological focal point of the two parallel sections of Gen. 1–11'.[32]

Scholars have also noted the import of the primaeval blessing in relation to the patriarchal narratives. Harland rightly observes, for example, that

> God's blessing is one of the great unifying themes of Genesis with animals (1.22),
> humanity (1.28), sabbath (2.3), Adam (5.2), Noah (9.1) and the patriarchs (12.3=J,
> 17.16, 20=P) all receiving God's benediction... Genesis is a book of the fulfilment of
> divine blessing: 1.28, 9.1, 17.16, 20, 28.3, 48.4 = P, 41.52 = J.[33]

Weimar maintains, in fact, that the blessing, represented in a stereotypical way by the three verbs ברך, פרה and רבה, is the leading thought of the Toledots.[34]

The primaeval blessing is also seen to be central to the plot of Genesis. Clines identifies Gen. 1.26-28 as the first divine 'announcement' which is central to the plot of the book. Clines then raises the question whether these injunctions actually are fulfilled, and if so, *when* they are fulfilled: 'For – must we not suppose? – if those are the three things that God tells humans to do on the first page of Genesis, the rest of the pages ought to be telling us how the humans carried out the commands, or – at the very least – how they failed to carry out the commands'.[35] Turner similarly understands Gen. 1.26-28 to be central to the plot of Genesis. As with Clines, he maintains that the reader is expected to trace the development of

---

31. Brueggemann, 'The Kerygma of the Priestly Writers', pp. 397–414 (401).

32. Smith, 'Structure and Purpose', pp. 307–19 (311).

33. P.J. Harland, *The Value of Human Life: A Study of the Story of the Flood (Genesis 6–9)* (VTSup, 64; Leiden: E.J. Brill, 1996), p. 104; cf. Mathews, *Genesis 1–11.26*, pp. 157–58, 174. See also Clines' summary of the promise of descendants in the patriarchal narratives (*The Theme of the Pentateuch*, pp. 32–33).

34. P. Weimar, 'Die Toledot-Formel in der priesterschriftlichen Geschichtsdarstellung', *BZ* 18 (1974), pp. 65–93 (89).

35. Clines, *What Does Eve Do to Help?*, p. 52.

the primaeval blessing in the ensuing narratives. When reading Gen. 1.26-28 for the first time, he suggests that the reader 'must be optimistic that these divine imperatives will be obeyed, in the light of creation's immediate and obedient response to God's previous commands in ch. 1. However, an investigation of their fate in chs. 1–11 reveals a much more complex picture'.[36] Turner maintains that since the primaeval blessing of Gen. 1.28 consists of imperatives, this opens up the possibility that these commands might be disobeyed. He suggests that the 'struggle of this blessing/command to translate itself into reality provides part of the connective tissue in the unfolding of the narrative's plot'.[37] Clines and Turner have highlighted the import of the primaeval blessing for the plot of Genesis and have raised the question whether humankind do, in fact, obey the commands. We may well enquire, therefore, whether there is any indication after the flood that Noah's descendants are carrying out the primaeval commands. Is the blessing fulfilled in the primaeval history?

36. Turner, *Announcements of Plot*, p. 22.
37. L.A. Turner, *Genesis* (Readings: A New Biblical Commentary; Sheffield: Sheffield Academic Press, 2000), p. 24.

Chapter 1

IS THE DISPERSAL IN GENESIS 9.19 TO BE INTERPRETED POSITIVELY?

1. *Introduction*

The reissuing of the primaeval blessing in Gen. 9.1 and 9.7 is immediately followed by details concerning the covenant God made with Noah and his descendants (Gen. 9.8-17). This provides the assurance to humanity that God would not send another flood. The narrative about Noah and his sons is resumed in Gen. 9.18-19: 'The sons of Noah who went out of the ark were Shem, Ham, and Japheth. Ham was the father of Canaan. These three were the sons of Noah; and from these the whole earth was peopled' (NRSV, Gen. 9.18-19). A number of scholars argue that 9.19 is the first indication after the flood that the primaeval blessing is fulfilled. First, it is noted that the statement, 'and from these the whole earth was peopled' (NRSV), looks back to the blessing announced in Gen. 9.1.[1] Secondly, Gen. 9.19 is understood to mark the fulfilment of the primaeval blessing since Noah's three sons have both increased and begun to disperse. Jacob notes, for example, that v. 19 emphasizes that the whole world is derived from only three men. Thus the blessing of v. 1 is fulfilled at this point in the narrative.[2] Turner similarly comments that the narrative following the primaeval blessing in Gen. 9.1 'indicates that the human family was faithful to its divine calling'.[3] As with Jacob and Turner, Sarna concludes that the primaeval blessing of Gen. 9.1 is fulfilled in 9.19.[4] Cassuto has also made the following comments on 9.19:

> Although they were only three, they succeeded in raising up descendants in such large numbers that from them there went forth and spread abroad all the people of the earth (this is the significance of the expression *the whole earth* in this verse and in xi 1), and by their dispersion they were able to fill the earth, in accordance with the blessing bestowed upon them by God (ix 1): *Be fruitful and multiply, and fill the earth.*[5]

According to this interpretation, the statement, 'and from these the whole earth was peopled', indicates that Noah's descendants are carrying out God's creational purposes.[6] Thus v. 19 is understood to be a *positive* statement which

---

1. Anderson, 'The Tower of Babel', pp. 165–78 (176); C. Westermann, *Genesis 1–11* (trans. J.J. Scullion; A Continental Commentary; Minneapolis: Fortress Press, 1994), p. 11 (= *Genesis*, Bd. I [BKAT; Neukirchen: Neukirchener Verlag, 1974], p. 16).
2. Jacob, *Genesis*, p. 67 (= *Das erste Buch der Tora*, p. 259); cf. Wenham, *Genesis 1–15*, p. 198.
3. Turner, *Announcements of Plot*, p. 29.
4. Sarna, *Genesis*, p. 65.
5. Cassuto, *Genesis*, Vol. 2, p. 149.
6. Wenham, *Genesis 1–15*, p. 198; cf. Mathews, *Genesis 1–11.26*, p. 427.

directly relates to the primaeval blessing. This interpretation deserves closer examination. Before considering whether Gen. 9.19 indicates that Noah's descendants are, indeed, filling the earth, it is first necessary to consider briefly the meaning of the primaeval commands in Gen. 1.28 and 9.1, in particular, the meaning of the third command, 'fill the earth'.

2. *The Meaning of the Command to 'Fill the Earth'*

a. *Genesis 1.28 in Its Literary Context*

The primaeval blessing in Gen. 1.28 reads: פרו ורבו ומלאו את־הארץ. The verb used in the third primaeval command is מלא, 'be full, fill' (Gen. 1.28; 9.1). It is evident from the context that אדם, male and female (Gen. 1.26-27),[7] are to do the 'filling' and הארץ is the place which is to be filled. If Gen. 1.28 is read in the context of the creation account, הארץ seems to refer to the entire earth which God makes productive and habitable for humans.[8] While it is not stated explicitly what humans are to fill the earth with, we may infer from the context that they are to fill it with themselves, that is, with other humans.[9] It appears, therefore, that the primaeval commands are to be realized through the proliferation of the species.

This idea is also suggested in Gen. 1.22. The blessing announced to humankind in Gen. 1.28 is almost identical to God's blessing upon the living creatures in v. 22:

God's blessing upon living creatures (1.22):	God's blessing upon humankind (1.28a):
ויברך אתם אלהים	ויברך אתם אלהים
לאמר	ויאמר להם אלהים
פרו ורבו ומלאו את־המים בימים	פרו ורבו ומלאו את־הארץ

As with v. 28, the verbs פרה, רבה and מלא occur together in v. 22. However, it is not the earth that is to be filled, but the waters in the sea. The context suggests that the living creatures are to fill the waters with themselves. Birds are

---

7.   Accordingly, the five imperatives in Gen. 1.28 are masculine *plural*.

8.   E.g. Gen. 1.1, 2, 10, 11, 12, etc. Sailhamer agrees that הארץ in Gen. 1.1 refers to the cosmos; however, he argues that הארץ in v. 2 ('the earth was formless and void') has a localized meaning, referring to the garden of Eden and the promised land. He concludes, therefore, that in Genesis 1 God is preparing the garden of Eden and the promised land for humankind (J. Sailhamer, *Genesis Unbound* [Sisters: Multnomah Books, 1996], pp. 68–96). This view is problematic as it requires that הארץ has two different meanings in Gen. 1.1-2. Furthermore, humankind's dominion given at creation seems to have the cosmos in view (cf. Ps. 8). D. Tsumura thus argues that הארץ in Genesis 1 and 2.5-6 refers to the earth, but suggests that there is a narrowing down of focus in Genesis 2 (cf. אדמה, 2.5, 6), so that the garden becomes the focal point (*The Earth and the Waters in Genesis 1 and 2: A Linguistic Investigation* [JSOTSup, 83; Sheffield: Sheffield Academic Press, 1989], pp. 17–43, 85–92).

9.   Snijders notes that a text does not always state explicitly what an object is filled with. Rather, this information is to be supplied from the context (L.A. Snijders, 'מלא', *TDOT*, Vol. 8, pp. 297–307 [298]). For example, we read that Rebekah went down to the spring and 'filled her jar' (Gen. 24.16). The context indicates that she filled it with *water*.

to *multiply* on the earth (v. 22b) and sea creatures are to 'be fruitful and multiply and *fill* the waters in the seas' (v. 22a). In both cases, emphasis seems to be on the proliferation of the species. The sea creatures were to fill the waters through pro-creation: as they multiplied, the waters would be filled with them. Thus Leupold writes regarding the living creatures, that they are to 'keep on multiplying until they fill the earth'.[10] Similarly, one could argue that humans were to fill the earth through procreation: as they multiplied, the earth would be filled with them.[11] Given that they were to fill the entire *earth*, it is evident that large numbers of humans would be required for the primaeval commands to be fulfilled.

While the early chapters of Genesis affirm that humankind *do* multiply (Gen. 4.1-2, 17-22, 25-26; 5.1-32; 6.1, etc.), it is important to note that no statement is made that they 'filled the earth'. Thus we may assume that the creation blessing has not been fully realized *prior* to the flood. To be sure, we do read in the flood narrative that the earth had been 'filled' (Gen. 6.11). This seems to be an ironic allusion to the primaeval commands, however. Humankind were to fill the earth with themselves, but they had filled it with *violence* (Gen. 6.11). Consequently, we are told that God wiped out humankind, save Noah and his family. Seen against the background of Gen. 1.28, the flood judgment clearly has an adverse effect on the realization of the blessing. Instead of the earth being filled with humans, God empties it of people except for Noah's family. That the blessing, 'Be fruitful and multiply, and fill the earth', is reissued after the flood is consistent with Snijders' observation, that it is often something *empty* that is to be filled.[12] Accordingly, Noah and his sons are commanded to *fill* the earth, or as some early English translations suggest, they were to 'replenish the earth'.[13] As with Gen. 1.28, we may conclude that the primaeval commands in 9.1 are to be realized through procreation. This idea may even be intimated in the repetition of the commands to Noah and his sons in Gen. 9.7.

b. *The Repetition of the Primaeval Blessing in Genesis 9.1 and 9.7*
The renewal of the commands after the flood reads as follows:

Gen. 9.1	פרו ורבו ומלאו את־הארץ
Gen. 9.7	ואתם פרו ורבו שרצו בארץ ורבו־בה

Before considering Gen. 9.7, it is worth noting that some scholars have emended v. 7, proposing that the final verb רבה, 'multiply, increase', should be changed to רדה, 'rule'.[14] Gen. 9.7 would thus read, 'And you, be fruitful and multiply, abound

---

10. Leupold, *Genesis*, Vol. 1, p. 81.

11. The view that humans are required to procreate in obedience to Gen. 1.28 is common in Jewish literature, as J. Cohen has shown ('*Be Fertile and Increase, Fill the Earth and Master It': The Ancient and Medieval Career of a Biblical Text* [Ithaca: Cornell University Press, 1989], pp. 125–65).

12. Snijders, 'מלא', *TDOT*, Vol. 8, pp. 297–307 (298).

13. E.g. Great Bible (1539); Bishops' Bible (1568); Douay (1609); KJV (1611); RV (1885); ASV (1901), etc. Other early English Bibles translated the command as 'fill the earth' (e.g. Tyndale [1530]; Geneva Bible [1560]; RSV [1952]).

14. R. Alter, *Genesis: Translation and Commentary* (New York: W.W. Norton & Co., 1996), p. 39;

on the earth and *rule it*'. Both Kittel's *Biblica Hebraica* and BHS suggest this reading, comparing Gen. 9.7 to 1.28 where the verb רדה occurs. Porten and Rappaport have examined the textual evidence for this emendation and conclude that, while there is some support for רדה, represented by the Greek reading, κατακυριεύω,[15] there is good evidence from Septuagint manuscripts (πληθύνω) and translations to support the MT.[16]

In addition, they have analysed the poetic structure in Gen. 9.7 and have identified the verbal pattern as an a→b→c→b (פרה→רבה→שרץ→רבה) sequence. They have demonstrated that this verbal sequential pattern is found on several occasions in the Old Testament.[17] In some instances, a sequence of imperatives is found as in Gen. 9.7.[18] An example of the sequence may be seen in Gen. 27.29a. As with Gen. 9.7, the verbal sequence is a→b→c→b (עבד→שחה→הוה→שחה):

יעבדוך עמים וישתחו לך לאמים הוה גביר לאחיך וישתחו לך בני אמך

Porten and Rappaport further observe that Gen. 1.22 also has an a→b→c→b verbal sequence (פרה→רבה→מלא→רבה), which they compare to Gen. 9.7: פרה→רבה→שרץ→רבה. They conclude, therefore, that Gen. 1.22 is the structural parallel to 9.7. The implication is that Gen. 1.28 should not be used as the basis for the emendation of 9.7, since the parallel text to Gen. 9.7 is not 1.28, but 1.22.[19]

In addition, Porten and Rappaport note that Gen. 1.28 and Exod. 1.7 both have a sequence of five non-identical verbs:

Gen. 1.28	פרה→רבה→מלא→כבש→רדה (a→b→c→d→e)
Exod. 1.7	פרה→שרץ→רבה→עצם→מלא (a→b→c→d→e)

Skinner, *Genesis*, p. 171; E.A. Speiser, *Genesis* (AB; New York: Doubleday, 1969), p. 57; Vawter, *On Genesis*, p. 133.

15. Some MSS of the Septuagint have κατακυριεύω, 'rule, gain dominion over', rather than πληθύνω, 'multiply, increase' (cf. B. Porten and U. Rappaport, 'Poetic Structure in Genesis IX 7', *VT* [1971], pp. 363–69).

16. Porten and Rappaport note that the MT is supported by: the 'Berlin Fragment' (H.A. Sanders and C. Schmidt, *The Minor Prophets in the Freer Collection and the Berlin Fragment of Genesis* [New York: Macmillan, 1927], p. 288); A.E. Brook and N. McLean, *The Old Testament in Greek* (London: Cambridge University Press, 1906), I-1, p. 21; A. Rahlfs (ed.), *Septuaginta*, Vol. 1 (Stuttgart: Deutsche Bibelgesellschaft, 1935), p. 68. Support for the MT is also found in the Samaritan Pentateuch, Targums Onkelos and Pseudo-Jonathan. See Porten and Rappaport, 'Poetic Structure in Genesis IX 7', pp. 364–65, for a comprehensive survey of the textual material. The MT is accepted by several commentators (U. Cassuto, *A Commentary on the Book of Genesis*, Vol. 1 [trans. I. Abrahams; Jerusalem: Magnes Press, 1961], p. 128; Mathews, *Genesis 1–11.26*, p. 406; Wenham, *Genesis 1–15*, p. 155).

17. E.g. Isa. 30.10 (ראה→חזה→דבר→הזה); Isa. 34.1 (שמע→קשב→שמע); see Porten and Rappaport for further examples ('Poetic Structure in IX 7', pp. 363–69).

18. Isa. 28.23 (עלה→צעק→נתן→צעק); Jer. 22.20 (אזן→שמע→קשב→שמע).

19. As with other scholars, R.S. Hendel proposes emending רבה in Gen. 9.7 on the basis of the parallel text in Gen. 1.28 (*The Text of Genesis 1–11: Textual Studies and Critical Edition* [Oxford: Oxford University Press, 1998], p. 57). He does not discuss the article by Porten and Rappaport, however.

They maintain, therefore, that the structural parallel to Gen. 1.28 is not 9.7, as is commonly assumed by scholars who emend the text, but Exod. 1.7. Porten and Rappaport have persuasively demonstrated that the poetic structure in Gen. 9.7 supports the MT.

If the MT of Gen. 9.7 is retained, then it appears that the command to 'fill the earth' in Gen. 9.1 has been replaced by the commands to 'abound on the earth and multiply in it', in v. 7. The two texts read as follows:

9.1 God blessed Noah…	'Be fruitful and multiply,
	and *fill* (מלא) *the earth*'.
9.7	'And you, be fruitful and multiply,
	abound (שרץ) *on the earth and multiply* (רבה) *in it'*.

It is noteworthy that the verbs שרץ and רבה have been used in v. 7 instead of מלא. As was noted earlier, Porten and Rappaport argue that the structural parallel to Gen. 9.7 is Gen. 1.22. The two verbal sequences are, in fact, identical, except for the verb in the third position:

Gen. 1.22:	רבה←מלא←רבה←פרה (a→b→c→b)
Gen. 9.7:	רבה←שרץ←רבה←פרה (a→b→c→b)

A comparison of these two texts shows that מלא occurs in the third position in Gen. 1.22, whereas שרץ is in the third position in 9.7. As is the case in Gen. 9.1 and 9.7, the verb שרץ is used instead of מלא. That the verbs שרץ, 'abound' (Gen. 1.22; 9.7), and רבה, 'increase, multiply' (Gen. 9.7), are interchangeable with מלא seems to support further the view that humankind were to fill the earth by multiplying.[20] They were to keep on increasing so that the land would be filled with them.[21] Given that the commands are reissued after the flood in Gen. 9.1, it is worth investigating whether there is any indication in the following chapters that the primaeval blessing is *fulfilled*. Did Noah's descendants keep on multiplying so that the land was filled with them?

3. *Language Used in Genesis 9.19*

As has been noted, scholars maintain that the statement in Gen. 9.19, 'and from these the whole earth was peopled' (NRSV), indicates that Noah's descendants are carrying out the primaeval commands. Accordingly, this verse is understood to

---

20. The close relationship between multiplying (רבה) and filling (מלא) is also seen in Ezek. 11.6: 'You have *multiplied* (רבה) your slain in this city, *filling* (מלא) its streets with them' (NASB). Similarly, רבה and מלא occur in 2 Kgs. 21.16a: 'Moreover, Manasseh shed *very much* (רבה) innocent blood, until he had *filled* Jerusalem (עד אשר־מלא את־ירושלם) from one end to another…' (NRSV). In this context, it is the multiplying of blood that resulted in Jerusalem's being *filled* with it.

21. This is in accordance with other texts where a place is said to be 'filled' with people or objects, due to high numbers of people or objects at a particular location. For example, in Ezek. 37.1 we are told that a valley was '*full* of bones' (והיא מלאה עצמות). Ezekiel passes through the valley, looking at the bones; he sees that 'there were *very many* (והנה רבות מאד) lying in the valley' (NRSV, Ezek. 37.2). In this case, the valley is full of bones because of the multitude of bones there. A number of other examples could be cited where a location is said to be *filled* with people due to the high numbers of people at the location (e.g. Exod. 1.7; Judg. 16.27; 1 Kgs. 20.27; 2 Kgs. 10.21; Jer. 23.10; Ezek. 36.38).

look back to the blessing in Gen. 9.1. It is worth noting at the outset, however, that the verbs used in the primaeval blessing, פרה, 'be fruitful', רבה, 'multiply', and ארץ + מלא, 'fill' + 'earth' (Gen. 1.28; 9.1) are absent in Gen. 9.19. In other words, we do not read that 'Noah's descendants were fruitful and multiplied' or that they 'filled the earth'. To be sure, מלא does appear in Targum Neofiti, ומאלין איתמלית כל ארעא (Gen. 9.19).[22] However, מלא is not present in the MT. Rather, the Hebrew text simply reads, ומאלה נפצה כל־הארץ (Gen. 9.19b). Since the verb נפץ, 'scatter, disperse', does not appear in the primaeval blessing in Gen. 1.28 or 9.1, we may conclude that the final author has not established a *direct* link between the primaeval blessing and 9.19. One cannot simply assume, therefore, that v. 19 looks back to Gen. 9.1.

In fact, it could be argued that the verb נפץ, 'scatter, disperse', in 9.19 actually looks *forward* to the scattering motif that follows (cf. פוץ, Gen. 10.18; 11.4, 8, 9). Accordingly, scholars note that v. 19 introduces the dispersal motif which is reiterated in the following two chapters.[23] Anderson points out, for example, that 'the dispersion verb (*pûṣ*, or its related form, *nāpaṣ*) is a motif that runs through the whole section, appearing in various modulations in 9.19 and 10.18, as well as three times in the Babel story (11.4, 8, 9)'.[24] The question may be asked, therefore, whether the verb נפץ, which is *not* used in Gen. 1.28 and 9.1, indicates that the primaeval blessing is being fulfilled. In other words, does 'scattering' relate in any way to the realization of the blessing? Is the dispersion in Gen. 9.19 to be understood in a *positive* light?

4. *The Meaning of the Verb* נפץ *in Genesis 9.19*

נפץ II appears only in the qal (four times) and has the meaning 'disperse, be scattered'[25] (Gen. 9.19; 1 Sam. 13.11; Isa. 11.12; 33.3). It is used in 1 Sam. 13.11 to describe the dispersal of Saul's army prior to the arrival of Samuel. When Samuel arrived, we are told that he questioned Saul about his offering. Saul responded saying,

'When I saw that the people were *slipping away* (נפץ) from me, and that you did not come within the days appointed, and that the Philistines were mustering at Michmash, I said, "Now the Philistines will come down upon me at Gilgal, and I have not entreated the favour of the Lord"; so I forced myself, and offered the burnt-offering' (NRSV, 1 Sam. 13.11b-12).

The NIV has translated 11b as 'When I saw that the men were *scattering*' (cf. KJV). Whether נפץ is translated by 'slipping away' or 'scattering', it is clear that it describes the people's dispersal from Saul (cf. פוץ, 1 Sam. 13.8). נפץ also occurs in Isa. 11.12: 'On that day the Lord will…raise a signal for the nations, and will

---

22. A. Díez Macho, *et al.* (eds.), *Biblia Polyglotta Matritensia IV: Targum Palaestinense in Pentateuchum*, L. 1: *Genesis* (Madrid: Consejo Superior de Investigaciones Científicas, 1988), p. 60.
23. Mathews, *Genesis 1–11.26*, p. 413; Wenham, *Genesis 1–15*, p. 198; Westermann, *Genesis 1–11*, p. 486 (= *Genesis*, Bd. I, p. 650).
24. Anderson, 'The Tower of Babel', pp. 165–78 (175).
25. BDB, p. 659; KB[3], Vol. 2, p. 711.

assemble the outcasts of Israel, and gather the *dispersed* of Judah from the four corners of the earth' (NRSV, Isa. 11.11-12). That נפץ refers to those who have been 'dispersed' is not surprising, given that the cognate verb פוץ is commonly used in reference to the exile.[26] As with 1 Sam. 13.11, נפץ means 'disperse' or 'scatter' in Isa. 11.12. Finally, נפץ occurs in the context of God's judgment in Isa. 33.3. The prophet speaks of YHWH's greatness, saying, 'At the sound of tumult, peoples fled; before your majesty, nations *scattered*' (NRSV, Isa. 33.3). In each of the afore-mentioned texts, נפץ seems to denote scattering or dispersing. Yet the NRSV trans-lates נפץ in Gen. 9.19 by 'was peopled' and the NASB by 'was populated'. In light of the meaning of נפץ in other texts, it is doubtful that the NRSV and NASB trans-lations of נפץ in Gen. 9.19 accurately reflect the meaning of the Hebrew verb. The idea of multiplying essential to these two English translations is difficult to sustain in every other text where נפץ occurs. How, then, should נפץ be translated?

Scholars are in agreement that Gen. 9.18-19 introduces the dispersal theme which is central to the following two chapters. Westermann notes, for instance, that the dispersion verb in Gen. 9.19 is found 'at the conclusion, 11.8, 9, as well as in 10.18, as a leitmotif going through the texts that follow the flood'.[27] The dis-persion verb, פוץ, is commonly translated by 'scatter' or 'scatter abroad' in the Babel story. Given that נפץ means 'scatter, disperse', and that Gen. 9.19 introduces the dispersal motif found in Genesis 10–11, we suggest that נפץ be translated by 'scatter'[28] (NIV), rather than 'people' (NRSV) or 'populate' (NASB). This accords not only with the meaning of נפץ in other texts, but also preserves the connection between נפץ in Gen. 9.19 and the scattering motif in Genesis 10–11 (פוץ, 10.18; 11.4, 8, 9), which scholars acknowledge is present in the Hebrew text. That the meaning of נפץ is similar to פוץ is supported by 1 Sam. 13 where both verbs are used to refer to the same event, namely, the scattering of Saul's army (פוץ: 13.8; נפץ: 13.11). Thus English translations of 1 Sam. 13.8, 11 do not use two *different* verbs to translate נפץ and פוץ, but one ('scatter', NASB, NIV, KJV; 'slip away', NRSV). We suggest, therefore, that נפץ should be translated either by 'scatter', or 'scatter abroad', which is how פוץ is translated in the Babel story. That נפץ should not be translated by 'people' or 'populate' is further supported by early translations of 9.19.

5. *Early and More Recent Translations of נפץ in Genesis 9.19*

It is noteworthy that the Septuagint employs the one Greek verb διασπείρω, 'scat-ter, disperse', for both נפץ in Gen. 9.19 and פוץ in Genesis 10–11 (Gen. 10.18; 11.4, 8, 9). Thus it is clear that the Septuagint does not differentiate between נפץ and פוץ, as is the case with modern English translations. Similarly, Targums Onqelos and Pseudo-Jonathan employ the one Aramaic verb בדר, 'scatter, strew',[29]

---

26. E.g. Neh. 1.8; Jer. 9.16; 13.24; 18.17; 30.11; Ezek. 11.16, 17; 12.15; 20.23, 34, 41; 22.15.

27. Westermann, *Genesis 1–11*, p. 486 (= *Genesis*, Bd. I, p. 650); cf. Anderson, 'The Tower of Babel', pp. 165–78 (175).

28. Cf. Mathews, *Genesis 1–11.26*, p. 413; Waltke, *Genesis*, p. 147.

29. M. Jastrow, *A Dictionary of the Targumim, the Talmud Babli and Yerushalmi, and the*

for both נפץ and פוץ. The Vulgate translates נפץ in 9.19 by *dissemino*, 'spread abroad, disseminate'.[30] It appears, therefore, that early translations do not support the rendering of נפץ as 'populate' (NASB, NKJV) or 'people' (NRSV).

Nor are the translations 'populate' and 'people' found in early English translations. Rather, נפץ is commonly translated by the verb 'overspread'. A summary of translations of Gen. 9.19 is set out in the following table.[31]

Translations	נפץ *(Gen. 9.19)*
LXX	διασπείρω
Vulgate	*dissemino*
Targums Onqelos, Ps-Jon	בדר
Targum Neofiti	מלא
Tyndale (1530)	overspred
Geneva Bible (1560)	overspred
Bishops' Bible (1568)	overspread
Douay (1609)	spred
KJV (1611)	overspread
RV (1885)	overspread
ASV (1901)	overspread
RSV (1952)	peopled
NASB (1970)	populated (marginal note: *lit.* scattered)
NIV (1978)	scattered
NKJV (1982)	populated
NRSV (1990)	peopled

It appears that it was not until the 1952 *Revised Standard Version* that the translation 'was peopled' first occurred. The NASB then translated נפץ by 'was populated', which is comparable to the RSV translation. The NASB acknowledges in the margin, however, that the literal meaning of נפץ is 'scattered'. The NKJV of 1982 followed the NASB, translating נפץ by 'was populated'. These more recent translations of נפץ are reflected in modern commentaries as well.

6. *Translations of Genesis 9.19 in Commentaries*

Early commentators translated נפץ by 'overspread, spread abroad, spread out'[32] or 'scatter'.[33] However, more recent scholars have followed either the NASB/NKJV

Midrashic Literature, Vol. 1 (New York: Pardes, 1950 [1886]), p. 141. As has been noted, Targum Neofiti translates נפץ in Gen. 9.19 by מלא. It also differs from Targums Onqelos and Pseudo-Jonathan in its translation of פוץ in Gen. 10.18 by פרש, which is the verb used to translate פרד in Gen. 10.5 and 10.32 (*Biblia Polyglotta*, Vol. IV, p. 64).

30. C. Lewis and C. Short, *A Latin Dictionary* (Oxford: Clarendon Press, 1975), p. 594.

31. The early English translations have been cited from L.A. Weigle (ed.), *The Genesis Octapla* (New York: Thomas Nelson and Sons, 1965), pp. 44–53.

32. G.G. Greenwood, *The Book of Genesis Treated as an Authentic Record*, Vol. 1 (London: The Church Printing Co., 2nd edn, 1904), p. 212; W.H. Griffith Thomas, *Genesis: A Devotional Commentary* (Grand Rapids: Eerdmans, 1946 [1907–1908]), p. 94; C.F. Keil and F. Delitzsch, *Commentary on the Old Testament: The Pentateuch*, Vol. 1 (trans. J. Martin; repr., Grand Rapids: Eerdmans, n.d. [1866]), p. 155; Leupold, *Genesis*, Vol. 1, p. 343.

33. Skinner, *Genesis*, p. 182.

('populated') or the NRSV ('peopled'). Wenham, for example, translates נפץ by 'was populated'. He then comments:

> Understanding 'was populated' from the root נפץ links this verse with 1 Sam 13.11, Isa 33.3, where it means 'scatter'. However, it must also be associated with another similar root, פוץ, which is frequent in Gen. 10–11; cf. 10.18; 11.4, 8, 9, again meaning to 'scatter'. So this remark anticipates the dispersal of mankind throughout the world as related in Gen. 10–11.[34]

Given that Wenham understands that נפץ means 'scatter' in 1 Sam. 13.11 and Isa. 33.3, and that פוץ also means 'scatter', why, then, has he translated נפץ in 9.19 by 'was populated'?

Westermann similarly affirms that נפץ in 9.19 has its setting in the Babel story and that the dispersion verb in 9.19 is a leitmotif which reappears in the following two chapters.[35] He also notes that he follows Gesenius, who proposes that נפצה in Gen. 9.19 is a niphal derived from the verbal root פצץ (= פוץ), and that פוץ means, 'to be shattered, to be scattered'. Given that נפץ is identified as the dispersion verb and that it has the same meaning as פוץ, why, then, does Westermann translate נפץ by 'bevölkern'[36] ('was peopled') in Gen. 9.19? His reason for this translation is based on his view that 9.19 goes back to the priestly blessing of 9.1[37] and that the scattering verb has a 'different echo, corresponding to which is a different concept of the dispersion of humankind over the earth'.[38] Is Westermann correct to assume, however, that the dispersion verb has a 'different echo' in 9.19? What evidence is there to support his interpretation? Since 9.19 is commonly understood to be J's introduction to Genesis 10–11, a distinction between נפץ and פוץ on source-critical grounds cannot be defended. Moreover, it was noted previously that the Septuagint and Targums Onqelos and Pseudo-Jonathan have employed the same verb to translate נפץ in Gen. 9.19 and פוץ in Genesis 10–11. Thus they do not support Westermann's view that the scattering verb has a 'different echo' in 9.19.

This inconsistency in the translation of נפץ in 9.19 and פוץ in the Babel story is also present in Cassuto's work. He translates נפץ by 'was peopled', yet remarks in parenthesis that the verb has the literal meaning 'was scattered'.[39] He then compares 9.19 with פוץ in 11.9, which he does translate as 'scatter'. Given that Cassuto understands that נפץ means, literally, 'was scattered' and that 9.19 introduces the main theme of the dispersion,[40] we may well question why he has translated נפץ by 'was peopled'. The same point may be made with respect to

---

34. Wenham, *Genesis 1–15*, p. 198.

35. Westermann, *Genesis 1–11*, p. 486 (= *Genesis*, Bd. I, p. 650).

36. Gen. 9.19b: 'und von ihnen aus hat sich die ganze Erde *bevölkert*' (Westermann, *Genesis*, Bd. I, p. 15).

37. Westermann, *Genesis 1–11*, p. 11 (= *Genesis*, Bd. I, p. 15).

38. Westermann, *Genesis 1–11*, p. 486 (= *Genesis*, Bd. I, p. 650).

39. Cassuto, *Genesis*, Vol. 2, p. 141. This same point is noted in the NASB translation, which has 'populated' in the main text, while the marginal note states that the verb is translated literally as 'scattered'.

40. Cassuto, *Genesis*, Vol. 2, p. 141.

Anderson's translation. He translates נפץ by 'repopulate', but then refers to נפץ as the 'scattering-verb'.[41] If נפץ is the 'scattering-verb', why not translate it as 'scatter'?

Turner, who similarly translates נפץ in Gen. 9.19 by 'peopled', notes that נפץ can have a negative connotation, such as shattering or dispersing. He concludes, however, that the *context* supports the traditional translation 'peopled'. Yet Turner cites 1 Sam. 13.11 and Isa. 33.3 to support the 'traditional translation'[42] even though the meaning of נפץ is clearly not 'peopled' in either of these texts, but 'scatter' or 'disperse'. Why do scholars consistently translate נפץ in 9.19 by 'populate' or 'people', even though they acknowledge that the verb means 'scatter, disperse' and that it is related to the cognate verb פוץ – which they do translate as 'scatter'?

It was noted earlier that there is scholarly consensus that the primaeval blessing is fulfilled in the Table of Nations and that 9.19 introduces the dispersal motif. Accordingly, 9.19 is understood to be a *positive* statement since the dispersion in the following Table marks the fulfilment of the blessing. Instead of translating נפץ by 'scatter', which we might expect in light of its meaning and association with the cognate verb פוץ (Gen. 11.4, 8, 9), the verbs 'people' and 'populate' seem to have been chosen as a translation of נפץ because these terms convey the dispersion in a *positive* light. It seems to be the case that these translations reflect a particular *interpretation* of Gen. 9.19 which sees a connection between 9.19 and the blessing in 9.1 and 9.7. This is especially seen in the NASB translation of Gen. 9.7 and 9.19, which translates both שרץ (9.7) and נפץ (9.19) by the verb 'populate':

Gen. 9.7	'And as for you, be fruitful and multiply;
	Populate[43] (שרץ) the earth abundantly and multiply in it'.
Gen. 9.19	These three were the sons of Noah; and from these the whole earth
	was *populated*[44] (נפץ).

The connection between Gen. 9.7 and 9.19 present in the NASB translation is not so evident, however, in the Hebrew text.

We have observed thus far that נפץ in v. 19 introduces the scattering motif found in the *following* chapters (פוץ, Gen. 10.18; 11.4, 8, 9). This thematic connection between 9.19 and the scattering motif present in the Hebrew text (and in the LXX and Targums Onqelos and Pseudo-Jonathan) is obscured by English translations which employ two *different* verbs for נפץ in 9.19 and פוץ in the Babel story. Instead of representing the connection between 9.19 and the *scattering* motif, the NASB translation 'was populated', and the NRSV 'was peopled' establishes a connection between Gen. 9.19 and the *primaeval blessing* (Gen. 9.1, 7) – even though the Hebrew text does not.

---

41. B.W. Anderson, 'From Analysis to Synthesis: The Interpretation of Genesis 1–11', *JBL* 97 (1978), pp. 23–39 (33 n. 33).

42. Turner, *Announcements of Plot*, p. 29 n. 2; cf. *idem*, *Genesis*, p. 56.

43. Italics mine. The NASB notes in the margin: Lit., *Swarm in the earth*.

44. Italics mine. The NASB notes in the margin: Lit., *scattered*.

We suggest that it is preferable to translate נפץ in Gen. 9.19 by the verb 'scatter' (NIV, NLT), rather than 'people' or 'populate'. This translation reflects more accurately the verb נפץ and highlights the thematic connection between Gen. 9.19 and the dispersal theme that follows (Gen. 10.18; 11.4, 8, 9). If נפץ is translated by 'scatter', it is not so evident that this verse looks back to the primaeval blessing as is commonly supposed. Rather, 9.19 anticipates the *scattering* of Noah's descendants, which is the focus of the following two chapters.[45]

It is important to note at this point that the new *English Standard Version* (ESV), completed in 2001, is different from the NASB/NKJV ('populate') and NRSV ('people') in its translation of נפץ by 'disperse'. The NASB/NKJV translation, 'populated', has simply been placed in the margin as an alternative reading. The ESV is thus similar to the NIV translation of 9.19 ('scatter'). The ESV also establishes a connection between 9.19 and the ensuing dispersal motif in its translation of פוץ in Genesis 10–11 by 'disperse' (10.18; 11.4, 8, 9). The strength of the ESV is that it has faithfully represented the verbal repetitions present in the Hebrew text. However, the ESV marks a significant departure from all the major English versions in its translation of פוץ in the Babel story. Instead of the usual translation, that YHWH *scattered* the Babelites (NRSV, NIV, NASB), according to the ESV, he simply *dispersed* them. The significance of this translation is underscored by comparing it with other renderings of פוץ in the ESV. Elsewhere in the Old Testament, when YHWH 'scatters' people as an act of judgment, the ESV translates פוץ by 'scatter'[46] (except in Ezek. 12.15[47]). It seems to be the case, therefore, that the ESV, in its translation of פוץ by 'disperse', has removed the negative connotation associated with 'scattering' and replaced it with a more positive term. This change seems to reflect the prevailing view that the dispersal in Gen. 11.1-9 fulfils the primaeval blessing. We have argued, however, that it is preferable to translate נפץ by 'scatter, scatter abroad' in accordance with how the NRSV, NIV, and NASB translate פוץ in the Babel story.[48] Whether נפץ and פוץ should be translated by 'disperse' or not will be discussed in Chapter 3. We may simply note at this point that נפץ does not mean 'people' or 'populate' and that the translation 'disperse' may well have been chosen in order to present a positive picture of the dispersal after the flood.

---

45. The connection between 9.19 and the Babel story is further underscored by the repetition of the subject, כל־הארץ (i.e. 'from these the *whole earth* scattered'), in Gen. 9.19, which occurs in Gen. 11.1 as well (i.e. 'now the *whole earth* had one language and the same words').

46. E.g. Deut. 4.27; 28.64; 30.3; Isa. 24.1; Jer. 9.16 [15]; 13.24; Ezek. 11.16; 22.15; 29.12. See Chapter 3 for a detailed discussion of פוץ.

47. In Ezek. 12.15, פוץ occurs in parallel with זרה (פוץ is translated by 'disperse' and זרה by 'scatter'). In Ezek. 12.15, 'disperse' has a negative connotation since it is in parallel with 'scatter'. פוץ and זרה occur in parallel in Exod. 20.23 as well. In this verse, פוץ is translated by 'scatter', and זרה by 'disperse'.

48. We have retained the term 'scatter' throughout our study in regard to the Babel story rather than follow the ESV translation. The reason for this will be discussed in Chapter 3.

7. *Conclusion*

We have noted that most recent English translations portray Gen. 9.19 in a positive light and that scholars interpret it against the background of the primaeval blessing. Yet we have observed that נפץ anticipates the scattering motif reiterated in the following chapters (10.18; 11.4, 8, 9); thus it is not so evident that Gen. 9.19 'looks back' to the blessing of 9.1. The question needs to be re-examined, therefore, whether the dispersal motif is, indeed, related to the realization of the primaeval blessing. It is also assumed by scholars that when the Babelites state that they do not want to be *scattered* (11.4), they are refusing to *fill* the earth. The question may be raised, however, whether 'scattering' is tantamount to filling the earth. When Noah's descendants build the city and tower so that they might not be scattered, does this mean that they do not want to fill the earth?

Chapter 2

ARE THE BABELITES REJECTING THE COMMAND TO FILL THE EARTH?

1. *Scholarly Views Regarding the Actions of the Babelites*

The scattering motif is unquestionably central to the Babel story. YHWH not only scatters the Babelites, but their fear of being scattered provides the motivation for the collective building activity in the first place. The people intend to build a city and tower and make a name for themselves, 'otherwise we shall be scattered abroad…' (NRSV, Gen. 11.4). Scholars maintain that this statement of purpose indicates that the Babelites 'resisted the divine command to "increase" and "fill the earth"'[1] and that the tower was 'an attempt to thwart God's command to be fertile and increase'.[2] Accordingly, the desire to congregate in the one place is understood to be a rejection of the primaeval commands.[3]

Scholars observe that this view was first espoused by Josephus,[4] who writes that God had commanded the Babelites to colonize so that the people might not quarrel with each other, but cultivate the earth. According to Josephus, the people refused to obey, thinking that God was plotting against them. God's dispersing the people thus resulted in every continent being filled with them.[5] Josephus also writes that Nimrod incited the people to build a tower so that they would not be washed away by another flood.[6] Thus according to Josephus, Nimrod did not build the tower in defiance of the primaeval commands, but as an act of revenge against God for the destruction of his forefathers.

More recent scholars argue, however, that the city and tower were built in defiance of God's command to 'fill the earth' (Gen. 9.1). God envisaged that humankind should disperse to all parts of the earth, but the people wanted to stay together. Thus they intend to build a city and a tower so that they might not be dispersed.[7] The sin of the builders, therefore, is disobedience to the primaeval

---

1. Mathews, *Genesis 1–11.26*, p. 474.
2. Harland, 'The Sin of Babel', pp. 515–33 (528).
3. Harland, 'The Sin of Babel', pp. 515–33 (527); Turner, *Announcements of Plot*, p. 31; Wenham, *Genesis 1–15*, p. 240; van Wolde, *Words Become Worlds*, p. 99.
4. Anderson, 'The Tower of Babel', pp. 165–78 (170–71); Cassuto, *Genesis*, Vol. 2, p. 230; Turner, *Announcements of Plot*, p. 30.
5. Josephus, *Ant.*, I.109-12, 120.
6. Josephus, *Ant.*, I.114, 116.
7. Cassuto, *Genesis*, Vol. 2, p. 243; Jacob, *Genesis*, p. 79 (= *Das erste Buch der Tora*, p. 301).

command to fill the earth.[8] This view was espoused by a few scholars in the nineteenth century,[9] but Holzinger objected to it, arguing against Dillmann in particular.[10] This interpretation is, as we have noted, widely accepted by scholars today. Sarna maintains, for example, that the purpose of the building activity – that the Babelites not be scattered (Gen. 11.4) – constitutes 'a direct challenge to the intent of God as expressed in the blessing to postdiluvial humanity: "Fill the earth". Man did not perceive this to be a blessing and so devised means to thwart its fulfilment'.[11] The building activity of the Babelites is understood, therefore, to be contrary to the divine intentions expressed in Gen. 1.28 and 9.1. Thus Cohn maintains that the 'tower generation failed to fill the earth and instead built a city to shut God out'.[12] This view is espoused by Turner as well, who argues that while humankind have been successful at multiplying,

> the purpose of such multiplication was to 'fill the earth' and 11.1-9 indicates that humans were not willing to do this... Thus the act of building a city and tower and settling down...has as its object the more modest but still serious aim of frustrating the divine will that humans should spread abroad and fill the earth.[13]

The sin of the people, therefore, lies in their attempt to unite in the one place instead of filling the earth. Is one to assume, therefore, that the building of the tower 'flies directly in the face of the divine commandment to multiply and fill the earth'?[14] Is this how we are to interpret the Babelites' actions?

Van Wolde has discussed this view in detail.[15] She argues that the city-builders are not seeking to penetrate into heaven, but to maintain their unity. Thus she categorizes the ambitions of the builders as *horizontal* rather than *vertical*.[16] Unlike others, however, she questions whether the people are actually committing any sin at all.[17] She contends that the builders are simply endeavouring to maintain

---

8. Cassuto, *Genesis*, Vol. 2, p. 243; Harland, 'The Sin of Babel', pp. 515–33 (527); Ross, *Creation and Blessing*, p. 234; Turner, *Announcements of Plot*, pp. 31–32. Other scholars maintain that the sin of the Babelites is two-fold: (a) they are disobeying the command to fill the earth and (b) they are prideful and acting independently of God in their seeking to make a name for themselves (Hamilton, *Genesis 1–17*, pp. 353, 356; Waltke, *Genesis*, p. 161; Wenham, *Genesis 1–15*, pp. 239–40, 245).

9. Alford, *The Book of Genesis*, p. 53; Dillmann, *Genesis*, Vol. 1, p. 202; Evans, *The Books of the Pentateuch*, p. 41.

10. H. Holzinger, *Genesis* (Freiburg: J.C.B. Mohr [Paul Siebeck], 1898), p. 112.

11. Sarna, *Genesis*, p. 83; cf. Anderson, 'The Tower of Babel', pp. 165–78 (168); Waltke, *Genesis*, p. 180.

12. Cohn, 'Narrative Structure', pp. 3–16 (7).

13. Turner, *Announcements of Plot*, p. 31. As has been noted, Clines also raises the question whether the primaeval commands are obeyed or not. In contrast to Turner, however, he does not discuss the interpretation presented above. His silence on this matter may well indicate that he does not espouse this view.

14. Hamilton, *Genesis 1–17*, p. 353.

15. Van Wolde, *Words Become Worlds*, pp. 85-109; *idem*, 'Facing the Earth: Primaeval History in a New Perspective', in P.R. Davies and D.J.A. Clines (eds.), *The World of Genesis: Persons, Places, Perspectives* (JSOTSup, 257; Sheffield: Sheffield Academic Press, 1998), pp. 22–47, especially pp. 37–45.

16. Van Wolde, *Words Become Worlds*, p. 100.

17. Van Wolde, *Words Become Worlds*, pp. 94, 103.

their unity. It is YHWH who seeks to disrupt this because his concern is for the land, that it be cultivated and filled. Van Wolde argues that the story has too often been read from a human perspective. The divine perspective, however, shows that YHWH's dispersing the people ensures that his intention for the whole earth (i.e. that the land be filled) is achieved.[18] Thus YHWH's scattering the people is not to be understood as his judgment, but as an act of creation. He is simply carrying out his divine purposes which he established in Gen. 1.28.

Harland has taken up van Wolde's view and similarly suggests that the striving of the Babelites is not vertical, but horizontal (although he does view their actions as sin). He maintains that if Gen. 11.1-9 is read from within its canonical context, the people 'sinned by an attempt to prevent themselves being scattered over the face of the whole earth in rebellion to the commands of Gen. i 28 and ix 1'.[19] Harland sees a direct link between the statement 'otherwise we shall be scattered abroad' (Gen. 11.4) and the commands given in Gen. 1.28 and 9.1. According to Harland, the people are motivated by fear and the desire to go against the divine will.[20] As with van Wolde, he concludes that the dispersion is willed by God and fulfils the purpose of Gen. 1.28. YHWH's scattering the builders thus ensures that the primaeval blessing is fulfilled.

According to this line of interpretation, the people are refusing to fill the earth. The statement made by the Babelites in Gen. 11.4 is central to this view: 'Then they said, "Come, let us build ourselves a city, and a tower with its top in the heavens, and let us make a name for ourselves; otherwise we shall be scattered abroad upon the face of the whole earth"' (NRSV, Gen. 11.4). It is clear from Gen. 11.4 that the Babelites do not want to be scattered. The question, however, is whether the statement, פֶּן־נָפוּץ עַל פְּנֵי כָל־הָאָרֶץ, means that the Babelites were disobeying the primaeval command to *fill* the earth.

2. *The Meaning and Import of the Conjunction* פֶּן *in Genesis 11.4*

The statement in Gen. 11.4, פֶּן־נָפוּץ עַל־פְּנֵי כָל־הָאָרֶץ, begins with the conjunction פֶּן, 'lest, so as not'. The conjunction usually signifies a negative purpose or result clause.[21] Sometimes this clause describes a situation that *will* result if the action of the main verb is not carried out.[22] In other cases, the situation described in the subordinate clause is a *potential* situation that may arise.[23] What is common in these negative purpose or result clauses is that the situation described in the subordinate clause is something *undesirable*; it is a 'dreaded thing, a thing to

---

18. Van Wolde, *Words Become Worlds*, pp. 102–104.
19. Harland, 'The Sin of Babel', pp. 515–33 (532).
20. Harland, 'The Sin of Babel', pp. 515–33 (527).
21. F.I. Andersen, *The Sentence in Biblical Hebrew* (The Hague: Mouton & Co., 1974), p. 27; cf. GKC, §152w; B.K. Waltke and M. O'Connor, *An Introduction to Biblical Hebrew Syntax* (Winona Lake: Eisenbrauns, 1990), p. 640.
22. E.g. Gen. 19.15; Exod. 19.22, 24; 20.19; 23.33; Deut. 22.9.
23. E.g. Gen. 26.7, 9; 32.11; 38.11; 42.4; Exod. 5.3; 13.17; Deut. 20.5, 6.

ward off'.[24] BDB thus suggests that פֶּן has an 'averting or deprecating' sense.[25] Dreaded situations include: dying,[26] being killed,[27] being swept away,[28] being smitten,[29] being struck with plagues,[30] and being consumed.[31] That the conjunction פֶּן occurs with יָרֵא, 'be afraid', underscores that the action described in the subordinate clause is often associated with fear.[32] The statement in Gen. 11.4, '*otherwise* we shall be scattered abroad', suggests, therefore, that the Babelites dread being scattered.

This point has been noted by a number of scholars. Harland observes, for example, that the conjunction פֶּן is frequently used to express fear and that what motivates the Babelites is fear of being scattered.[33] He further suggests that this fear 'could be interpreted as disobedience to the command of i 28 and ix 1. The people rebel against God, even if out of ignorance of his will'.[34] Ross similarly draws the conclusion that 'the tower, on the one hand, is born from the people's fear of being scattered across the earth; and on the other hand it is an attempt to frustrate God's plan to fill the earth (Gen. 9.1)'.[35] Whether the Babelites are seeking to frustrate God's intention is yet to be established. The point to note is that the statement, '*otherwise* we shall be scattered', indicates that the Babelites dread or are fearful of being scattered. But if scattering is tantamount to filling the earth, which is how this text has been interpreted by scholars, then the Babelites are fearful of the command to fill the earth. It is precisely their negative assessment of the *command* that provides the motivation for the collective building activity. This raises the question whether there is any evidence to indicate that Noah's descendants dread the command to fill the earth. When God reissued the primaeval blessing to Noah and his sons after the flood (Gen. 9.1), did it evoke fear in them?

3. *Are the Builders Fearful of the Primaeval Commands?*

Given that the primaeval commands were given to humankind in Gen. 1.28, it may be helpful to consider first whether humans viewed them in a negative light

---

24. Joüon, §168g. Negative result clauses are commonly used in Proverbs to provide motivation for right behaviour (e.g. Prov. 5.8-10; 9.8; 20.13; 24.17-18; 25.9-10). The conjunction פֶּן can also occur with verbs that may not in themselves have negative connotations. In these cases, it is the *context* which indicates that the verb has a negative sense (e.g. Exod. 1.10).

25. BDB, p. 815.

26. מוּת: Gen. 3.3; 26.9; Exod. 20.19; Lev. 10.7, etc.

27. הרג: Gen. 26.7.

28. ספה: Gen. 19.15, 17.

29. נכה: Gen. 32.11 [12].

30. נגע: Exod. 5.3.

31. אכל: Exod. 33.3.

32. E.g. Gen. 26.7; 31.31; 32.11 [12]; cf. GKC, §152w.

33. Harland, 'The Sin of Babel', pp. 515–33 (527); cf. Anderson, 'The Tower of Babel', pp. 165–78 (171).

34. Harland, 'The Sin of Babel', pp. 515–33 (531); cf. Brueggemann, *Genesis,* p. 98.

35. Ross, 'The Dispersion of the Nations', pp. 119–38 (119).

before the flood. Is there any evidence that Adam and Eve were fearful of the primaeval commands? Did they in some way reject them? Kikawada and Quinn suggest that the attempt of Adam and Eve to hide themselves in the garden may indicate that they no longer wanted to fulfil God's command to be fruitful and multiply.[36] Nothing in the narrative, however, indicates that this is the case. On the contrary, the genealogies testify that human beings *are* obeying the commands (cf. Gen. 4.1-2, 17-22; 5.1-32; Gen. 6.1). Thus there is no indication that they were fearful of the primaeval commands *before* the flood. The question remains, however, whether Noah's descendants are resisting the primaeval commands *after* the flood.

a. *The Primaeval Commands Are God's Blessing*
It is important to note at this point that, while the primaeval blessing consists of imperatives, they are clearly identified as the *blessing* of the creator. The blessing given to humankind in Gen. 1.28 is preceded by God's blessing on the living creatures in 1.22:

ויברך אתם אלהים לאמר
פרו ורבו ומלאו את־המים בימים

In v. 22, the verbal form לאמר, 'saying, in order to say', identifies the following commands, 'Be fruitful and multiply and fill the waters in the seas', as the *content* of God's blessing.[37] In other words, God did not bless the animals *and* give them commands. Rather, the imperatives are his blessing. In Gen. 1.28 and 9.1 the *wayyiqtol* form of אמר is used:

Gen. 1.28	Gen. 9.1
ויברך אתם אלהים	ויברך אלהים את־נח ואת־בניו
ויאמר להם אלהים	ויאמר להם
פרו ורבו ומלאו את־הארץ	פרו ורבו ומלאו את־הארץ

The variation in verbal form in Gen. 1.28 and 9.1 may simply be due to stylistic reasons;[38] however, the different verbal form in the blessing upon humans may be intended to underscore the unique relationship God has with them.[39] The point relevant to the present discussion is that the *content* of the blessing is introduced by the *wayyiqtol* form of אמר in Gen. 1.28 and 9.1.[40] The imperatives, 'Be fruitful and multiply, and fill the earth', are, therefore, to be identified as God's

36. Kikawada and Quinn, *Before Abraham Was*, p. 68.
37. An example of this construction may be seen in Jacob's blessing on Ephraim and Manasseh: 'So he blessed them that day saying (לאמור), "By you Israel will invoke blessing…" ' (Gen. 48.20). As with Gen. 1.22, the *content* of the blessing is introduced by לאמר.
38. Joüon gives examples where ויאמר is being used exactly like לאמר (§118*j*).
39. In Gen. 1.28 the speaker, אלהים, is mentioned twice, as is the recipient of the blessing. Westermann concludes that this difference underscores that, unlike the living creatures, God has created humankind as his counterpart with whom he can speak (*Genesis 1–11*, p. 160 [= *Genesis*, Bd. I, p. 221]).
40. For other examples where a blessing is introduced by the verbal sequence ויאמר + ויברך, see Gen. 14.19; 24.60; 27.27; 35.9-10; 48.3-4, etc.

blessing. That the content of the blessing concerns fecundity is not surprising, given that fruitfulness and increase are repeatedly associated with the divine blessing in Genesis.[41] Westermann thus concludes that the promise of increase, which commonly follows the blessing, is an explication of the divine blessing.[42] Accordingly, the Psalmist affirms that when God blesses people, they multiply (ויברכם וירבו מאד; Ps. 107.38). Conversely, decrease in numbers is associated with God's curse (Deut. 28.62). We may conclude, therefore, that the primaeval commands, 'Be fruitful and multiply, and fill the earth' (Gen. 1.28; 9.1, 7), constitute God's blessing.[43]

b. *Did the Babelites* Perceive *God's Blessing in a Negative Light?*

We may return, then, to the question posed previously – whether there is any indication that Noah's descendants viewed the primaeval blessing in a *negative* light. Was it something they dreaded or were fearful of? To begin with, when the blessing was spoken to Noah and his sons (Gen. 9.1, 7), there is no indication that they perceived it negatively. Neither is there any suggestion that Noah's descendants are refusing to be fruitful and multiply.[44] The Table of Nations (Gen. 10.1-32) and the Shemite genealogy (Gen. 11.10-26) clearly indicate that they did increase after the flood.[45] There is no indication, therefore, that Noah's descendants are afraid of the commands to 'be fruitful and multiply' (cf. Gen. 10.1-32; 11.10-26). Are we to assume, then, that they are fearful of the command to fill the earth? If the command to fill the earth was God's judgment, it would be understandable why Noah's descendants would be fearful of it, as Cain was, for instance, when YHWH's judgment was pronounced against him (cf. Gen. 4.14).

It is important to underscore at this point that, even though the primaeval blessing is in the form of *imperatives*, this should not obscure the fact that filling the earth constitutes God's *blessing*. We may compare Gen. 27.29, for instance, where Isaac blesses Jacob saying, '*Be lord* (imv.) over your brothers' (NRSV, Gen. 27.29). The presence of a command does not preclude Isaac's blessing from being viewed positively. Similarly, when Moses blessed Naphtali saying, '*possess* (imv.) the west and the south' (NRSV, Deut. 33.23b), the imperatival form does not preclude this from being a *blessing*. Analogously, since the command to '*fill* the earth' in

---

41. For example, פרה (Gen. 1.22, 28; 9.1; 17.20; 28.3; 48.3-4) and רבה (Gen. 17.20; 22.17; 26.3-4, 24; 28.3; 48.3-4; cf. Deut. 1.10-11; 7.13, etc.); cf. C. Westermann, *The Promises to the Fathers: Studies on the Patriarchal Narratives* (trans. D.E. Green; Philadelphia: Fortress Press, 1980), pp. 19–21, 152–53 (= *Die Verheißungen an die Väter: Studien zur Vätergeschichte* [Göttingen: Vandenhoeck & Ruprecht, 1976], pp. 25–26, 141–43).

42. Westermann, *The Promises to the Fathers*, p. 19 (= *Die Verheißungen an die Väter*, p. 25).

43. This is not to deny that the primaeval blessing also includes the commands to 'subdue the earth' and 'have dominion' over the living creatures (Gen. 1.28). We have limited our discussion to the first three commands, however.

44. Cohen notes that, according to some midrashic sources, the Babelites are said to be 'subverting the divine injunction to procreate, either by reproducing recklessly or by neglecting procreation and thereby failing to fill the earth' (*'Be Fertile and Increase'*, pp. 78–79). Nothing in the text indicates that this is the case, however.

45. Clines, *What Does Eve Do to Help?*, p. 52.

Gen. 9.1 is God's *blessing* upon Noah's descendants, it is doubtful that they would have seen it in a negative light or rejected it.

Yet Sarna argues that Noah's descendants 'did not perceive this to be a blessing and so devised means to thwart its fulfillment'.[46] We may well question, however, whether a blessing, bestowed on an individual or on people by God himself, would actually be *perceived* in such a negative light, as Sarna claims. There is no indication in Genesis that individuals who are blessed by God[47] or by a father[48] perceive the blessing to be something *other* than a blessing, or as something undesirable. On the contrary, a blessing seems to be greatly sought after (cf. Jacob: Gen. 27.1-46; 32.24-26; Esau: Gen. 27.34, 36, 38) – even when it is in the form of an imperative (Gen. 27.29). We suggest, therefore, that Noah's descendants are not fearful of the commands to 'be fruitful and multiply, and fill the earth', since they constitute God's *blessing*. What they are fearful of, however, is being *scattered*, and being scattered is not to be equated with filling the earth.

4. *Is the Scattering Motif to be Identified with Filling the Earth?*

There has been a tendency in Old Testament scholarship to associate 'scattering' in the primaeval history with 'filling the earth' (Gen. 9.1). To begin with, we have already observed that English translations of the scattering verb, נפץ, in Gen. 9.19 establish a connection between v. 19 and the blessing of 9.1, even though the Hebrew text does not. This has resulted in an artificial association of 'scattering' with the primaeval blessing. Accordingly, Farmer can refer to the primaeval commands in Gen. 9.1-7 simply as the 'command to scatter',[49] yet the scattering verb does not occur in these verses. Similarly, Harland notes that 'after the flood the narrative is particularly concerned with the motif of scattering (ix 1, 7, x 18, 32)'.[50] According to Harland, the *scattering* motif is present in Gen. 9.1 and 9.7 – even though פוץ is not. Given that scholars assume that the primaeval blessing includes the notion of scattering, it is not surprising that YHWH's 'scattering' the Babelites is seen to restore the order intended from the beginning. Similarly, when the Babelites state that they do not want to be scattered, this is interpreted to mean that they do not want to fill the earth.

It is worth underscoring, however, that God never commanded Noah's descendants to *scatter*. That נפץ and פוץ do not occur in the primaeval blessing is not surprising, given that scattering is commonly associated with divine *punishment* in the Old Testament.[51] Scattering is even identified as one of the curses of the Mosaic covenant (Deut. 28.64). We may also observe that פוץ is used in parallel with verbs such as: נום, 'flee',[52] שגה, 'err, go astray',[53] נהג, 'drive away',[54] נדח,

---

46. Sarna, *Genesis*, p. 83.
47. For example, Gen. 12.2; 17.20; 22.17; 26.24.
48. For example, Gen. 27.4, 7, 27; 28.3.
49. Farmer, 'What Is "This" They Begin to Do?', pp. 17–28 (22).
50. Harland, 'The Sin of Babel', pp. 515–33 (532).
51. See the following chapter for a detailed discussion of פוץ.
52. Num. 10.35; Ps. 68.1 [2].

'banish, drive away',[55] רחק, 'remove',[56] זרה, 'scatter, disperse',[57] and חלק, 'divide'.[58] We maintain, therefore, that it is inaccurate and somewhat misleading to suggest that the primaeval commands, which constitute God's *blessing*, include the notion of *scattering*. Accordingly, when Noah's descendants say that they do not want to be scattered, this does not mean that they do not want to fill the earth. What they are afraid of is scattering, not the divine blessing.

5. *Conclusion*

Scholars argue that the Babelites are rejecting the command to fill the earth. We noted, however, that if Gen. 11.4 is interpreted in this way, then the Babelites are *fearful* of the primaeval command. Yet there is no indication that humankind were fearful of God's commands, which constitute his *blessing*. The only suggestion that Noah's descendants are refusing to fill the earth is the statement made in Gen. 11.4, 'otherwise we shall be scattered abroad'. It was noted, however, that the verb used in 11.4 is not מלא, but פוץ. Since God did not command Noah's descendants to scatter, we cannot simply assume that Gen. 11.4 means that the Babelites do not want to fill the earth. That 'scattering' is not to be identified with the command to fill the earth is supported by the fact that scattering is commonly associated with judgment; thus we would not expect the primaeval *blessing* to include a command to scatter. It was concluded, therefore, that the Babelites are not disobeying the command to fill the earth when they say, 'otherwise we shall be scattered abroad'. The question still needs to be considered, however, whether YHWH's scattering the Babelites does, in any sense, ensure that the primaeval blessing is fulfilled.

53. Ezek. 34.6.
54. Deut. 4.27.
55. Jer. 23.2; cf. Isa. 11.12 where נפץ is in parallel with נדח.
56. Ezek. 11.16.
57. Ezek. 12.15; 20.23; 22.15; 29.12, etc.
58. Gen. 49.7.

Chapter 3

DOES YHWH'S SCATTERING NOAH'S DESCENDANTS FULFIL THE PRIMAEVAL BLESSING?

1. *Scholarly Views of YHWH's Scattering Noah's Descendants*

It is evident from Gen. 11.4 that the descendants of Noah do not want to be scattered, yet the Babel story indicates that this is precisely what happened: 'So the LORD scattered them abroad from there over the face of all the earth, and they left off building the city. Therefore it was called Babel, because there the LORD confused the language of all the earth; and from there the LORD scattered them abroad over the face of all the earth' (NRSV, Gen. 11.8-9). As has been noted, there is scholarly consensus that YHWH's scattering Noah's descendants ensures that the command to fill the earth is *fulfilled*.[1] It is argued that even though the people are disobeying the command, YHWH's intervention guarantees that it is carried out. Some scholars conclude, therefore, that YHWH actually *compels* the people to obey. Leupold maintains, for instance, that through YHWH's intervention, the Babelites 'must even obey His command, "replenish the earth", though they certainly never intended to do so'.[2] As with Leupold, Harland concludes that 'it may be appropriate not only to speak of God punishing in xi 8 and 9 but also compelling obedience, and ensuring that his will is obeyed'.[3] Mann similarly argues that those scattered at Babel are '*coerced* by God to fill the earth'.[4] This raises the question whether YHWH does, indeed, compel Noah's descendants to obey his command to fill the earth. Are there other examples where YHWH enforces his will upon humans? YHWH does not, it seems, take action to ensure that Adam and Eve obey his command given in Gen. 2.17 (cf. Gen. 3.6, 17). Some scholars have also observed that YHWH's judgments in the primaeval history have a negative effect on the realization of the blessing.[5] YHWH's destroying

---

1. Brueggemann, *Genesis*, pp. 98–99; Farmer, 'What Is "This" They Begin to Do?', pp. 17–28 (26); Garrett, *Rethinking Genesis*, p. 110; Kikawada, 'The Shape of Genesis 11.1-9', pp. 18–32 (32); Kikawada and Quinn, *Before Abraham Was*, p. 51; Mathews, *Genesis 1–11.26*, p. 467; Ross, *Creation and Blessing*, p. 247; *idem*, 'The Dispersion of the Nations', pp. 119–38 (119, 133); van Wolde, *Words Become Worlds*, pp. 102–103; Vawter, *On Genesis*, p. 157.

2. Leupold, *Genesis*, Vol. 1, p. 391.

3. Harland, 'The Sin of Babel', pp. 515–33 (531); cf. Kikawada and Quinn, *Before Abraham Was*, p. 71.

4. Mann, ' "All the Families of the Earth" ', pp. 341–53 (347).

5. Clines, *What Does Eve Do to Help?*, p. 52. Turner, *Announcements of Plot*, pp. 23, 41; *idem*, *Genesis*, p. 33.

humankind through the flood, save Noah and his family, further indicates that he does not always ensure that the primaeval commands are carried out. Are we to assume, then, that YHWH now compels obedience to his commands in the Babel story?

Scholars further argue that YHWH's scattering Noah's descendants restores the created order which God intended from the beginning. Mathews writes, for example, that 'it was this very onus of dispersal that enabled them to fulfill the divine dictate to "fill the earth" (Gen. 9.1, 7; 1.28), which chap. 10 shows occurred (vv. 5, 18, 20, 30-32)'.[6] Scattering, therefore, is understood to be in accordance with God's purposes expressed in Gen. 1.28 and 9.1. Even though the Babelites are seeking to thwart God's plan for his creation, their being scattered ensures that the divine intention for creation will be realized.[7] Kikawada thus concludes that the 'motif of scattering in our story would then fulfil the blessing given in Genesis 1, since the third element of that blessing is, "Be fruitful and multiply and *fill the earth*", (1.28). Dispersion may be the means of accomplishing this blessing'.[8] It is evident that according to these views, scattering is in accordance with the created order: it ensures that the divine blessing set forth in Gen. 1.28 and 9.1 is fulfilled.

Kikawada concludes, in fact, that YHWH's scattering the people is to be interpreted as a *blessing* rather than a punishment since it fulfils the primaeval commands.[9] As with Kikawada, Jacob also concludes that 'scattering' is not a punishment, but an unavoidable consequence of the primaeval commands.[10] If God's scattering the Babelites ensures that the primaeval blessing is fulfilled, then 'scattering' is not only to be interpreted positively in the context of Genesis 1–11, but can even be understood as an act of creation itself. Accordingly, van Wolde argues that when God scatters the people, he is 'executing something that belongs to creation and in that sense the story of the Tower of Babel concludes the history of creation'.[11] While it is true that the primaeval *blessing* 'belongs to creation', it is worth bearing in mind that 'scattering' (פוץ) does not. פוץ does not occur in any of the blessings pronounced upon the creatures (Gen. 1.22; cf. 8.17) or upon humans (Gen. 1.28; 9.1, 7; cf. Exod. 1.7). Neither does scattering constitute a divine or human blessing anywhere else in the Old Testament.

2. *Scattering and the Curses of the Mosaic Covenant*

We have noted that being scattered is, indeed, one of the curses of the Mosaic covenant.[12] Deuteronomy 28.64a states, for example, 'The LORD will *scatter*

6.　Mathews, *Genesis 1–11.26*, p. 469.

7.　Brueggemann, *Genesis*, pp. 98–99; Vawter, *On Genesis,* pp. 156–57.

8.　Kikawada, 'The Shape of Genesis 11.1-9', pp. 18–32 (32).

9.　Kikawada, 'The Shape of Genesis 11.1-9', pp. 18–32 (32 n. 22); cf. Farmer, 'What Is "This" They Begin to Do?', pp. 17–28 (26).

10.　Jacob, *Genesis*, p. 79 (= *Das erste Buch der Tora*, p. 301).

11.　Van Wolde, *Words Become Worlds*, pp. 102–103.

12.　For a discussion of scattering as one of the curses of the covenant, see P.M. Head, 'The Curse

(פוץ) you among all peoples, from one end of the earth to the other' (NRSV; cf. Deut. 4.27). The same idea is expressed by the verb זרה, 'scatter', in Lev. 26.33: 'And you I will *scatter* among the nations…your land shall be a desolation, and your cities a waste' (NRSV).[13] Accordingly, the prophets repeatedly speak of YHWH's judgment against Israel, that he would 'scatter them among the nations' because of their disobedience. In fact, more than one third of all the occurrences of פוץ are used in reference to the exile.[14] Thus 'scattering' clearly constitutes the divine judgment against Israel – it is not a blessing, neither does it fulfil any blessing. God's scattering Israel is, in fact, the means by which the divine judgment (i.e. curse) is meted out. Are we to assume, then, that YHWH's scattering the Babelites is to be interpreted as God's *blessing* or a fulfilment of his blessing, when scattering is one of the *curses* of the Mosaic covenant?

3. *Scattering and Judgment*

An examination of פוץ shows that the verb is not only used in reference to the exile, which clearly speaks of divine judgment, but also occurs in other contexts of judgment. For example, in Isa. 24.1 YHWH's judgment against the earth is proclaimed: 'Now the LORD is about to lay waste the earth and make it desolate, and he will twist its surface and *scatter* its inhabitants' (NRSV, Isa. 24.1).[15] It is important to note that more than one third of the occurrences of פוץ are used in the context of judgment – whether it be in reference to the exile[16] or to YHWH's judging nations.[17] פוץ also seems to have negative connotations when used in a military context, since it is those who have been *defeated* who usually scatter.[18] Moreover, it is not insignificant that when YHWH is the one who causes people to scatter (expressed by the hiphil form of פוץ), as he does in Gen. 11.8 and 11.9, it is commonly an act of *judgment*.[19] It cannot simply be assumed, therefore, that

of Covenant Reversal: Deuteronomy 28.58-68 and Israel's Exile', *Churchman* 111 (1997), pp. 218–26 (222–23). Similarly, YHWH's judgment against the nations is associated with the notion of curse (Isaiah 24.1-6).

13. זרה is frequently used in reference to the judgment of exile (e.g. Ps. 106.27; Jer. 31.10; Ezek. 5.2, 10, 12; 6.8; 12.15; 20.23; 22.15). Ezekiel uses זרה and פוץ in parallel when referring to YHWH's judgment against Israel (Ezek. 12.15; 20.23; 22.15; 36.19) and against Egypt (Ezek. 29.12; 30.23, 26).

14. Deut. 4.27; 28.64; 30.3; Neh. 1.8; Jer. 9.16 [15]; 13.24; 18.17; 30.11; Ezek. 11.16, 17; 12.15; 20.23, 34, 41; 22.15; 28.25; 34.12; 36.19. We have included prophetic texts which use פוץ to denote the scattering of God's 'sheep' since this is a metaphor for the exile (e.g. Jer. 10.21; 23.1, 2; Ezek. 34.5 [2×], 6, 12).

15. Cf. Ezek. 29.12, 13; 30.23, 26.

16. Deut. 4.27; 28.64; 30.3; Neh. 1.8; Jer. 9.16 [15]; 10.21; 13.24; 23.1, 2; 30.11; 40.15; Ezek. 11.16, 17; 12.15; 20.23, 34, 41; 22.15; 28.25; 29.13; 34.5, 6, 12, 21; 36.19; 46.18; Zeph. 3.10. As noted above, זרה is commonly used to refer to the exile.

17. Isa. 24.1; Ezek. 29.12, 13; 30.23, 26. זרה is also used in reference to God's judging nations (e.g. Jer. 49.32, 36; Ezek. 29.12; 30.23, 26).

18. Num. 10.35; 1 Sam. 11.11; 2 Sam. 22.15; 1 Kgs. 22.17; 2 Kgs. 25.5; 2 Chron. 18.16; Pss. 18.14 [15]; 68.1 [2]; 144.6; Jer. 52.8; Hab. 3.14; Zech. 13.7.

19. Deut. 4.27; 28.64; 30.3; Neh. 1.8; Isa. 24.1; Jer. 9.16 [15]; 13.24; 18.17; 30.11; Ezek. 11.16;

when YHWH scatters the Babelites, this is to be understood as the divine *bless-ing*. Neither can we conclude that the primaeval blessing is *fulfilled* through the scattering of Noah's descendants.

a. *Jacob's 'Scattering' Simeon and Levi in Genesis 49.7*

That scattering is not to be identified with the divine blessing is further suggested in Genesis 49 which describes Jacob's death-bed blessing on his sons. Genesis 49.7 is important as it marks the only occurrence of פוץ in Genesis outside the primaeval history. While Jacob's last words in Genesis 49 are referred to as his 'blessing' (49.28), Wenham rightly observes that the 'blessing' of Jacob contains curses as well as blessings,[20] noting that there are curses on Reuben, Simeon and Levi.[21] In v. 7 Jacob pronounces judgment against Simeon and Levi because of their massacring the men of Shechem: 'Cursed be their anger, for it is fierce, and their wrath, for it is cruel! I will divide them in Jacob, and *scatter* them in Israel' (NRSV, Gen. 49.7; cf. Gen. 34). Scholars are in agreement that Jacob's announce-ment, that he will *scatter* Simeon and Levi, is a word of judgment against them.[22] Hamilton has commented on the verb פוץ in Gen. 49.7, noting that it is 'fre-quently used in the Old Testament to describe the dispersal of Israel among the nations (Deut. 4.27; 28.64; Jer. 9.15; Ezek. 11.16; 12.15; 20.23; 22.15; 36.19 [all *pûṣ* in the hiphil followed by *b^e*])'.[23] He further notes that 'the verb was used in Gen. 11.4 (qal), 9 (hiphil), for the dispersal of the tower builders'.[24] If Jacob's scat-tering Simeon and Levi is a word of *judgment*, are we to assume, then, that scatter-ing in the primaeval history constitutes God's creational *blessing*? An examination of Gen. 49.7 and how it may relate to our understanding of the scattering motif in the Babel story is notably absent from discussions of Gen. 11.1-9. If Gen. 49.7 is included in the discussion, the question may well be raised whether YHWH's scattering the Babelites would be perceived in such a positive light as is supposed by a number of scholars.

4. *Lack of Attention to the Language of 'Scattering'*

It is not insignificant that a number of scholars, who argue that scattering is *not* an act of judgment but God's blessing, give no attention to the meaning of פוץ. Van Wolde, for example, who maintains that YHWH's scattering the Babelites

12.15; 20.23; 22.15; 29.12; 30.23, 26; 36.19. The hiphil form of פוץ is used in each of these texts, as it is in Gen. 11.8 and 11.9.

20. G.J. Wenham, *Genesis 16–50* (WBC; Dallas: Word Books, 1994), p. 468; cf. V.P. Hamilton, *The Book of Genesis: Chapters 18–50* (NICOT; Grand Rapids: Eerdmans, 1995), p. 653.

21. Wenham, *Genesis 16–50*, p. 470. He notes that the curse pronounced on their anger is a curse on the people who displayed this anger (p. 475).

22. H. Gunkel, *Genesis* (from the 9th German Impression, 1977 = 3rd edn, 1910; trans. M.E. Biddle; Macon: Mercer University Press, 1997), p. 455; Hamilton, *Genesis 18–50*, pp. 651–52; von Rad, *Genesis*, p. 424 (= *Das erste Buch Mose*, p. 348); Wenham, *Genesis 16–50*, p. 475.

23. Hamilton, *Genesis 18–50*, p. 652.

24. Hamilton, *Genesis 18–50*, p. 652, n. 17.

restores the created order, devotes a whole chapter to the Babel story.[25] Yet she does not discuss in any way the meaning of פוץ or the context in which it occurs. Instead, she simply translates פוץ by 'disperse', and maintains that the dispersion is not presented as a punishment.[26] Van Wolde seems to have avoided the terms 'scatter, scatter abroad' (cf. NRSV, NIV, NASB, KJV) in her discussion of the Babel story since they have negative connotations, whereas 'disperse' does not. As with van Wolde, Kikawada also concludes that YHWH's scattering the Babelites is not to be understood as a punishment, but a blessing.[27] Yet he does not discuss in any way the meaning of פוץ or the context in which it occurs. If, however, the meaning of פוץ and its context are taken into consideration, one would not simply assume that scattering is God's blessing in the Babel story.

5. *Is Scattering to be Understood Positively because of the Positive* Context?

A number of scholars *have* acknowledged that פוץ can have negative connotations. However, they argue that the verb is being used *positively* in Gen. 11.1-9. Brueggemann, for example, remarks on פוץ:

> Now there is no doubt that in some contexts 'scatter' refers to exile and is a negative term (Ezek. 11.17; 20.34, 41; 28.25). But here another denotation must be considered. Especially in chapter 10, as we have seen that 'spreading abroad' (v. 32) is blessed, sanctioned, and willed by Yahweh. It is part of God's plan for creation and the fulfillment of the mandate of 1.28.[28]

This view is reiterated by Harland who notes that פוץ 'can be used in a negative sense in Ezek. xi 17, xx 34, 41 and xxviii 25, but can also be employed positively as in Gen. x 18. In x 32, where the root *prd* is used, this spreading abroad is willed by God and fulfils the aim of i 28. Consequently fear of scattering is resistance to the purpose of God'.[29] Turner writes along similar lines:

> While the verb 'to scatter' (*pûṣ*) used in 11.4, 8, 9 can have negative connotations, e.g. Ezek. 11.17; 20.34, 41; 28.25, when used within the context of Gen. 1–11 it expresses the positive aspect of God's command 'to fill' the earth. In fact the verb has been used with these positive connotations in 10.18, 'Afterwards the families of the Canaanites spread abroad' (*nāpāsû*).[30]

This raises the question whether the *context* is as 'positive' as these scholars claim. Support for this supposed positive view is found in Gen. 9.19 (נפץ), 10.18 (פוץ), and 10.5 (פרד) and 10.32 (פרד). These texts deserve closer examination.[31]

---

25. Van Wolde, *Words Become Worlds*, pp. 84–109.
26. Van Wolde, *Words Become Worlds*, p. 102.
27. Kikawada, 'The Shape of Genesis 11.1-9', pp. 18–32 (32 n. 22).
28. Brueggemann, *Genesis*, p. 98.
29. Harland, 'The Sin of Babel', pp. 515–33 (528).
30. Turner, *Announcements of Plot*, p. 32. Hamilton also notes that the dispersal is positive in 9.19 and 10.18 (*Genesis 1–17*, p. 356, n. 19).
31. פרד will be discussed in the following chapter.

a. *Does פוץ in Genesis 9.19 Have 'Positive' Connotations?*

To begin with, it has been noted that the dispersion in Gen. 9.19 is usually interpreted in a positive light. Anderson maintains, for example, that 'this transitional passage has no suggestion of scattering being an act of divine judgment, as in the Babel story (see also Isa. 33.3)'.[32] He argues that פוץ is positive in 9.19 since it fulfils the blessing of 9.1. It is important to note, however, that even though Anderson makes reference to 'scattering' in 9.19, he evidently understands that פוץ has the sense of human increase and population expansion. He first translates Gen. 9.19b as, 'and from them the whole earth was scattered'.[33] He then translates 9.19 as, 'these three sons of Noah – yet from them the whole earth was repopulated',[34] arguing that this is the sense of the verb. It has been noted, however, that this meaning cannot be sustained in any other text in which פוץ occurs. Anderson's translation of 9.19 establishes an artificial reading of this verse, thereby portraying the dispersal in a positive light. As has been noted, we have suggested that the translation 'scatter' or 'scatter abroad' is preferable as it shows the connection between 9.19 and the ensuing scattering motif (Gen. 10.18; 11.4, 8, 9). Given that scattering is God's judgment in the Babel story, as Anderson himself concurs, and that 9.19 introduces the scattering motif, it may well be the case that 9.19 has ominous overtones.

As with Anderson, Waltke maintains that the descendants of Noah are multiplying under God's blessing in the Table of Nations, whereas they are scattered under God's wrath in the Babel story.[35] Accordingly, the dispersion is positive in Gen. 10.1-32, but negative in 11.1-9. Waltke differs from Anderson, however, in his translation of פוץ by the verb 'scatter' (cf. NIV). He then clarifies how he understands פוץ in 9.19: '"scattering" entails that God blesses them and makes them fruitful'.[36] According to Waltke, scattering is positive in 9.19 because it entails the divine blessing. Yet he later discusses the import of the scattering verb, פור, in Gen. 10.18, noting that the narrator 'reserves the key word for judgment, "scattered" (*pûṣ*), for the curse-laden Canaanites (10.18; 11.4, 8-9)'.[37] If פור is identified as the 'key word for judgment' in Genesis 10-11, are we to assume, then, that the cognate verb, פוץ, 'scatter', entails God's *blessing* in 9.19? These supposed different connotations of פוץ and פור – positive in 9.19 and negative in 10.18; 11.1-9 – cannot be defended on the basis of different authors, since Waltke attributes both texts to the one author.[38] It could be argued, therefore, that 'scattering' has negative connotations in 9.19, as it does in Genesis 10-11.

32. Anderson, 'The Tower of Babel', pp. 165–78 (176).
33. Anderson, 'The Tower of Babel', pp. 165–78 (175).
34. Anderson, 'The Tower of Babel', pp. 165–78 (176). Given that the translation 'repopulate' does not appear in major English translations (cf. 'peopled', NRSV; 'populated', NASB), this seems to reflect Anderson's own translation.
35. Waltke, *Genesis*, pp. 161–62.
36. Waltke, *Genesis*, p. 147.
37. Waltke, *Genesis*, p. 163.
38. Waltke, *Genesis*, pp. 24–28.

b. *Is נפץ in Genesis 9.19 a* Leitwort?

Anderson has suggested that the repetition of the names of Noah's three sons in Gen. 9.19 (they are already mentioned in v. 18) has a special function: 'namely, *resumption* – harking back to the beginning of the story for the purpose of carrying the narrative forward'.[39] Anderson notes that the resumptive verse includes the additional remark that 'yet from these the whole earth was repopulated', and suggests that the resumption advances the story by underscoring the human increase and population expansion that took place in accordance with 9.1. But if נפץ means 'scatter', the function of v.19 is to introduce the scattering motif that is prominent in Gen. 10-11 (cf. פוץ: Gen. 10.18; 11.4, 8, 9)? Since scattering is YHWH's judgment in 11.1-9, it seems unlikely that it would be positive in 9.19. In fact, we have suggested that it may even have negative connotations. Given that the scattering motif is first introduced in 9.19, נפץ could even be identified as a *Leitwort*.

Waltke has noted that the literary device of a *Leitwort*, 'lead word' or 'key word', is an important feature in Genesis.[40] He cites the word ציד, 'game', in Gen. 25.28 as an example, noting that it reads, literally, 'Isaac loved Esau because of the *game in his mouth*' (ציד בפיו). Waltke further observes that, two chapters later, the narrator employs the word ציד eight times in the story of Isaac's blessing on Jacob.[41] Waltke concludes, therefore, that the narrator's employment of ציד in Gen. 25.28 'foreshadows Isaac's defining moment of failure' in Genesis 27.[42] We may return to Waltke's observation regarding פוץ in Gen. 10.18 at this point, that the narrator has reserved the key word for judgment, פוץ, for the 'curse-laden Canaanites (10.18; 11.4, 8-9)'.[43] He concludes, in fact, that פוץ in 10.18 'foreshadows the punitive judgment' on the tower builders.[44] If נפץ in 9.19 is identified as a *Leitwort*, is it not possible that the Babel judgment is already foreshadowed in 9.19?

Alter has also commented on the importance of verbal repetition (*Leitwort*) and notes that the repetition of the word-root 'can often intensify the dynamic action of the repetition'.[45] He continues that 'word-motifs' in larger narrative units are used to 'sustain a thematic development and to establish instructive connections between seemingly disparate episodes'.[46] This is in accordance with our view that נפץ in Gen. 9.19 is a *Leitwort* which introduces the scattering motif. Alter reiterates the import of verbal repetition in the introduction to his translation of Genesis, concluding that the 'translator's task, then, is to mirror the repetitions as

---

39. Anderson, 'The Tower of Babel', pp. 165–78 (176).
40. Waltke, *Genesis*, p. 34; cf. M. Buber, 'Leitwort Style in Pentateuch Narrative', in M. Buber and F. Rosenzweig (eds.), *Scripture and Translation* (trans. L. Rosenwald and E. Fox; Bloomington and Indianapolis: Indiana University Press, 1994), pp. 114–28.
41. Gen. 27.3, 5, 7, 19, 25, 30, 31, 33.
42. Waltke, *Genesis*, p. 34.
43. Waltke, *Genesis*, p. 163.
44. Waltke, *Genesis*, p. 171.
45. R. Alter, *The Art of Biblical Narrative* (New York: Basic Books, 1981), p. 93.
46. Alter, *The Art of Biblical Narrative*, p. 94.

much as feasible'[47] and that 'a translation that respects the literary precision of the biblical story...cannot be free to translate a word here one way and there another, for the sake of variety or for the sake of context'.[48] In light of Alter's comments, his *different* translations of the scattering verb in Genesis 9–11[49] are somewhat surprising:

Gen. 9.19b   and from these three the whole earth *spread out* (נפץ)
Gen. 10.18   Afterward the clans of the Canaanite *spread out* (פוץ)
Gen. 11.4   lest we *be scattered* (פוץ) over all the earth
Gen. 11.8   And the LORD *scattered* (פוץ) them from there
Gen. 11.9   And from there the LORD *scattered* (פוץ) them

Given Alter's view, that a translator is not free to translate a word in different ways for the sake of variety or the sake of context, we may raise the question why he has translated נפץ in 9.19 and the cognate verb פוץ in 10.18 as 'spread out', while translating פוץ in the following chapter as 'scatter'. Assuming that he has not used different terms for the sake of variety, it would appear that he has chosen different verbs for the sake of *context*. Given that scholars assume that scattering is positive in Genesis 9–10, but negative in the Babel story, it would appear that the prevailing view of the dispersal has influenced Alter's translation. Alter has not only failed to represent the verbal repetitions in these chapters, but has also chosen words that convey a *positive* meaning in Gen. 9.19 and 10.18, while maintaining a *negative* meaning in the Babel story. If the verbal repetitions present in the Hebrew text *are* retained in English translations, then 9.19 would not be seen in such a positive light, as is commonly the case. We suggest that scattering does not entail God's blessing in 9.19. Rather, it already has ominous overtones since it foreshadows the divine judgment. Given that 9.19 may well have negative connotations, this verse does not support the view that the *context* of the Babel story is positive, as some scholars suppose.

c. *Does* פוץ *in Genesis 10.18 Have 'Positive' Connotations?*

As has been noted, פוץ in Gen. 10.18 is also cited by a number of scholars to support a positive view of the dispersal. Harland maintains, for example, that while פוץ can be used in a negative sense, it is being used positively in 10.18.[50] Westermann also argues that פוץ in 10.18 is a 'neutral idea with no judgment value attached and describes the natural process of expansion of a group that began with a family and grows from one generation to another'.[51] Similarly, Turner maintains that although פוץ can have negative connotations, the verb 'has been used with these positive connotations in 10.18'.[52] It is noteworthy that Turner

---

47. Alter, *Genesis*, p. xxvii.
48. Alter, *Genesis*, p. xxix.
49. Alter, *Genesis*, pp. 40, 43, 45, 46.
50. Harland, 'The Sin of Babel', pp. 515–33 (528).
51. Westermann, *Genesis 1–11*, p. 523 (= *Genesis*, Bd. I, p. 698).
52. Turner, *Announcements of Plot*, p. 32; cf. Anderson, 'The Tower of Babel', pp. 165–78 (176); Brueggemann, *Genesis*, p. 98; Hamilton, *Genesis 1–17*, p. 356, n. 19; Harland, 'The Sin of Babel', pp. 515–33 (528).

then cites the NRSV translation of v. 18, 'Afterwards the families of the Canaanites spread abroad', to support his interpretation (cf. NASB). As with Westermann and Alter, the NRSV translates פוץ by 'spread abroad' in 10.18 (cf. NASB), but by 'scatter abroad' in the Babel story. The NRSV translation of the scattering verb in Genesis 9–11 is outlined as follows:

Gen. 9.19b	and from these the whole earth *was peopled* (נפץ)
Gen. 10.18b	Afterwards the families of the Canaanites *spread abroad* (פוץ)
Gen. 11.4b	otherwise we shall *be scattered abroad* (פוץ)
Gen. 11.8a	So the LORD *scattered* (פוץ) them *abroad* from there
Gen. 11.9b	and from there the LORD *scattered* (פוץ) them *abroad*

Given that scholars are in agreement that פוץ (and its related form נפץ) represents a motif that runs through Genesis 9–11, why has פוץ been translated by 'spread abroad' in 10.18, but by 'scatter abroad' in 11.1-9? It is important to note that these supposed different connotations of נפץ and פוץ cannot be defended on source-critical grounds, since these texts are usually attributed to J. It seems to be the case, therefore, that the translations 'was peopled' (9.19) and 'spread abroad' (10.18) have been chosen because they portray the dispersion in a *positive* light, even though there is no indication in the Hebrew text that נפץ in 9.19 and פוץ in 10.18 have connotations different from פוץ in the Babel story. Preference for a neutral term seems to have influenced the translation of פוץ in Gen. 10.18. These two *different* translations of פוץ – as 'spread abroad' in 10.18, but 'scatter abroad' in 11.1-9 – provide support for the view that the dispersal is positive in Gen. 10.1-32 but negative in 11.1-9, even though the Hebrew text does not. As has been noted, the Septuagint uses the *same* verb, διασπείρω, 'scatter, disperse', to translate both נפץ (9.19) and פוץ (10.18; 11.4, 8, 9). Similarly, Targums Onqelos and Pseudo-Jonathan employ the one Aramaic verb, בדר, 'scatter, strew'[53] for נפץ (9.19) and פוץ (10.18; 11.4, 8, 9). We suggest, therefore, that נפץ (9.19) and פוץ (10.18) be translated as 'scatter' or 'scatter abroad', in accordance with most English translations of פוץ in 11.1-9. Given that פוץ is commonly associated with judgment, and that it is negative in Gen. 11.1-9, the claim that פוץ is *positive* in Gen. 10.18 needs to be reconsidered.

It is noteworthy that פוץ is used with reference to the *Canaanites* in 10.18. Scholars usually assert that Gen. 10.1-32 is being viewed positively as the fulfilment of the primaeval blessing, yet it is worth bearing in mind that the Table of Nations does not follow immediately after the blessing in 9.1. Genesis 9.25-27 indicates that Canaan was cursed by Noah. In light of this, we may well question whether the judgment against Canaan is in some way alluded to in the ensuing genealogy.[54] Van Wolde suggests that the story of Noah's drinking 'results in a

---

53. Jastrow, *A Dictionary of the Targumim*, Vol. 1, p. 141.

54. Westermann argues that the cursing of Canaan is only to be understood in the context of the family; thus it does not have any negative implications with regard to the Canaanites (*Genesis 1–11*, pp. 490–92 [= *Genesis*, Bd. I, pp. 655–57). While not denying the family context of Gen. 9.25-27, this does not preclude a blessing or curse on an individual from having consequences for his progeny (e.g. Gen. 3.17; 5.29). The birth narrative of Jacob and Esau demonstrates the close association between individuals and the nations they represent (Gen. 25.23); cf. Brueggemann, *Genesis*, pp. 90–91.

difference in the evaluation of these three sons' and that 'this forms the preparation for the subsequent genealogy in 10.1-32, which describes the descendants of Noah's sons as the forefathers of many peoples on the earth'.[55] Similarly, Turner comments on Gen. 9.25-27, maintaining that in the Table of Nations the 'hierarchical relationships will potentially be played out'.[56] So in what way does Noah's cursing Canaan prepare the reader for the following genealogy? Does the judgment upon him influence how the Canaanites are portrayed in the Table? Mathews suggests that it does. He maintains that פוץ, 'scatter, disperse', in 10.18 anticipates the judgment of 11.1-9 and that there is an implied association between the Canaanites and the Babelites that 'echoes Noah's invocation against Canaan'.[57] A similar view is expressed by Wenham, who notes that although פוץ in Gen. 10.18 'is apparently used in a neutral, innocent sense, it may yet be foreshadowing the judgment to befall all mankind at Babel. The Canaanites are often viewed in the Pentateuch as *the* sinful nation who deserve God's wrath'.[58] It has been noted that Waltke similarly suggests that the 'key word for judgment' has been reserved for the 'curse-laden' Canaanites.[59] Given that Canaan has been cursed by his father in Gen. 9.25 and that פוץ has negative connotations in the Babel story, it is possible that פוץ is negative in 10.18. Since פוץ *could* have negative connotations in 10.18, it is not so evident that this verse provides support for a positive view of the dispersion. In short, Gen. 9.19 and 10.18 do not provide conclusive evidence that the dispersal is positive in these verses.

6. *YHWH's Scattering the Babelites and the Primaeval Blessing*

That YHWH's scattering the Babelites is not positive and does not fulfil the primaeval blessing is further suggested by examining the verb פוץ in more detail. A survey of פוץ shows that when YHWH causes people to scatter, it seems to result in their becoming *few* rather than many. Deuteronomy 4.27 states, for example, 'The LORD will scatter you among the peoples; only a few of you will be left among the nations where the LORD will lead you' (NRSV). Similarly, scattering is associated with becoming few in Deuteronomy 28: 'Although once you were as numerous as the stars in heaven, you shall be left few in number, because you did not obey the LORD your God... The LORD will scatter you among all the peoples...' (NRSV, Deut. 28.62, 64). P.M. Head has commented on the motif of 'numerical reversal' in Deuteronomy 28. He suggests that the exile would mean a reversal of the promise of fecundity given to Abraham and his seed.[60] If one of the results of Israel's being scattered was that they become *few*

---

55. Van Wolde, *Words Become Worlds*, pp. 108–109.
56. Turner, *Genesis*, p. 57.
57. Mathews, *Genesis 1–11.26*, p. 457.
58. Wenham, *Genesis 1–15*, p. 226.
59. Waltke, *Genesis*, p. 163.
60. Head, 'Covenant Reversal', pp. 218–26 (220–21). The idea of a 'remnant' may also point to this concept, since YHWH's scattering Israel resulted in their being few (i.e. a remnant). On the reversal of the covenant curses, see H.M. Wolf, 'The Transcendent Nature of Covenant Curse

in number, is it likely that the scattering of Noah's descendants would fulfil the primaeval blessing? A decrease in population through scattering is also suggested in Isaiah 24. In this context, YHWH announces his judgment on the nations: 'Now the Lord is about to lay waste the earth and make it desolate, and he will twist its surface and scatter its inhabitants... Therefore a curse devours the earth, and its inhabitants suffer for their guilt; therefore the inhabitants of the earth dwindled, and few people are left' (NRSV; Isa. 24.1, 6). Similarly, Ezekiel announces that YHWH would make the land of Egypt a desolation; their cities would be laid waste and the Egyptians would be scattered (Ezek. 29.12). Egypt would thus be 'uninhabited' for forty years (Ezek. 29.11). Since scattering seems to result in populations being depleted rather than increasing, are we to assume that the injunction to 'be fruitful and multiply, and fill the earth' will be fulfilled through YHWH's scattering the Babelites? Seybold has suggested that YHWH's action in the Babel story may even foresee a thinning out of humankind.[61] Even Jacob acknowledges that when people are scattered among nations, this usually leads to their decreasing in number and even to their perishing – although he argues that this type of scattering is not in view in Gen. 11.1-9.[62] Given that scattering causes a place to become empty of people, that is, a wasteland, a place with no human beings, one could argue – contrary to Jacob – that YHWH's scattering Noah's descendants does have an *adverse* effect on the realization of the primaeval blessing. The negative results of 'scattering' in the *exile* have been underscored by Brueggemann.

a. *The Babel Story and the Exile*
Brueggemann has elaborated on the adverse effect of scattering in the *exile*. He notes that

> Israel is 'scattered' (*pûṣ*), a new term in Israel's Yahwistic vocabulary, of which
> Yahweh is characteristically the active subject. Israel is scattered to the winds, away
> from the promised place, and away from its resources for identity. Exile is indeed the
> complete defeat, loss, and forfeiture of life with Yahweh.[63]

According to Brueggemann, scattering is *negative* in the exile since it constitutes God's judgment, but *positive* in the primaeval history since it fulfils the priestly blessing. It is important to note, however, that, according to Brueggemann, the

Reversals', in A. Gileadi (ed.), *Israel's Apostasy and Restoration: Essays in Honor of Roland K. Harrison* (Michigan: Baker Book House, 1988), pp. 319–25.

61. K. Seybold, 'Der Turmbau zu Babel: Zur Entstehung von Genesis XI 1-9', *VT* 26 (1976), pp. 453–79 (475).

62. Jacob maintains that the dispersion of humankind in Gen. 11.1-9 is to be distinguished from the dispersion of a people among nations, which usually has an adverse effect on people. He argues that the dispersion in the primaeval history is to be interpreted positively because it fulfils the primaeval blessing (*Das erste Buch der Tora*, p. 301). We have raised the question, however, whether YHWH's scattering the Babelites in 11.1-9 does, indeed, fulfil the blessing of 9.1.

63. W. Brueggemann, *Theology of the Old Testament: Testimony, Dispute, Advocacy* (Minneapolis: Fortress Press, 1997), p. 435.

priestly message was for the *exilic* community.[64] Clines similarly suggests that the primaeval history 'is not just about the nations, nor about God and man, but is heard in exile as a story of God and Israel. The dispersion of the nations (ch. 11) is Israel's own diaspora'.[65] An important question arises, therefore. Would the people in exile, who have themselves been 'scattered' by God as a result of his judgment,[66] interpret God's 'scattering' Noah's descendants as his creational *blessing*? Given that scattering has a negative effect on Israel in the exile, as the complete defeat, loss, and forfeiture of life with YHWH, from the time of the exile onwards, scattering would resound with associations of YHWH's judgment.[67] We conclude, therefore, that the scattering motif in the primaeval history is not positive. Neither does it fulfil the primaeval blessing. On the contrary, we maintain that YHWH's scattering Noah's descendants, which is foreshadowed in 9.19, is negative in the Babel story and that it may even have an adverse effect on the realization of the blessing. We suggest, therefore, that נפץ and פוץ in Genesis 9–11 should be translated by 'scatter' rather than 'disperse' (ESV), since the language of 'scattering' has negative connotations and accords with other texts where 'scattering' is used in the context of judgment.

7. *Conclusion*

It is commonly argued by scholars that YHWH's scattering Noah's descendants in Gen. 11.1-9 ensures that the command to 'fill the earth' is fulfilled. Some scholars maintain, therefore, that YHWH's scattering the people is to be understood as a *blessing* or an act of creation. An examination of פוץ has shown, however, that 'scattering' is commonly associated with judgment and is one of the curses of the Mosaic covenant. It was noted that, even within the book of Genesis, פוץ is associated with judgment (Gen. 49.7). Yet some scholars maintain that scattering is positive in Gen. 11.1-9 because of the positive *context*. Four verses are cited to support this view: Gen. 9.19 (נפץ), 10.18 (פוץ), 10.5 (פרד) and 10.32 (פרד).[68] It was observed that, while a positive view of Gen. 9.19 is suggested by English translations ('people', 'populate'), these translations do not accurately reflect the Hebrew text. If נפץ is translated by 'scatter', which we have argued is a preferable translation, then it is not so evident that Gen. 9.19 is positive. On the contrary, we have suggested that נפץ in 9.19 is a *Leitwort* which already has ominous overtones, foreshadowing the Babel judgment. It was further noted that English translations of פוץ in Gen. 10.18 ('spread out', 'spread abroad') affirm this supposed 'positive' view of the dispersal, but the Hebrew text does not. It was suggested that the 'scattering' of the Canaanites may well have negative connotations (cf. Gen. 9.25); thus Gen. 10.18 cannot be used to support a positive reading of 'scattering'. We

---

64. Brueggemann, 'The Kerygma of the Priestly Writers', pp. 397–414 (397–98, 412).

65. Clines, 'Theme in Genesis 1–11', pp. 483–507 (505).

66. As has been noted, more than one third of the occurrences of פוץ are used in reference to the exile.

67. See also Wolf, 'Covenant Curse Reversals', pp. 319–325 (323–24).

68. As has been noted, פרד will be examined in the following chapter.

maintain, therefore, that there is no conclusive evidence to support a positive view of the dispersal in 9.19 and 10.18. Since 'scattering' is commonly associated with judgment, which is particularly evident in the exile, it seems unlikely that scattering would be perceived positively in the Babel story, as some scholars suppose. Thus we conclude that נָפַץ and פּוּץ should be translated by 'scatter' rather than 'disperse' (ESV).

We have discussed 9.19 and 10.18 in detail, but two verses still need to be examined. Scholars argue that the 'spreading out' of the nations in Gen. 10.5 and 10.32 marks the fulfilment of the primaeval blessing after the flood. Not surprisingly, these verses are understood to support a positive view of the dispersal. The question still remains, therefore, whether the 'spreading out' of Noah's descendants does, indeed, indicate that the primaeval blessing has been fulfilled.

Chapter 4

IS THE PRIMAEVAL BLESSING FULFILLED IN THE TABLE OF NATIONS?

1. *Scholarly Views of the Primaeval Blessing in Relation to the Table*

There is widespread scholarly agreement that the primaeval blessing is fulfilled in the Table of Nations.[1] It is worth underscoring at the outset, however, that the question is not whether the blessing is in the *process* of being realized in the Table, which is clearly the case since Noah's descendants are multiplying, but whether the blessing is *fulfilled* in Gen. 10.1-32. Scholars commonly answer in the affirmative and cite three verses to support this view:

> From these the coastland peoples *spread* (פרד). These are the descendants of Japheth in their lands, with their own language, by their families, in their nations (NRSV, Gen. 10.5).

> Afterwards the families of the Canaanites *spread abroad* (פוץ, NRSV, Gen. 10.18b).

> These are the families of Noah's sons, according to their genealogies, in their nations; and from these the nations *spread* abroad (פרד) on the earth after the flood (NRSV, Gen. 10.32).

The common element in these verses (according to English translations) is the verb 'spread abroad'. Scholars maintain that the 'spreading abroad' of Noah's descendants indicates that the primaeval commands are being carried out. Harland remarks on פרד in Gen. 10.32, for example, that 'this spreading abroad is willed by God and fulfils the aim of i 28'.[2] Several scholars argue that the placement of Gen. 10.1-32 *before* the Babel story indicates that the Table of Nations is being viewed positively as the fulfilment of the primaeval blessing.[3] This positive approach to Genesis 10 has implications for how the emergence of nations is interpreted. Anderson maintains, for instance, that ethnic diversity represented in the Table of Nations is not to be understood as the result of divine

---

1. Brueggemann, *Genesis*, pp. 93–94; Cassuto, *Genesis*, Vol. 2, p. 247; Clines, 'Theme in Genesis 1–11', pp. 483–507 (494); Hamilton, *Genesis 1–17*, pp. 330, 347; Jacob, *Genesis*, p. 75 (= *Das erste Buch der Tora*, p. 294); Nacpil, 'Between Promise and Fulfilment', pp. 166–81 (169); von Rad, *Genesis*, p. 144 (= *Das erste Buch Mose*, p. 109); Ross, *Creation and Blessing*, p. 221; Sarna, *Genesis*, p. 65; Smith, 'Structure and Purpose', pp. 307–19 (312–13); Vawter, *On Genesis*, p. 156; Wenham, *Story as Torah,* p. 36.

2. Harland, 'The Sin of Babel', pp. 515–33 (528); cf. Turner, *Announcements of Plot*, p. 29; Vawter, *On Genesis*, p. 156.

3. Clines, 'Theme in Genesis 1–11', pp. 483–507 (494); cf. Harland, 'The Sin of Babel', pp. 515–33 (532); Hamilton, *Genesis 1–17*, p. 347. See Chapter 6 for a discussion of the placement of Gen. 10.1-32 and 11.1-9.

judgment, but the 'fruit of the divine blessing given at the creation (1.28) and renewed in the new creation after the flood (9.1, 7)'.[4] The emergence of nations, therefore, is understood to mark the fulfilment of God's intention outlined in Gen. 1.28 and 9.1.[5] As has been noted, this interpretation is based on a positive appraisal of Gen. 10.1-32. What evidence is there to support the view that the primaeval blessing is *fulfilled* in the Table?

2. *Is Language from the Primaeval Blessing Used in the Table of Nations?*

It is worth noting that the verbs פרה, רבה and מלא (+ ארץ), used in the primaeval blessing (Gen. 9.1; cf. 1.28), are absent in Gen. 10.1-32. Thus we do not read that Noah's descendants 'were fruitful and multiplied, and filled the earth'. Instead, the verb פרד appears in Gen. 10.5 and 10.32 and פוץ in 10.18. We may conclude, therefore, that no *direct* verbal link has been made between the blessing of Gen. 9.1 and the Table of Nations.[6] Furthermore, it is evident from other texts in Genesis that the final author *could* have established a direct literary relationship. For example, the verbs פרה and רבה appear together fifteen times in the Old Testament[7] and are most commonly applied to Abraham's progeny.[8] Similarly, the verb ברך, which occurs in Gen. 1.28 and 9.1, is frequently associated with Abraham and his seed.[9] Language from the primaeval blessing is notably absent, however, in the Table of Nations and in its introduction at 9.19. We can conclude, therefore, that the final author has not established any formal link between the blessing of 9.1 and the dispersal of the nations in 10.1-32. The question may thus be raised concerning the language which *is* used, whether it indicates that the blessing of 9.1 is in any sense fulfilled in the Table of Nations.

To begin with, we have already discussed Gen. 10.18 in detail, concluding that פוץ should be translated as 'scatter' rather than 'spread abroad', in accordance with translations of פוץ in the Babel story. It was noted that since Noah's descendants were not commanded to *scatter*, one cannot simply assume that the intention of creation comes to fulfilment in v. 18. It was further suggested that 10.18 may even have negative connotations, foreshadowing the Babel judgment. Thus it was concluded that 10.18 does not provide evidence for a 'positive' view of the

---

4.   Anderson, 'The Tower of Babel', pp. 165–78 (176); cf. Cassuto, *Genesis,* Vol. 2, p. 175; Harland, 'The Sin of Babel', pp. 515–33 (532).

5.   Mathews, *Genesis 1–11.26*, p. 429; Nacpil, 'Between Promise and Fulfilment', pp. 166–81 (169).

6.   We have argued that, while פוץ in 10.18 is associated with the scattering motif (9.19; 11.4, 8, 9), it is not to be identified with the command to fill the earth in 9.1 (cf. Chapter 2).

7.   Gen. 1.22, 28; 8.17; 9.1, 7; 17.20; 28.3; 35.11; 47.27; 48.4; Exod. 1.7; Lev. 26.9; Jer. 3.16; 23.3; Ezek. 36.11.

8.   E.g. פרה: Abraham (Gen. 17.6), Isaac (Gen. 26.22) and Joseph (Gen. 41.52; 49.22); רבה: Sarah (Gen. 16.10), Abraham (Gen. 17.2; 22.17; 26.4), Isaac (Gen. 26.24) and Israel (Gen. 47.27).

9.   E.g. Abraham (Gen. 12.2, 3; 18.18; 22.17, 18; 24.1; 24.35), Sarah (Gen. 17.16), Ishmael (Gen. 17.20); Isaac (Gen. 25.11; 26.3, 4, 12, 24, 29) and Jacob/Israel (Gen. 27.29, 33; 28.3, 14; 30.27; 32.26, etc.).

dispersal. The question remains, however, whether Gen. 10.5 and 10.32 indicate that the primaeval blessing has been fulfilled.

3. *The Meaning of* פרד *in Genesis 10.5 and 10.32*

The 'spreading abroad' of Noah's descendants is central to the aforementioned interpretation. That פרד conveys the idea of spreading abroad is reflected in the NIV translation ('spread out', Gen. 10.5, 32) and the NRSV/ESV translation ('spread', Gen. 10.5; 'spread abroad', Gen. 10.32). This idea that Noah's descendants were 'spreading out' is also reflected in recent commentaries and monographs.[10] Alternative translations of פרד, however, include: 'branched out',[11] 'were separated'[12] (NASB, NEB) and 'divided'[13] (KJV, JB). The NASB translation reads, for example:

> From these the coastlands of the nations *were separated* into their lands, every one according to his language, according to their families, into their nations (10.5).

> These are the families of the sons of Noah, according to their genealogies, by their nations; and out of these the nations *were separated* on the earth after the flood (10.32).

It is noteworthy that scholars do not argue that the 'separation' (NASB) or 'division' (KJV) of Noah's descendants marks the fulfilment of the primaeval blessing. Rather, it is their 'spreading abroad' (NRSV) which fulfils it. This view, therefore, is based primarily on the NRSV ('spread, spread abroad') and NIV translations ('spread out'), not on the NASB ('separate') or KJV translations ('divide').

---

10. D. Atkinson, *The Message of Genesis 1–11* (The Bible Speaks Today; Leicester: Inter-Varsity Press, 1990), p. 175; Brueggemann, *Genesis*, p. 98; Mathews, *Genesis 1–11.26*, pp. 439, 442, 465; Ross, *Creation and Blessing*, pp. 226–27; J. Sailhamer, *The Pentateuch as Narrative* (Library of Biblical Interpretation; Grand Rapids: Zondervan, 1992), pp. 130, 134; S. Tengström, *Die Toledot-formel und die literarische Struktur der priesterlichen Erweiterungsschicht im Pentateuch* (Lund: Gleerup, 1981), p. 23; Turner, *Announcements of Plot*, p. 32; Waltke, *Genesis*, pp. 168, 174.

11. Hamilton, *Genesis 1–17*, p. 343; Holzinger, *Genesis*, p. 93; Speiser, *Genesis*, pp. 64–65; Wenham, *Genesis 1–15*, p. 211. The RSV has been used in the English version of von Rad's commentary; hence the verbs 'spread' (10.5) and 'spread abroad' (10.32) appear in it (*Genesis*, p. 139). However, the idea of 'branching out' is reflected in the *German* edition of von Rad's commentary: Gen. 10.5, 'Von diesen zweigten sich die Inseln der Völker ab', and 10.32b, 'und von ihnen haben sich die Völker auf der Erde nach der Flut verzweigt' (*Das erste Buch Mose*, p. 105). Similarly, Westermann translates פרד by '(sich) abzweigen' (10.5), 'branch, branch off', and by '(sich) verzweigen' (10.32), 'branch' (*Genesis*, Bd. I, pp. 663, 665), whereas the English translation of his commentary cites the RSV rendering, 'spread' (*Genesis 1–11*, pp. 496–97).

12. Dillmann, *Genesis*, Vol. 1, p. 338; W. Paul, *The Hebrew Text of the Book of Genesis* (Edinburgh: W. Blackwood & Sons, 1852), p. 92; Ross, *Creation and Blessing*, pp. 226–27.

13. Alford, *The Book of Genesis*, pp. 45, 52; B.J. Bacon, *Genesis of Genesis* (Hartford: Student Publ. Co., 1893), pp. 116, 118; J. Calvin, *A Commentary on Genesis* (ed. and trans. J. King; Edinburgh: Banner of Truth, 1965 [1554]) pp. 311–12; Keil and Delitzsch, *The Pentateuch*, p. 164; Driver, *Genesis*, pp. 117, 132; J.P. Lange, *A Commentary on the Holy Scriptures: Genesis* (trans. P. Schaff; Grand Rapids: Zondervan, 1864), pp. 344–45; F. Lenormant, *The Book of Genesis* (London: Longmans, Green & Co., 1886), pp. 33, 35; M. Luther, *Luther's Commentary on Genesis*, Vol. 1 (trans. J.T. Mueller; Grand Rapids, Zondervan, 1958), pp. 180, 188; Griffith Thomas, *Genesis*, p. 100.

That there are *different* translations of פרד raises a question regarding the mean-ing of the verb. Does פרד mean 'spread out' or 'separate, divide'?

The verb פרד occurs another six times in Genesis,[14] once more in the Penta-teuch (Deut. 32.8), and a further seventeen times in the Old Testament.[15] The niphal form of פרד is first used in Gen. 2.10 with reference to the river that flowed from Eden and is translated in the NRSV by 'divides' (cf. NASB), in the NIV by 'was separated', and in the KJV by 'was parted'. The niphal form of פרד commonly refers to a person's separating from (מן) another.[16] For example, פרד occurs on three occasions in reference to Lot's separating from Abram:

> 'Is not the whole land before you? *Separate* yourself *from* me. If you take the left hand, then I will go to the right; or if you take the right hand, then I will go to the left'... So Lot chose for himself all the plain of the Jordan, and Lot journeyed east-wards; thus they *separated* from each other... The LORD said to Abram, after Lot had *separated from* him, ... (NRSV, Gen. 13.9, 11, 14a).

It is worth noting that, while the separation of two people could require moving to different geographical locations, as is the case with Lot (cf. Judg. 4.11), פרד refers to the act of separation, that is, a person separating *from* another. Accord-ingly, the niphal form of פרד is usually translated by verbs such as 'separate', 'part company', and 'divide'.[17] Leaving aside Genesis 10 for a moment, there is only one occasion in the Old Testament where the NRSV and NIV translate פרד by 'spread out' (Ezek. 1.11).[18] Given that פרד usually denotes separation or division, we may enquire why the NRSV and NIV have translated the verb as 'spread, spread abroad' (NRSV) and 'spread out' (NIV) in Genesis 10 instead of 'divide' (KJV) or 'separate' (NASB, NEB). A survey of translations may be helpful at this point.

4. *Translations of* פרד *in Genesis 10.5 and 10.32*

The Septuagint renders פרד in Gen. 10.5 by ἀφορίζω, 'separate, take away', and by διασπείρω, 'scatter, disperse' in 10.32. The Vulgate translates פרד by *divisio,* 'division, separation', in Gen. 10.5 and 32. Targums Onqelos, Pseudo-Jonathan and Neofiti render פרד by פרש, 'separate, divide' (Gen. 10.5, 32). It is note-worthy that the idea of 'spreading out' present in recent English translations is

---

14. Gen. 2.10; 13.9, 11, 14; 25.23; 30.40.

15. E.g. Judg. 4.11; Ruth 1.17; 2 Sam. 1.23; 2 Kgs. 2.11; Neh. 4.19 [13].

16. E.g. Gen. 13.9, 11, 14; 25.23; Judg. 4.11; 2 Sam. 1.23.

17. Translations of the niphal form of פרד by the NIV include: 'separate' (Gen. 2.10; 25.23; Neh. 4.19 [13]), 'part, part company' (Gen. 13.9, 11, 14; 2 Sam. 1.23); 'leave' (Judg. 4.11); 'desert' (Prov. 19.4) and 'pursue selfish ends' (Prov. 18.1). The NRSV translations include: 'divide' (Gen. 2.10; 25.23; 2 Sam. 1.23); 'separate' (Gen. 13.9, 11, 14; Judg. 4.11; Neh. 4.19 [13]); 'be left friendless' (Prov. 19.4); 'lives alone' (Prov. 18.1).

18. This is the only attestation of the qal form of פרד. The qal passive participle is translated by the NRSV as 'their wings were spread out above' (Ezek. 1.11a; cf. NIV). BDB suggests that the passive participle in Ezek. 1.11 means 'divided, i.e. spread, of wings' (p. 825); KB[3] suggests 'spread out, creatures spreading their wings' (KB[3], Vol. 3, p. 962).

not represented in early translations of פרד, although the idea of dispersal is present in the LXX in 10.32.[19]

Early English translations of Gen. 10.5 and 10.32 do not reflect the idea of 'spreading out' either. Rather, they commonly render פרד by 'divide'. A summary of translations of פרד is set out in the following table.[20]

Translations	10.5 (פרד)	10.32 (פרד)
LXX	ἀφορίζω, 'separate'	διασπείρω, 'scatter'
Vulgate	*divisio*, 'separate, divide'	*divisio*, 'separate, divide'
Targums[21]	פרש, 'separate, divide'	פרש, 'separate, divide'
Tyndale Bible (1530)	[of these] came	[of these] came
Geneva Bible (1560)	divide	divide
Bishops' Bible (1568)	divide	divide
KJV (1611)	divide	divide
RV (1885)	divide	divide
ASV (1901)	divide	divide
RSV (1952)	spread	spread abroad
NASB (1971)	separate	separate
NIV (1978)	spread out	spread out
NKJV (1982)	separate	divide
NRSV (1989)	spread	spread abroad
ESV (2001)	spread	spread abroad

The translation 'spread' (Gen. 10.5), 'spread abroad' (Gen. 10.32) first appeared in the RSV translation of 1952. The NIV, which was published in 1978, seems to have followed the RSV by translating פרד by 'spread out' (Gen. 10.5, 32). The RSV translation is also represented in the NRSV translation, 'spread' (Gen. 10.5) and 'spread abroad' (Gen. 10.32), and most recently in the ESV translation.

5. *Translations of* פרד *in Commentaries*

As with early translators, commentators prior to the RSV usually translated פרד by 'divide',[22] 'separate',[23] or 'branch out'.[24] Accordingly, the summary statements in

19. The Septuagint translates פרד by διασπείρω only on three occasions (Gen. 10.32; Deut. 32.8; Esth. 3.8). Διασπείρω may have been used in Gen. 10.32 in order to connect v. 32 with the ensuing Babel story where the same verb occurs (Gen. 11.4, 8, 9; cf. Gen. 9.19). If it is accepted that διασπείρω is negative in 9.19; 10.18 and 11.1-9, this would suggest that v. 32 is negative as well.

20. Early English translations are found in *The Genesis Octapla*, pp. 46–51.

21. Targums Onqelos, Pseudo-Jonathan and Neofiti.

22. Alford, *The Book of Genesis*, pp. 45, 52; Bacon, *Genesis of Genesis*, pp. 116, 118; Calvin, *A Commentary on Genesis*, pp. 311–12; Driver, *Genesis*, p. 132; Keil and Delitzsch, *The Pentateuch*, p. 164; Lange, *Genesis*, pp. 344–45; Lenormant, *Genesis*, pp. 33, 35; Luther, *Genesis*, pp. 180, 188; Thomas, *Genesis*, p. 100.

23. Dillmann, *Genesis*, Vol. 1, p. 338; Paul, *The Hebrew Text of the Book of Genesis*, p. 92. H.G. Mitchell differs, however, in his translation of פרד by 'disperse themselves' (*The World before Abraham* [Cambridge, MA: Houghton, Mifflin and Co., 1901], pp. 91, 93).

24. Baumgartner suggests that the niphal form of פרד in Gen. 10.5 and 10.32 means 'sich abzweigen (genealogisch), separate (in genealogy)' (*Lexicon in Veteris Testamenti libros*, Vol. 2 [ed. L. Koehler; Leiden: E.J. Brill, 1953], p. 776). As with Baumgartner, Holzinger translated פרד by

Gen. 10.5 and 10.32 focus on the division or separation of Noah's sons. For example, Rabbi Moshe ben Nachman (1195–1270) comments on Gen. 10.5: 'from there they were parted', suggesting that the meaning of this statement is that 'the children of Japheth are those who dwell on the isles of the sea, and they are separated, each one of his sons residing singly on another isle, and their countries are far from each other'.[25] Similarly, Dillmann renders פרד as 'have separated', explaining that the people 'detached as well as expanded, *themselves*'.[26] W. Paul suggests that the verb in Gen. 10.5 means 'were separated or descended', which he then compares with Gen. 25.23, 'Two nations shall be separated from your womb'. He suggests that the idea is that they 'shall be descended from thee'.[27] Keil and Delitzsch also refer to the separation of Noah's sons when commenting on Gen. 10.5: '*"From these have the islands of the nations divided themselves in their lands"*; i.e. from the Japhetites already named, the tribes on the Mediterranean descended and separated one from another as they dwell in their lands, *"everyone after his tongue, after the families, in their nations"*'.[28] They later remark on Gen. 10.32, noting that it 'prepares the way for the description of that event which led to the division of the one race into many nations with different languages'.[29]

This is very different from current views on this verse, however, that the 'spreading out' of Noah's sons is willed by God and fulfils the aims of Gen. 1.28. It is noteworthy that, while Keil and Delitzsch and others acknowledge that Noah's descendants dispersed into different geographical regions, they understood that פרד conveyed the idea of separation or division of people. The KJV, JB and the NASB retain this idea of division in their translations ('divide', KJV, JB; 'separate', NASB). Similarly, BDB suggests that פרד means 'divide, separate', and that in Gen. 10.5 and 32 the sense is 'of peoples separating from (מִן) parent stock'.[30] The 1953 edition of Baumgartner's Lexicon states that the meaning of פרד in Gen. 10.5 and 10.32 is '*sich abzweigen (genealogisch)*, separate (in genealogy)'.[31] The RSV translation 'spread, spread abroad' is clearly a departure from

---

'sich abzweigen' (*Genesis*, p. 93). Holzinger does use the verb 'ausbreiten', 'spread out', later in his commentary. However, it is in reference to Dillmann, who argues that people were to 'spread out' (p. 112). Jacob notes that פרד in Gen. 10.5 means 'abzweigen' and translates 10.5a as: 'Von diesen schieden sich die Meerlande der Völker' and 10.32b as: 'und von diesen schieden sich die Völker auf der Erde nach dem mabbul' (*Das erste Buch der Tora*, pp. 279, 294). Von Rad translates פרד by '(sich) zweigen' in Gen. 10.5 and by '(sich) verzweigen' in 10.32 (*Das erste Buch Mose*, p. 105). Westermann translates פרד in Gen. 10.5 by '(sich) abzweigen' and by '(sich) verzweigen' in 10.32 (*Genesis*, Bd. I, pp. 663, 665).

25. Rabbi Moshe ben Nachman, *Ramban (Nachmanides): Commentary on the Torah, Genesis* (trans. Rabbi C.B. Chavel; New York: Shilo Publishing House, Inc., 1971), p. 144.

26. Dillmann, *Genesis*, Vol. 1, p. 338.

27. Paul, *The Hebrew Text of the Book of Genesis*, p. 92.

28. Keil and Delitzsch, *The Pentateuch*, p. 164.

29. Keil and Delitzsch, *The Pentateuch,* p. 172.

30. BDB, p. 825.

31. Baumgartner, *Lexicon in Veteris Testamenti libros*, p. 776. The 3rd German edition of the lexicon states that פרד in 10.5 and 10.32 means: 'Völker von ihrem Ursprung' (L. Koehler and

the traditional rendering of פרד in Gen. 10.5 and 10.32, which was subsequently followed by the NRSV and the NIV, as well as by later commentators. We may thus raise the question regarding what transpired between the RV/ASV (1881/1901) translation, 'divide', and the RSV (1952) translation, 'spread, spread abroad'.

6. *James Moffatt's Translation of Genesis 10.5 and 10.32*

In 1924 James Moffatt completed his 'new translation' of the Old Testament.[32] In contrast to the aforementioned translations, which represent the work of teams of scholars, Moffatt's translation is the work of a single author.[33] Moffatt's view, that the Masoretic text is replete with corruptions, led to a number of emendations which were somewhat conjectural.[34] In certain places he also changed the text on the basis of more general theoretical considerations. For example, Moffatt transposed Gen. 2.4a, 'This is the story of how the universe was formed', placing it at the beginning of the book of Genesis. On other occasions, Moffatt's translation is evidently interpretative. For instance, he translates בני־האלהים in Gen. 6.2 as 'angels', which is a departure from the ASV, 'sons of God'. He also translates Gen. 1.26a as: 'Let us make man in our own likeness, to resemble us' (cf. ASV: 'Let us make man in our image, after our likeness'). Moffatt's translation again seems to reflect his interpretation of the Hebrew text.

Moffatt's work is important for the present discussion as his translation seems to be the first in which the verb 'spread' – the translation that appeared in the RSV (1952) – occurs as a rendering of פרד in Gen. 10.5 and 10.32. His translations of Gen. 9.19, 10.5, 10.18 and 10.32 are outlined in the following table.[35]

RV/ASV (1885/1901)	*Moffatt's New Translation (1924)*[36]
9.19b and of these was the whole earth *overspread*	9.19b and from them people of the earth *spread* all over the earth
10.5 Of these were the isles of the nations *divided* in their lands	10.5 from whom the seaboard nations *spread*

W. Baumgartner, *Hebräisches und Aramäisches Lexicon zum Alten Testament*, Bd. III [revised by W. Baumgartner and J.J. Stamm; Leiden: E.J. Brill, 1983], p. 906. The recent English edition of the lexicon states that the niphal form of פרד means 'diverge, separate, be scattered, separated', and suggests that פרד in Gen. 10.5 and 10.32 means 'nations spreading away from their homelands' (KB[3], Vol. 3, p. 962). When the RSV was first published, however, Baumgartner's German lexicon did not reflect the RSV rendering. The translator of the most recent English edition, M.E.J. Richardson, notes that he consulted the NRSV (1989) and the REB (1992) when translating biblical quotations.

32. J. Moffatt, *The Old Testament: A New Translation by James Moffatt*, Vol. 1 (New York: George H. Doran Co., 1924).

33. For a discussion of inherent weaknesses in translations by individuals, see H.P. Scanlin, 'Bible Translation by American Individuals', in E.S. Frerichs (ed.), *The Bible and Bibles in America* (Atlanta: Scholars Press, 1988), pp. 43–82 (43–44).

34. For an array of examples of these emendations and a critical analysis of Moffatt's translation, see O.T. Allis, 'Dr. Moffatt's "New Translation" of the Old Testament', *PTR* 23 (1925), pp. 267–317.

35. Italics mine.

36. Moffatt, *The Old Testament*, Vol. 1, pp. 9–10.

10.18 and afterward were the families of the Canaanite *spread abroad.*	10.18 after that the Canaanite families *spread abroad*
10.32 and of these were the nations *divided* after the flood	10.32 from whom the nations on the earth *spread*

While Moffatt maintained the RV/ASV notion of 'overspread' in Gen. 9.19, he seems to have enhanced the text by adding that 'people of the earth spread *all over the earth*'. According to the Hebrew text, ומאלה נפצה כל־הארץ, the subject is כל־הארץ (in agreement with the feminine singular verb נפצה, from the root נפץ); thus the location to which people spread is not given. Moffatt's addition, therefore, that people spread *all over the earth* seems to amplify the dispersal of the people.[37] It is noteworthy that Moffatt uses the verb 'spread' in Gen. 10.5 and 10.32 as a translation for פרד. Thus the *one* English verb 'spread' was used to translate נפץ (Gen. 9.19), פוץ (Gen. 10.18) and פרד (Gen. 10.5, 32). This is not so surprising, however, as Allis has observed that inconsistency is a characteristic of Moffatt's translation which makes it, according to Allis, a 'very unreliable version'. He concludes that Moffatt's translation is 'very loose and inexact, so inexact that it is often difficult to tell whether what Dr. Moffatt gives us is his free translation of the Hebrew or an attempt to improve on it'.[38] The result of Moffatt's translation of Genesis 9–10 is that the *different* meanings of key verbs is obscured and an artificial connection is established between Gen. 9.19 (נפץ), 10.5 (פרד), 10.18 (פוץ), and 10.32 (פרד), which is not present in the Hebrew text. This also means that the thematic relationship between 9.19, 10.18, and the scattering motif in the Babel story is *not* represented in Moffatt's translation since he translates פוץ in the Babel story by 'scatter'. The dispersal is, therefore, presented in a positive light in Genesis 9–10, but negative in the Babel story.

In view of the fact that Moffatt's translation is somewhat interpretative, the question can be raised whether Moffatt's departure from the usual rendering of פרד as 'divide' is another example of his interpretation. The idea that Noah's children were to 'spread over the whole earth' is mentioned in a few commentaries prior to Moffatt. H. Alford, for example, wrote on Gen. 11.4 in his commentary on Genesis published in 1872:

> *Their* purpose seems to have been to gain a centre of permanent habitation, and also a distinguishing memorial or mark by which their repute might be handed down. There doubtless is something of a rebellion against *God's* purposes implied in their determination. He would have them spread over the whole earth, while they resolved to be gathered in one spot.[39]

Dillmann similarly wrote of Gen. 9.1 and its relationship to the Babelites: 'evidently, as in chs. ix. 1 and i. 28 from *A*, the spreading of men over the earth is presupposed as agreeable to nature and in accordance with the divine will. But

---

37. This may also be seen in Gen. 11.9b, which Moffatt translates as, 'there the Eternal scattered men all over the wide earth'. Here the adjective *wide* is added to emphasize the extensiveness of the dispersal.

38. Allis, 'Dr. Moffatt's "New Translation" of the Old Testament', pp. 267–317 (273).

39. Alford, *The Book of Genesis*, p. 53.

men wish to oppose this tendency, to defy the divine arrangement...'.[40] Evans also wrote that 'God's command to Noah and his descendants to scatter and people the earth was evidently disobeyed...the building of the tower of Babel was a manifestation of the defiance of God's command...'.[41] It may well be the case that this interpretation influenced Moffatt's translation of פרד. The 'spreading' of Noah's descendants shows that the primaeval blessing is being realized in these verses (Gen. 9.19; 10.5, 32).

7. *Genesis 10.5 and 10.32 in* An American Translation

Another translation of the Old Testament was completed in 1927 entitled *An American Translation*. This was the work of four scholars: A.R. Gordon, T.J. Meek, J.M. Powis Smith and L. Waterman. T.J. Meek translated the Pentateuch, and later revised the entire Bible.[42] Like Moffatt's translation, this new translation is replete with emendations.[43] The translators have rearranged verses, supposedly to improve the sense of the text.[44] According to the translators, the Hebrew text is variously 'ungrammatical', 'unintelligible', 'obviously wrong', 'untranslatable', 'meaningless', and 'makes no sense'.[45] This work is relevant to the present discussion inasmuch as it reflects another new translation of Gen. 10.5 and 10.32 which reads as follows:

> It was from these that the coast-lands of the nations *were populated*, country by country, each with its respective language, according to the various clans, nation by nation (Gen. 10.5).

> These were the clans descended from Noah, arranged according to their descendants by nationalities; and from these the nations of the earth *were populated* after the flood (Gen. 10.32).[46]

This seems to be the first occasion where פרד in Gen. 10.5 and 10.32 is translated by the verb 'populate'. This English verb may have been chosen since it conveys the idea of increase, which is congruent with the primaeval blessing of Gen. 9.1. Yet the meaning 'populate' cannot be sustained in any other text where פרד occurs. Accordingly, this meaning is not attested for פרד in any of the standard Hebrew lexicons. This translation is represented, however, in the *New Living*

---

40. Dillmann, *Genesis*, Vol. 1, p. 202. Holzinger, however, objected to Dillmann's view, arguing that YHWH was not provoked by their unity. Rather, it was because the Babelites started to act with joint force and power (*Genesis*, p. 112).

41. Evans, *The Books of the Pentateuch*, p. 41.

42. *The Old Testament: An American Translation*, translated by A.R. Gordon, T.J. Meek, J.M. Powis Smith and L. Waterman (ed. J.M. Powis Smith; Chicago: The University of Chicago Press, 1939).

43. For numerous examples of emendations and a review of the translation, see O.T. Allis, 'An "American" Translation of the Old Testament', *PTR* 26 (1928), pp. 109–41 (116–28).

44. Allis cites numerous examples of this ('An "American" Translation', pp. 109–41 [116–25]).

45. Allis, 'An "American" Translation', pp. 109–41 (130).

46. *An American Translation*, p. 8 (italics mine). Gen. 9.19 was translated as 'and from them *sprang* the whole world', and Gen. 10.18 as 'Later the Canaanites scattered'.

Translation of 1996 (Gen. 10.32: 'The earth was populated with the people of these nations after the Flood'). We may recall at this point that the verb 'populate' appeared in the RSV translation of Gen. 9.19 in 1952. The question may well be asked whether *An American Translation* influenced English translations of these chapters in any way.

8. *Leupold's Genesis Commentary and Translation of Genesis 10.5 and 10.32*

H.C. Leupold evidently consulted *An American Translation* when writing his commentary on Genesis.[47] Volume 1 of Leupold's commentary was published in 1942, ten years prior to the publication of the RSV translation. Leupold translated Gen. 10.5: 'It is of these that the islands of the nations were populated according to their countries'.[48] It appears that Leupold accepted the rendering of *An American Translation* for this verse. He translates Gen. 10.32b, however, as 'from these were the nations of the earth spread abroad after the flood'.[49] Verse 32 seems to reflect Moffatt's translation ('spread'), with some modification. Leupold underscored the expansion of Noah's progeny with his translation, 'spread *abroad*', as Moffatt had done previously in Gen. 9.19 (i.e. 'from them people of the earth spread *all over the earth*'). Given that v. 5 is in close proximity to v. 32 and that both verses are usually attributed to the same author, we may question why Leupold translates פרד by 'populate' in Gen. 10.5, but by 'spread abroad' in Gen. 10.32. These two *different* translations of פרד within the one chapter are somewhat inconsistent.

This inconsistency is underscored by examining Leupold's translations of פרד in other texts and his definition of the verb. Elsewhere in his commentary on Genesis, Leupold translates פרד by 'divide' (Gen. 2.10), 'part, part company' (Gen. 13.9, 11, 14) and 'separate' (Gen. 25.23). Similarly, he entitles Gen. 13.1-18 – where פרד occurs three times – as the 'Separation from Lot'.[50] Furthermore, on two occasions he comments on פרד, maintaining that the niphal in Gen. 13.9 'is here used reflexively: separate yourself = "part"',[51] and that in Gen. 25.23 the verb 'carries the emphasis in the sense that the two nations shall have nothing in common. They shall "separate" because they are so radically different and shall remain apart forever'.[52] Leupold's remarks on פרד in these passages represent the way scholars had interpreted פרד in Gen. 10.5 and 10.32. So, given Leupold's own definitions of the verb, why did he not translate פרד in Gen. 10.5 and 10.32 as 'divide'? Why the two new translations – 'populate' in Gen. 10.5 and 'spread abroad' in 10.32?

47. Leupold, *Genesis*, Vol. 1, p. 32.
48. Leupold, *Genesis*, Vol. 1, p. 362.
49. Leupold, *Genesis*, Vol. 1, p. 380.
50. Leupold, *Genesis*, Vol. 1, pp. 430–44.
51. Leupold, *Genesis*, Vol. 1, p. 436.
52. H.C. Leupold, *Exposition of Genesis*, Vol. 2 (Grand Rapids: Baker Book House, 1953), p. 704.

Leupold's comments on the primaeval commands in Gen. 9.1 are worth noting. After expounding on the first two elements, 'Be fruitful and multiply', he then comments on the command to 'fill the earth', stating that 'mankind is not to concentrate in some few spots but is to spread out so that the earth presents no unoccupied and uncultivated areas'.[53] Later in his discussion of Gen. 11.4 he refers to the injunction to 'replenish the earth' (Gen. 9.1) and notes that 'this, of necessity, involved spreading abroad'.[54] He suggests that the city builders were refusing to obey this command and that YHWH's scattering them ensured that the command was carried out.[55] It seems to be the case that Leupold's interpretation of Gen. 11.1-9 – that Noah's children were to 'spread out' and that YHWH's scattering them ensured that the primaeval command is realized – has influenced his translation of פרד in Gen. 10.5 and 10.32. The verb 'populate' in v. 5 shows that God's command to 'be fruitful and multiply' has been carried out, whereas the verb 'spread abroad' indicates that the command to 'fill the earth' has been accomplished. While this interpretation is represented prior to Leupold,[56] his commentary is important as it seems to be the first occasion when this view was accompanied by a new translation that supported it. In other words, Leupold not only argued that Noah's descendants were to spread abroad (Gen. 9.1), but his *translation* of Gen. 10.32, 'from these were the nations of the earth spread abroad after the flood', confirmed that the blessing was fulfilled in v. 32. Thus an English translation emerged that supported the interpretation espoused by Leupold and others. Ten years later, the translations 'spread' (Gen. 10.5) and 'spread abroad' (Gen. 10.32) appeared in the RSV translation, and subsequently in the NRSV and the NIV ('spread out') as well. It is not surprising to find, therefore, that it is precisely the 'spreading out' of Noah's descendants that is understood to mark the fulfilment of the primaeval blessing. We may recall Harland's comments on Gen. 10.32, for instance, that 'this spreading abroad is willed by God and fulfils the aim of i 28'.[57] But if פרד does not mean 'spread abroad', would it be so evident that Gen. 10.5 and 10.32 fulfil the aim of Gen. 1.28?

9. *Implications of English Translations for Interpretation*

In sum, two significant changes took place with the publication of the RSV translation in 1952. First, נפץ in Gen. 9.19 was translated by 'was peopled'. This translation required changing the subject, כל־הארץ, from being a reference to the *inhabitants* of the earth (cf. RV, 'the whole earth overspread'), to a *geographical region*, 'from these the whole earth was peopled'.[58] Genesis 9.19 was

---

53. Leupold, *Genesis*, Vol. 1, p. 328.

54. Leupold, *Genesis*, Vol. 1, p. 387.

55. Leupold, *Genesis*, Vol. 1, p. 391.

56. E.g. Alford, *The Book of Genesis*, p. 53; Dillmann, *Genesis*, Vol. 1, p. 202; Evans, *The Books of the Pentateuch*, p. 41.

57. Harland, 'The Sin of Babel', pp. 515–33 (528).

58. If נפץ means 'scatter' or 'disperse', as we have argued thus far, then כל־הארץ clearly refers to the inhabitants of the earth, as it does in Gen. 11.1.

subsequently translated by the NASB as 'from these the whole earth was populated'. The NKJV, 'was populated', reflects this new translation as well. The
translations 'was peopled' and 'was populated' establish a connection between
9.19 and the primaeval blessing, even though the Hebrew text does not.

The other important change that took place with the publication of the RSV in
1952 was that פרד in Gen. 10.5 and 10.32 was translated by 'spread' (10.5),
'spread abroad' (10.32). As has been noted, Moffatt seems to have been the first
scholar who translated פרד in this way. Yet Moffatt's translation is highly interpretative. Allis has examined Moffatt's work in detail and concludes that his new
translation

> is momentous because it is, we believe, the boldest and most ambitious attempt that has
> yet been made to *rewrite* the Bible in the light of rationalistic criticism, to introduce
> purely conjectural changes into a *translation* of the Old Testament not merely without
> explaining or justifying them, but even without *indicating* their presence in any way.[59]

Given that Moffatt's translation of Gen. 10.5 and 10.32 is represented in the RSV
translation, it is worth considering whether his work influenced the RSV in any
way. One scholar has noted that Moffatt's work 'enjoyed a phenomenal sale with
numerous reprints'.[60] Another scholar suggests that Moffatt's translation 'became
the most popular such translation between the two World Wars (1914–1945)'.[61]
The influence of his translation is illustrated by the fact that several commentators evidently consulted it.[62] Moreover, it is not insignificant that Moffatt served
as the executive secretary of the committee preparing the RSV translation until his
death in 1944[63] and was one of the translators who worked on the RSV.[64] It may
not be coincidental, therefore, that Moffatt's translation of פרד as 'spread', which
was a departure from the RV/ASV rendering, 'divide', appeared in the RSV translation of 1952.

Once the translation 'peopled' (RSV, NRSV) or 'populated' (NASB, NKJV) had
been accepted as a rendering for נפץ, and 'spread abroad' (NRSV) or 'spread out'
(NIV) for פרד in Gen. 10.5 and 10.32,[65] it is not surprising to find the commonly
held view that the primaeval blessing is *fulfilled* in the Table of Nations. Waltke,
for example, refers to the primaeval commands, noting that the rule established
is: 'to spread out and fill the earth'.[66] Thus the one Hebrew verb, מלא, has come

---

59. Allis, 'Dr. Moffatt's "New Translation" of the Old Testament', pp. 267–317 (314); cf. P.D.
Wegner, *The Journey from Texts to Translations: The Origin and Development of the Bible*
(Michigan: Baker Books, 1999), pp. 346–48.

60. J.P. Lewis, 'English Versions', *ABD*, Vol. 6 (1992), pp. 816–34 (827).

61. Wegner, *The Journey from Texts to Translations*, p. 346.

62. Some scholars note that they consulted Moffatt's translation. For example, the translator of
Cassuto's commentary on Exodus, I. Abrahams, acknowledges that he consulted it (Cassuto, *A
Commentary on the Book of Exodus* [trans. I. Abrahams; Jerusalem: Magnes Press, 1967], p. VII). D.
Kidner also consulted Moffatt's translation (*Genesis* [TC; Chicago: Inter-Varsity Press, 1967], p. 45).

63. Lewis, 'English Versions', *ABD*, Vol. 6, pp. 816–34 (827).

64. Wegner, *The Journey from Texts to Translations*, p. 348.

65. Mathews, for example, translates פרד by 'spread out', but notes that the verb means 'divide'
(*Genesis 1–11.26*, p. 442).

66. Waltke, *Genesis*, p. 191.

to mean fill the earth *and* spread out.[67] As has been noted, it is precisely the 'spreading out' of Noah's descendants that marks the fulfilment of the primaeval blessing (Gen. 10.5, 18, 32). Brueggemann writes, for instance, that 'especially in chapter 10, we have seen that "spreading abroad" (v. 32) is blessed, sanctioned, and willed by Yahweh. It is part of God's plan for creation and the fufillment of the mandate of 1.28'.[68] He also comments on פוץ in Gen. 10.18 and suggests that the intent of creation finally comes to fulfilment in the spreading out of the Canaanites.[69] Atkinson underscores the significance of the 'spreading out' of the nations: 'A key word is "spread". *From these the coastland peoples spread (10.5); the families of the Canaanites spread (10.18); the nations spread abroad on the earth after the flood (10.32)'.*[70] Atkinson cites the RSV translation, which employs the one English verb 'spread' for the two *different* Hebrew verbs (i.e. פרד: Gen. 10.5, 32; פוץ: 10.18). He concludes, therefore, that 'the spread of the people points to God's blessing'.[71] The question may well be asked whether this interpretation would be assumed if פרד in Gen. 10.5 and 10.32 refers to the separation or division of Noah's sons.

It is not insignificant that, while the view that the primaeval blessing is *fulfilled* in the Table of Nations is well attested in recent literature, it is not well represented in early commentaries on Genesis. It is not mentioned, for instance, in the commentaries of Keil and Delitzsch (1888), Dillmann (1892), Holzinger (1898), Gunkel (1901), Driver (1904), Procksch (1913), König (1919) or Skinner (1930).[72] This is not so surprising, given that פרד was translated by 'divide' or 'separate' prior to the RSV translation in 1952. It may be helpful to summarize at this point arguments in favour of the traditional rendering of פרד in Gen. 10.5 and 10.32 as 'separate' or 'divide'.

10. *Support for the Meaning of* פרד *as 'Separate' or 'Divide'*

First, this rendering is in accordance with the usual meaning of the niphal form of פרד as 'divide, separate'.[73] As already noted, apart from Genesis 10, there is only

---

67. The verb 'spread' has even appeared in the NEB translation of Gen. 6.1a which is translated 'when mankind began to increase and to spread all over the earth...'. The Hebrew text, however, simply reads: ויהי כי־החל האדם לרב על־פני האדמה. The NEB has used the two English verbs 'to increase' *and* 'to spread' to translate the one Hebrew infinitive לרב.

68. Brueggemann, *Genesis*, p. 98.

69. Brueggemann, *Genesis*, p. 98; cf. Turner, *Announcements of Plot,* p. 29.

70. Atkinson, *The Message of Genesis 1–11*, p. 173.

71. Atkinson, *The Message of Genesis 1–11*, p. 175.

72. Although some earlier commentators articulated the view that Noah's sons were to spread out in accordance with Gen. 9.1, they do not state that the primaeval blessing is fulfilled in Gen. 10.1-32. Rather, the Table of Nations is usually seen to be describing the division of humankind. As far as I can tell, B. Jacob (1934) seems to be the first scholar who espoused this view, arguing that the command to 'fill the earth' has become a reality in the Table (*Das erste Buch der Tora*, p. 294). Jacob translates פרד by 'scheiden', 'separate' (pp. 279, 294), however. As with Jacob, von Rad argues that the commands to 'be fruitful and multiply' are fulfilled in the Table (*Genesis*, p. 144 [= *Das erste Buch Mose*, p. 109]).

73. BDB, p. 825.

one occasion where the verb (qal passive participle) is translated by 'spread out' (Ezek. 1.11) in the NRSV and NIV.

Secondly, the idea of division is suggested in Deut. 32.8, which marks the only occurrence of פרד in the Pentateuch outside Genesis. This text may even have Gen. 10.1-32 as its background.[74] In Deut. 32.8, the hiphil form of פרד is used:

> Remember the days of old, consider the years long past; ask your father, and he will inform you; your elders, they will tell you. When the Most High apportioned the nations, when he divided humankind (בהפרידו בני אדם), he fixed the boundaries of the peoples according to the number of the gods (NRSV, Deut. 32.7-8).[75]

If Gen. 10.1-32 and Deut. 32.8 are both referring to the primaeval division of humankind, then we may question why the NRSV and the NIV translate פרד by 'divide' in Deut. 32.8 (NASB, 'separate'), but render the same verb in Gen. 10.5 and 10.32 by 'spread, spread abroad'. These different translations are particularly noticeable in the case of the NIV, since its footnote indicates that the translators saw a connection between these two texts. Why, then, are there two *different* translations of the one Hebrew verb? This inconsistency is also reflected in commentaries. Mathews notes, for example, that the term פרד means 'divide' and that it

> anticipates the divine action against the Babel builders. Significantly, the term also occurs in the Song of Moses ('when he divided all mankind', Deut. 32.8), which shows the intended linkage between the sovereign pattern for the nations (seventy in number) and the descendants of Israel (seventy sons of Jacob; cf. 46.27; Exod. 1.5; Deut. 10.22).[76]

It is evident that Mathews translates פרד by 'divide' in Deut. 32.8 and is of the opinion that Deut. 32.8 has the Table of Nations in view, yet he translates פרד in Gen. 10.5 and 10.32 by 'spread out'. If פרד means 'divide' in Deut. 32.8 and there is an intended linkage between this text and Gen. 10.1-32, why not translate פרד by 'divide' in Gen. 10.5 and 10.32 as well? Cassuto also cites Deut. 32.8 in relation to Gen. 10.32: 'The connection between this verse and our chapter becomes quite clear from the parallelism observable in the use of the expressions common to both – not only of general terms like *nations* and *bounds* [or *borders*], but also of characteristic words such as the stem פָּרַד *pāradh* ["separate"]'.[77] While the RSV translation, 'spread', is retained in Cassuto's commentary, he makes the

---

74. Cassuto, *Genesis*, Vol. 2, p. 175; E.H. Merrill, *Deuteronomy* (NAC; Nashville: Broadman & Holman, 1994), p. 413; Sailhamer, *The Pentateuch as Narrative*, p. 131; J.A. Thompson, *Deuteronomy* (TC; Leicester: Inter-Varsity Press, 1974), p. 299.

75. The NRSV, 'according to the number of the *gods*', is based on Qumran fragments, which appear to be represented in the LXX reading, ἀγγέλων Θεοῦ. P. Sanders argues that the LXX reflects the original reading, noting that it is supported by two Qumran fragments (4QDt^j: בני אלהים; 4QDt^t: [...] בני אל; see Sanders, *The Provenance of Deuteronomy 32* [Leiden: E.J. Brill, 1996], pp. 156–57). The MT reading, בני ישראל, is supported by Targum Onqelos, the Vulgate and the Peshitta. The NASB, NIV and JB follow the MT.

76. Mathews, *Genesis 1–11.26*, pp. 442–43.

77. Cassuto, *Genesis*, Vol. 2, p. 177.

following comments with regard to Gen. 10.5: '*Spread* [נִפְרְדוּ *niphr^edhū*,
literally, 'were separated, divided'.]'.[78] He suggests that the reader compare Gen.
2.10 where he translates פרד by 'divide'. He then writes: 'Just as the river that
went forth from Eden divided – that means, split and ramified – into four branch-
streams, even so from the aforementioned offspring of Japheth there branched
out many more different nations. Compare also Deut. xxxii 8: *when He*
SEPARATED [בְּהַפְרִידוֹ *b^ehaphrīdhō] the sons of men*'.[79] According to Cassuto,
the literal meaning of פרד is 'separate, divide'. Thus even though the RSV translations, 'spread' (10.5) and 'spread abroad' (10.32), appear in his commentary,[80]
Cassuto's *definition* of פרד and his understanding of the verb in Deut. 32.8
accord with our view of פרד in Gen. 10.5 and 10.32, that it means 'divide,
separate'. In short, if Gen. 10.5, 32 and Deut. 32.8 are not presenting *different*
views, then it may be preferable for English translations to reflect this, translating
פרד by 'divide' in Gen. 10.5 and 10.32, in accordance with translations of פרד in
Deut. 32.8.[81]

Thirdly, as noted above, the rendering 'separate' or 'divide' has the support of
early translations including the Septuagint (ἀφορίζω, 'separate', Gen. 10.5), the
Vulgate (*divisio,* 'division, separation', Gen. 10.5, 32), and Targums Onqelos and
Pseudo-Jonathan (פרש, 'separate, divide', Gen. 10.5, 32). It was also shown that
English translations and commentators prior to Moffatt's translation of 1924
reflect this idea of division. The translation 'were separated' is retained in the
NASB and NEB translations.

If, then, Gen. 10.5 and 10.32 refer to the division or separation of people from
Noah's three sons, which is how these verses traditionally have been understood,
then the summary statement in v. 32, ומאלה נפרדו הגוים בארץ, indicates that the
nations of the earth *separated* from the families of Noah's sons. Analogous to
this would be the *separation* of Jacob and Esau, ושני לאמים ממעיך יפרדו (Gen.
25.23); two peoples would be separated from one womb. Thus from the one
family two nations would emerge.[82] In Genesis 10, seventy nations emerge from
three families.[83] Keil and Delitzsch suggest, in fact, that Gen. 10.32 'prepares the
way for the description of that event which led to the division of the one race into
many nations with different languages'.[84] Evans similarly notes that Genesis 10

78. Cassuto, *Genesis*, Vol. 2, p. 195.
79. Cassuto, *Genesis*, Vol. 2, pp. 195–96.
80. The translator of Cassuto's commentary, I. Abrahams, notes that he used the RSV translation
as the basis for his biblical translation (Cassuto, *Genesis*, Vol. 1, p. IX). It is difficult to say with
certainty whether Cassuto accepted this translation or not, although his comment in Gen. 10.5, that
פרד means, literally, 'were separated, divided', suggests that his view of 10.5 differed from the literal
meaning of the verb.
81. Cf. S.R. Driver, *Deuteronomy* (ICC; Edinburgh: T&T Clark, 1896), p. 355; Keil and Delitzsch,
The Pentateuch, pp. 469–70; Merrill, *Deuteronomy*, p. 413.
82. Cf. Gen. 2.10 (ומשם יפרד והיה לארבעה ראשים) where one river divides and becomes four
rivers.
83. Or seventy-one, depending on how one reckons the figure. The number seventy requires
excluding one member of the genealogy, possibly Nimrod (Sarna, *Genesis*, p. 69).
84. Keil and Delitzsch, *The Pentateuch*, p. 172.

'sets forth the beginning of nations. We have here the unity, division, and dispersion of the race... All mankind has sprung from one common source'.[85] It may
well be that the division referred to in Gen. 10.5 and 10.32 is the beginning of a
process that is developed in the patriarchal narratives. Skinner, for example, suggests that Genesis 12–50 'is a collection of narratives concerning the immediate
ancestors of the Hebrew people, showing how they were gradually separated
from the surrounding nations and became a chosen race, and at the same time
how they were related to those tribes and nationalities most nearly connected
with them'.[86] The view that פרד in Gen. 10.5 and 10.32 denotes division or separation is congruent with the overall purpose of Genesis in that it describes the
division of the one family into many nations; hence the appropriate title, the
'Generation of the Division'.[87] Genesis 10 may even be paradigmatic of how God
will act with respect to Israel in that he will separate one people from the nations.

11. *Conclusion*

Scholars argue that the 'spreading out' of the nations in Gen. 10.5 and 10.32
marks the fulfilment of the primaeval blessing. An examination of פרד has shown,
however, that the verb commonly means 'separate' or 'divide' and that early translations of 10.5 and 10.32, including the LXX, Vulgate and Targums Onqelos and
Pseudo-Jonathan, and early English translations, understood פרד in this way. It
was noted that an important change took place in 1952 with the publication of the
RSV, which translated פרד by 'spread, spread abroad' instead of 'divide' (KJV, RV,
ASV). It was suggested that the RSV was influenced by Moffatt, whose English
translation in 1924 seems to mark the first occasion where פרד was translated by
'spread'. Having examined פרד in detail, we concluded that פרד in Gen. 10.5
and 10.32 may well refer to the division or separation of Noah's descendants.

   Several implications follow from this conclusion. First, the view that the primaeval blessing is fulfilled in Gen. 10.5 and 10.32 may be questioned. If Gen.
10.5 and 10.32 are describing the separation of Noah's descendants, it is not so
evident that these verses refer back to Gen. 9.1 since God did not command
Noah's sons to *separate*. Secondly, if the primaeval blessing is not fulfilled in the
Table, then the view that the dispersal is being presented in a positive light needs
to be reconsidered. It may well be the case that the separation of Noah's descendants is being presented in something of a neutral sense in the Table, although, if
the ensuing Babel story is taken into consideration,[88] it would have negative
connotations since the division in Gen. 10.1-32 is the result of divine judgment.
Thirdly, it cannot simply be assumed that the 'emergence of the nations is depicted
as meeting the goal of God's blessing'[89] or that 'ethnic diversity is understood to
be the fruit of the divine blessing given at creation (1.28) and renewed in the new

85. Evans, *The Books of the Pentateuch,* p. 41.
86. Skinner, *Genesis,* p. iii; cf. Leupold, *Genesis,* Vol. 1, p. 12.
87. Cassuto, *Genesis,* Vol. 2, p. 243.
88. The relationship of Gen. 10.1-32 to 11.1-9 will be examined in Chapter 6.
89. Mathews, *Genesis 1–11.26,* p. 429.

creation after the flood (9.1, 7)',[90] since there is no indication that when God blessed humankind, they were required to 'separate'. In conclusion, we have argued thus far that the primaeval blessing is in the *process* of being realized in the Table, but is not fulfilled there. Rather, there is the expectation of a *future* fulfilment of the blessing. Given that the primaeval blessing is reissued to Noah and his three sons (Gen. 9.1), we may well raise the question whether the blessing will be taken up by all *three* sons – Shem, Ham and Japheth. Is there, then, any indication *within* the Table that would intimate how the primaeval blessing advances after the flood?

---

90. Anderson, 'The Tower of Babel', pp. 165–78 (176). For a similar view, see Blenkinsopp, *The Pentateuch,* p. 144; Harland, 'The Sin of Babel', pp. 515–33 (532); Hartley, *Genesis*, p. 117.

Chapter 5

THE PRIMAEVAL BLESSING AND THE SHEMITE GENEALOGY

1. *The Placement of Shem's Genealogy in the Table of Nations*

The Table of Nations lists the descendants of Noah's three sons. The order in which Noah's sons appear is consistently Shem, Ham and Japheth (Gen. 5.32; 6.10; 9.18). This order is repeated at the outset of the Table (10.1), yet the genealogies are then presented in the *reverse* order (Japheth: 10.2-5; Ham: 10.6-20; Shem: 10.21-31). Scholars have rightly concluded that the placement of Shem's genealogy *after* Japheth and Ham, even though Ham is the youngest son (Gen. 9.24), draws attention to Shem's line.[1]

Focus on Shem is also indicated by the additional introductory comments in 10.21.[2] The genealogies of Noah's three sons are each introduced by an enumerative formula: Japheth: בני יפת (10.2), Ham: ובני חם (10.6) and Shem: בני שם (10.22). Shem's genealogy, however, is preceded by the following introduction:

ולשם ילד גם־הוא אבי כל־בני־עבר אחי יפת הגדול

This introduction draws attention to Shem's genealogy in particular. The identification of Shem as the 'father of all the children of Eber' focuses on Eber – who marks the fourth generation from Shem and the fourteenth generation from Adam – and his sons. The names of Eber's two sons, Peleg and Joktan, are then given in v. 25. That Joktan has thirteen sons shows him to be the most prolific son in the Table, yet this is somewhat of a foil in view of the following Shemite genealogy where Peleg's descendants are listed (Gen. 11.18-26).[3] Given that Shem is identified as the father of *all* the sons of Eber, this statement appears to be broader in scope than simply Gen. 10.25-29. It may even have in view the

---

1.   N.A. Bailey, 'Some Literary and Grammatical Aspects of Genealogies in Genesis', in R.D. Bergen (ed.), *Biblical Hebrew and Discourse Linguistics* (SIL; Winona Lake: Eisenbrauns, 1994), pp. 267–82 (274); Cassuto, *Genesis*, Vol. 2, pp. 198, 217; Dillmann, *Genesis*, Vol. 1, pp. 312, 323; Hamilton, *Genesis 1–17*, p. 343; R.B. Robinson, 'Literary Functions of the Genealogies of Genesis', *CBQ* 48 (1986), pp. 595–608 (603); Sarna, *Genesis*, p. 69; Tengström, *Die Toledotformel*, p. 26; Turner, *Genesis*, p. 58.

2.   Mathews, *Genesis 1–11.26*, p. 460; Sailhamer, *The Pentateuch as Narrative*, p. 133; Sarna, *Genesis*, p. 69; Tengström, *Die Toledotformel*, pp. 26–27.

3.   Tengström notes that it is unusual that Peleg's sons are not mentioned in the Table, especially in view of the strong emphasis placed on Eber's descendants in v. 21. He suggests that this omission can only be explained in light of Gen. 11.10-26 where Peleg's genealogy is resumed (Tengström, *Die Toledotformel*, p. 24). Thus the 'gap' in the genealogy points forward to Gen. 11.10-26.

ensuing Shemite genealogy, in which the descendants of Eber's son, Peleg, are given (Gen. 11.18-26). Finally, the identification of Shem as אחי יפת הגדול (Gen. 10.21) focuses attention on Shem's relationship to his brother Japheth. Depending on which noun the adjective modifies, Shem could be the elder brother of Japheth, in which case Shem would be identified as Noah's firstborn son (i.e. Shem-Japheth-Ham).[4] Alternatively, Japheth is the elder brother of Shem (i.e. Japheth-Shem-Ham).[5] Given that Ham is the youngest of the three sons (Gen. 9.24), we can conclude that the placement of the genealogies of Japheth, Ham and Shem in the Table cannot be chronological. The question might rightly be asked then, whether the reversal of primogeniture in the Table has any theological significance.

2. *Is the Reversal of Order in Genesis 10.1-32 Theologically Significant?*

Robinson observes that this reversal of order not only highlights Shem, but also places Shem's genealogy directly before the Babel story. He remarks that the 'sorry events of Babel are recounted, then the genealogy of Shem is taken up again and leads, now as a linear genealogy, father to son, father to son, to Terah, father of Abraham. Genealogies of Shem effectively bracket the account of the building of the tower. To what end?'[6] Robinson concludes that the placement of Shem's genealogy both before (10.21-31) and after the Babel story (11.10-26) underscores the irony of the Babelites' striving for a name. He suggests that there is a wordplay on שם: the people are striving for a שם, but God has already provided a שם through the process of procreation (cf. בני שם, 10.22; שם שם, 11.10).[7] This play on שם is also seen in Gen. 12.2: in contrast to the illegitimate striving of the Babelites to 'make a name for themselves', YHWH promises that he will make Abram's שם great.[8] While scholars have rightly drawn attention to the play

---

4.   According to this view, the adjective is modifying אחי; cf. Hamilton, *Genesis 1–17*, p. 343; Robinson, 'Literary Functions', pp. 595–608 (603); Sarna, *Genesis*, p. 78; Skinner, *Genesis*, p. 219; Wenham, *Genesis 1–15*, p. 228; Westermann, *Genesis 1–11*, p. 525 (= *Genesis*, Bd. I, p. 700). While this view accords with the priority given to Shem (Gen. 5.32; 6.10; 9.18; 10.1), Gen. 9.24 shows that the order is not chronological since Ham, who is the youngest of Noah's sons, is not listed last. Moreover, it cannot be inferred from Gen. 11.10-26 that Shem is Noah's firstborn, since Seth, who is included in the Gen. 5 genealogy, is Adam's third son.

5.   According to this view, the adjective גדול is modifying יפת; cf. LXX (ἀδελφῷ 'Ιάφεθ τοῦ μείζονος); Cassuto, *Genesis*, Vol. 2, p. 218.

6.   Robinson, 'Literary Functions', pp. 595–608 (603).

7.   Robinson, 'Literary Functions', pp. 595–608 (603); cf. Bailey, 'Genealogies in Genesis', pp. 267–82 (275).

8.   A.K. Jenkins, 'A Great Name: Genesis 12.2 and the Editing of the Pentateuch', *JSOT* 10 (1978), pp. 41–57 (45). See also Clines, 'The Significance of the "Sons of God" Episode (Genesis 6.1-4) in the Context of the Primeval History (Genesis 1–11)', *JSOT* 13 (1979), pp. 33–46 (38); Hamilton, *Genesis 1–17*, p. 372; L. Ruppert, '"Machen wir uns einen Namen…"' (Gen. 11, 4): Zur Anthropologie der vorpriesterschriftlichen Urgeschichte', in R. Mosis and L. Ruppert (eds.), *Der Weg zum Menschen: zur philosophischen und theologischen Anthropologie: für Alfons Deissler* (Freiburg: Herder, 1989), pp. 28–45; Turner, *Genesis*, p. 63.

on םש in these chapters, it is worth examining whether there is more to the fact that Shem is featured last in the Table.

It is noteworthy that the patriarchal narratives show evidence of a literary structure that presents the less prominent son first, whereas the son belonging to the main line is featured last.[9] According to the Toledot structure, Ishmael's Toledot (Gen. 25.12-18) precedes Isaac's (Gen. 25.19–35.29), and Esau's Toledot (Gen. 36.1-43) precedes Jacob's (Gen. 37.1–50.26). Weimar has observed this feature, noting that the priestly writer starts with the 'side line' (*Nebenlinie*) and then continues with the 'main line' (*Hauptlinie*). He suggests that this is the central theological purpose of the priestly writer.[10] Mathews similarly maintains that 'this reversal of the custom of primogeniture becomes a thematic essential in Genesis, especially the patriarchal accounts (Isaac and Ishmael, Jacob and Esau, Ephraim and Manasseh)'.[11] It is worth considering at this point whether this literary feature, which presents the secondary lines first and the primary line last, is in any way present in the final redaction of the primaeval history.[12]

To begin with, one observes that Cain's genealogy (Gen. 4.17-24) is presented prior to Seth's genealogy (Gen. 4.25-26). The Sethite genealogy is then resumed in the following chapter (Gen. 5.1-32). If the placement of Seth's genealogy (Gen. 4.25-26) after Cain's (Gen. 4.17-24) is analogous to the Toledots of Isaac (Gen. 25.19–35.29) and Jacob (Gen. 37.1–50.26), which both appear *after* their respective brothers (Ishmael: Gen. 25.12-18; Esau: Gen. 36.1-43), then it may even indicate that Cain's genealogy is the secondary line and Seth's genealogy is the main line.[13] It is not surprising, therefore, that the primaeval blessing is recalled

9. Cassuto, *Genesis*, Vol. 2, p. 198; Mathews, *Genesis 1–11.26*, p. 440; Sarna, *Genesis*, p. 69; J. Scharbert, 'Der Sinn der Toledot-Formel in der Priesterschrift', in H.J. Stoebe (ed.), *Wort-Gebot-Glaube: Beiträge zur Theologie des Alten Testaments: W. Eichrodt FS* (Zurich: Zwingli Verlag, 1979), pp. 45–56 (45).

10. Weimar, 'Die Toledot-Formel', pp. 65–93 (70); cf. *idem*, 'Aufbau und Struktur der priesterschriftlichen Jakobsgeschichte', *ZAW* 86 (1974), pp. 174–203 (201).

11. Mathews, *Genesis 1–11.26*, p. 280, n. 297.

12. It is worth pointing out that the terms 'main line' and 'secondary line' are being used to denote the prominence given to a particular line in relation to Israel. These designations are to be distinguished, however, from Noth's identification of genealogies as either 'primary' or 'secondary', which is based on whether a genealogy is thought to have existed independently of the narrative (primary) or whether it was a secondary expansion of a narrative (M. Noth, *A History of Pentateuchal Traditions* [trans. B.W. Anderson; Atlanta: Scholars Press, 1981], pp. 214–19; see R.R. Wilson's discussion of these categories in *Genealogy and History in the Biblical World* [YNER, 7; New Haven: Yale University Press, 1977], pp. 201–202).

13. This point has been made by several scholars (T.D. Andersen, 'Genealogical Prominence and the Structure of Genesis', in R.D. Bergen [ed.], *Biblical Hebrew and Discourse Linguistics* [SIL; Winona Lake: Summer Institute of Linguistics, 1994], pp. 242–63 [260]; Hamilton, *Genesis 1–17*, p. 251; Mathews, *Genesis 1–11.26*, p. 261; Wenham, *Genesis 1–15*, p. 97), although there are differences in the terminology used to identify the two genealogies. We have preferred not to use terms such as 'elect' and 'non-elect', or 'chosen' and 'rejected', as these categories seem to be derived from reading into the primaeval history concepts that are present in the patriarchal narratives. We prefer to identify a genealogy as either the 'main' line or a 'secondary' line (there can be several secondary lines, but only one main line).

at the outset of *Seth's* genealogy (Gen. 5.2), since in the patriarchal narratives it is the main line that takes up the Abrahamic blessing.[14]

When considering the significance of the reversal of order in the Table of Nations, it is worth noting that there are several instances within Gen. 10.1-32 where the order of names is *maintained*. For example, the sons of Japheth are listed in Gen. 10.2 (Gomer, Magog, Madai, Javan, Tubal, Meshech and Tiras). The sons of Japheth's firstborn, Gomer, are given in v. 3, and the sons of his fourth son, Javan, in v. 4. While this is selective in that only the children of the first and fourth sons are mentioned, the order in which they are presented is in accordance with v. 2. Similarly, the sons of Ham are given in v. 6 (Cush, Mizraim, Put and Canaan). The sons of Cush (10.7), Mizraim (10.13-14) and Canaan (10.15-18) are then given in the same order in which they appeared in v. 6 (this time Put's sons are not mentioned). That the order of the sons is maintained in these verses seems to underscore that the reversal of order in the broader structure of Gen. 10.1-32 is an intentional literary device.

Moreover, a closer examination shows that, while the order of primogeniture is retained in the genealogies of Japheth and Ham, reversal of order is present in Shem's genealogy (Gen. 10.22-29). The sons of Shem are listed in Gen. 10.22 (Elam, Asshur, Arpachshad, Lud and Aram). In the following verse, however, the sons of Shem's fifth son, Aram, are given first (v. 23). The genealogy of his third son, Arpachshad, is then given in v. 24 (Arpachshad-Shelah-Eber). While the genealogy is again selective in that only the sons of Aram and Arpachshad are listed, the order of the two sons has been reversed. A second reversal may even be seen in vv. 25-29. The two sons of Eber, Peleg and Joktan, are listed in v. 25. The sons of Joktan are then given in vv. 26-29. Even though Peleg's sons are not mentioned until Gen. 11.18, the presentation of Joktan's sons prior to those of his brother seems to be indicative of another reversal.[15] We may conclude, therefore, that the reversal of Shem, Ham and Japheth in the broader structure of Gen. 10.1-32 is also evident at the micro-level in Shem's genealogy. What, then, is the theological import of these reversals in Gen. 10.1-32 and in Shem's genealogy in particular?

At this point we should recall Robinson's observation, that the reversal of the order of Shem, Ham and Japheth and the placement of Shem's genealogy after Gen. 11.1-9 means that the Shemite genealogy brackets the Babel story. He concludes that the theological purpose of the literary structure is to highlight the irony of the Babelites' striving for a name. But if this is the reason, why the reversal of Arpachshad and Aram, and Peleg and Joktan in Shem's genealogy? While Robinson's view accounts for the broader structure of Gen. 10.1-32, it does not account for the same feature occurring within the genealogy of Shem.[16]

---

14. That Cain's genealogy is a secondary line may even be suggested in the first chapter of Chronicles, which recalls the primaeval and patriarchal genealogies. It is noteworthy that Cain's genealogy is not mentioned. Instead, the Chronicler begins immediately with Seth's genealogy (1 Chron. 1.1). See below for a discussion of the genealogies in 1 Chronicles 1.

15. This reversal of order can be seen more clearly in 1 Chron. 1.20-26 where there is no Babel story to separate the genealogies.

16. Similarly, Robinson's view does not account for the reversal of order of Shem, Ham and

Other scholars have suggested that the reason for the reversal in Gen. 10.1-32 is that the people who have least significance for Israel are mentioned first. Ross argues, for example, that the descendants of Japheth are given first because they were less involved in Israel's history than the descendants of Ham.[17] Similarly, Jacob suggests that the order of Noah's sons corresponds to their distance from Israel. Thus Japheth, who has no direct relations with Israel, is most remote.[18] It is important to observe, however, that Aram's descendants are mentioned *prior* to the descendants of Arpachshad in the Table. Yet scholars have noted that the Arameans are prominent in the patriarchal narratives: Isaac's wife, Rebekah, is the daughter of Bethuel, the Aramean (Gen. 25.20). Similarly, Jacob's wives, Rachel and Leah, are daughters of Laban, the Aramean (Gen. 29.1-32; cf. Gen. 28.5; 31.20, 24). Mathews thus suggests that Aram's descendants have probably been included in Gen. 10.23 because of their *importance* for the history of the Hebrews.[19] The point to note is that Aram's descendants are not mentioned first because the Arameans are only remotely related to Israel. Thus, as with Robinson's view, this interpretation accounts for the broader structure, but does not explain the reversal *within* Shem's genealogy.

3. *Presentation of the Secondary Lines First and the Main Line Last*

The literary device used in the patriarchal narratives, which presents the secondary line prior to the main line, can account, however, for the reversals in both the broader structure of the Table of Nations[20] and the micro-structure of the Shemite genealogy (Gen. 10.21-31). The presentation of Japheth's and Ham's genealogies prior to Shem's in the Table would indicate that they are secondary lines and that Shem's genealogy is the main line. Accordingly, the main line is then resumed in Gen. 11.10-26. The placement of Aram's genealogy (Gen. 10.23) prior to Arpachshad's (Gen. 10.24) in Shem's genealogy can be understood in a similar way. It would indicate that Aram is the secondary line and Arpachshad is the main line.[21] Thus it is not Aram's genealogy, but Arpachshad's that is resumed in the linear Shemite genealogy. Similarly, Joktan's descendants are given first in the Table (Gen. 10.26-29), which would indicate that his is the secondary line. Accordingly, it is not Joktan's genealogy, but Peleg's which is taken up in the ensuing Shemite genealogy (cf. Gen. 11.18). This feature is observed by

Japheth (and Peleg and Joktan) in the genealogies of 1 Chronicles 1 where the Babel story is not even mentioned.

17. A.P. Ross, 'The Table of Nations in Genesis 10 – Its Content', *BSac* 138 (1981), pp. 22–34 (22).

18. Jacob, *Genesis*, p. 71 (= *Das erste Buch der Tora*, p. 273).

19. Mathews, *Genesis 1–11.26*, p. 462.

20. Several scholars have seen a connection between the reversal of Shem, Ham and Japheth in the Table of Nations and the placement of the Toledots of Ishmael and Isaac, and Esau and Jacob (Andersen, 'Genealogical Prominence', pp. 242–63 [254–55]; Cassuto, *Genesis*, Vol. 2, p. 198; Keil and Delitzsch, *The Pentateuch*, pp. 37, 163; Wenham, *Genesis 1–15*, p. 97).

21. Accordingly, the Chronicler does not even mention Aram's descendants. Instead, focus is on Arpachshad's genealogy (1 Chron. 1.18).

Keil and Delitzsch who make the following comments on the reversal motif in the primaeval narratives:

> families which branched off from the main line are noticed first of all; and when they have been removed from the general scope of the history, the course of the main line is more elaborately described, and the history itself is carried forward. According to this plan, which is strictly adhered to, the history of Cain and his family precedes that of Seth and his posterity; the genealogy of Japhet and Ham stands before that of Shem...[22]

A similar observation has been made by Cassuto who notes that 'the Torah first completes the genealogy of Japheth and Ham so as to dispose of the subject and avoid the need to revert to it later; whereas the account of Shem's offspring, who are central to the narrative, will continue in the subsequent chapters'.[23] According to this pattern, the descendants of the secondary lines are presented first (Gen. 10.1-20), thereby drawing attention to the main line which is presented last (Gen. 10.21-31). The main line is then resumed in Gen. 11.10-26. The primary and secondary genealogies are represented in the following diagram:

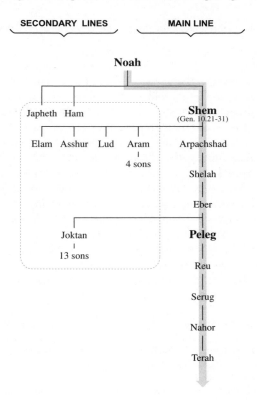

---

22. Keil and Delitzsch, *The Pentateuch*, p. 37.

23. Cassuto, *Genesis*, Vol. 2, p. 198; cf. Bailey, 'Genealogies in Genesis', pp. 267–82 (274); Kidner, *Genesis*, p. 105.

At a structural level, therefore, there is a narrowing down of focus from the 'Toledot of Shem, Ham and Japheth' (Gen. 10.1) to the 'Toledot of Shem' (Gen. 11.10). It may well be the case that the reversal of order in the Table of Nations is analogous to the Toledot structure of Ishmael and Isaac, and Esau and Jacob, that is, it is an intentional literary device that presents the secondary line first, and then focuses on the main line by presenting it last.

That Shem has a pre-eminent position in the Table is not so surprising, given that YHWH is identified as the 'God of Shem' in Gen. 9.26 (NIV, NASB, NKJV).[24] Wenham suggests, in fact, that 9.26 is the 'first intimation that the line of God's election blessing is going through Shem (cf. 4.26)'.[25] Mathews similarly maintains that the blessing 'first shows that the elect line of promise will be Shem's offspring, which is spelled out in the genealogy of 11.10-26, ending in the appointed "Abram" (Gen. 12.1-3)'.[26] We suggest that already in the Table, the reversal of primogeniture intimates that Japheth and Ham are secondary lines and that Shem is the main line.

4. *Presentation of Genealogies from Genesis in 1 Chronicles 1*

It is noteworthy that this reversal of order is also evident in the first chapter of 1 Chronicles where genealogies from the primaeval history and patriarchal narratives have been placed together.[27] 1 Chronicles 1 begins with the Genesis 5 genealogy and then moves directly to Noah's three sons: 'Adam, Seth, Enosh; Kenan, Mahalel, Jared; Enoch, Methuselah, Lamech; Noah, Shem, Ham, and Japheth' (NRSV, 1 Chron. 1.1-4). The omission of Cain's genealogy by the Chronicler is in agreement with what we have argued so far, that Cain is being portrayed as a secondary line. Accordingly, the Chronicler has simply begun with the main line by reiterating (as briefly as possible) the Sethite genealogy (cf. Gen. 5.1-32). The order of Noah's three sons is Shem, Ham and Japheth in 1 Chron. 1.4. Yet as with Gen. 10.1-32, the genealogies of the three sons are then given in the *reverse* order in the following verses (Japheth: 1.5-7; Ham: 1.8-16; Shem: 1.17-23). This literary feature can even be observed in the presentation of the patriarchs. The names of Abraham's two sons are introduced as 'Isaac and Ishmael' (1 Chron. 1.28); however, their genealogies are given in the reverse order (Ishmael: 1 Chron. 1.29-31; Isaac: 1 Chron. 1.34). Similarly, Esau's genealogy (1 Chron. 1.35-54) is

---

24. The NRSV translates the statement, ברוך יהוה אלהי שם, as: 'Blessed *by* the LORD my God be Shem'. We prefer the NIV/NASB translation, however (cf. LXX: εὐλογητὸς Κύριος ὁ Θεὸς τοῦ Σήμ); cf. Cassuto, *Genesis*, Vol. 2, p. 166; Driver, *Genesis*, p. 110; Hamilton, *Genesis 1–17*, p. 325; Sarna, *Genesis*, p. 67; Westermann, *Genesis 1–11*, p. 492 (= *Genesis*, Bd. I, p. 659).

25. Wenham, *Genesis 1–15*, p. 202.

26. Mathews, *Genesis 1–11.26*, p. 423.

27. Scholars are in agreement that the Chronicler has used Genesis for his source (R. Braun, *1 Chronicles* [WBC; Waco: Word Books, 1986], pp. 13, 15; S. Japhet, *I & II Chronicles* [OTL; Westminster: John Knox Press, 1993], pp. 52–53; J.A. Thompson, *1 Chronicles* [NAC; Nashville: Broadman and Holman, 1994], p. 49; H.G.M. Williamson, *1 and 2 Chronicles* [NCBC; London: Marshall, Morgan & Scott, 1982], p. 40).

given prior to Israel's genealogy (1 Chron. 2.1-2). Williamson has commented on
the Chronicler's pattern, concluding that 'details of secondary lines within a
family are consistently treated first (vv. 5-16, 20-23, 29-33, 35-54), each section
thus finishing with the line that was to lead eventually to Israel'.[28] According to
Williamson, Japheth and Ham (vv. 5-16) are being presented as secondary lines
in 1 Chronicles 1, as is the case with the sons of Ishmael (vv. 29-31) and Esau
(vv. 35-54). Williamson also notes that 'even within this latter section, Eber's
son Joktan is treated first (19-23), before (with partial recapitulation) the direct
line is traced from Shem to Abraham (24-27)'.[29] Thus he concludes that Joktan is
also being presented as a secondary line (vv. 20-23). Williamson's observations
are congruent with our analysis of the reversal of primogeniture in the Table of
Nations. Japhet similarly notes that the peripheral elements are dealt with first,
forming the background against which the main genealogical line is developed.
Japhet has examined the Chronicler's employment of the genealogies from Genesis and concludes that 'in all this, Chronicles follows the content, order and structure of Genesis'.[30] Thompson has also observed this reversal in 1 Chronicles 1, yet
he maintains that the idea of a main line and secondary lines is the *Chronicler's*
view:

> Following his usual pattern, he dealt first with what to him were secondary lines within
> the family of humankind: first the Japhethites (vv. 5-7), then the Hamites (vv. 8-16),
> and finally what to him was the major family – the Semites (vv. 17-27), narrowing
> down this family to Abraham and his sons (v. 28).[31]

We suggest, however, that this view did not originate with the Chronicler, but
that he was simply following the pattern already laid out in Genesis.[32] His
omissions of some of the Genesis material, such as Cain's genealogy (Gen. 4.17-
24) and Aram's sons (Gen. 10.23), do not effect any significant changes to the
pattern, but actually emphasize it.[33] If, then, the placement of the genealogies in
the Table of Nations shows Shem to be the main line, the question may be raised
whether this has any implications for how the primaeval blessing will be realized.

28. Williamson, *1 and 2 Chronicles*, p. 40. See also Japhet, *I & II Chronicles*, p. 53; M.D.
Johnson, *The Purpose of the Biblical Genealogies* (SNTS, 8; Cambridge, England: Cambridge University Press, 1969), p. 73, n. 4.

29. H.G.M. Williamson, *Israel in the Books of Chronicles* (Cambridge, England: Cambridge
University Press, 1977), p. 63; cf. J.G. McConville, *I & II Chronicles* (Philadelphia: Westminster
Press, 1984), p. 9.

30. Japhet, *I & II Chronicles*, p. 53.

31. Thompson, *1 Chronicles*, p. 49. Williamson suggests that the Chronicler has taken over
material from Genesis, while noting that 'its schematic presentation is the Chronicler's' (*Israel in the
Books of Chronicles*, p. 62).

32. Another indication that the pattern of Genesis has been retained is that the order of the sons in
the secondary line has not been reversed in 1 Chronicles 1, as pointed out by Williamson (*Israel in
the Books of Chronicles*, p. 63). See also Japhet, *I & II Chronicles*, p. 53.

33. Williamson, *1 and 2 Chronicles*, p. 40.

5. *The Main Line of Shem and the Primaeval Blessing*

In the patriarchal narratives, it is not the secondary line that takes up the Abrahamic blessing (Ishmael: Gen. 25.12-18; Esau: Gen. 36.1-43), but the main line (Isaac: Gen. 25.19–35.29; Jacob: Gen. 37.1–50.26). In light of this, is it possible that the placement of Shem's genealogy last in the Table has theological significance? The presentation of Japheth and Ham as secondary lines may even indicate that the primaeval blessing announced to Noah's three sons (Gen. 9.1) will be taken up by Shem's line in particular, in the same way that the Abrahamic blessing is not taken up by the secondary lines, but by the main line.

Scholars are of the opinion, however, that the primaeval blessing is fulfilled in the Table of Nations through Noah's *three* sons. It is not insignificant that scholars who espouse this view – such as Anderson, Brueggemann, Clines, Harland, Kikawada and von Rad – do not discuss the placement of Shem's genealogy in the Table and the implications it may have for how the primaeval blessing is being realized. Accordingly, scholars do not conclude that Japheth and Ham are secondary lines and that Shem is the main line. Von Rad, in fact, observes that the term 'Israel' is not mentioned in the Table and maintains that there is no centre to which the nations are related.[34] He suggests that Israel is represented by *Arpachschad* – a name which he contends is completely neutral for Israel's faith and sacred history. Thus according to von Rad, Shem's line is not given any prominence in the Table. He further argues that in the primaeval history, the genealogical line is not drawn from Noah to Shem, but from Noah to the *nations* (i.e. Gen. 10.1-32). In other words, there are no secondary lines in the Table; all three sons, therefore, would constitute the main line. Accordingly, the nations are the goal of the Table, not Israel.[35]

Von Rad has rightly noted that the term Israel does not occur in Gen. 10.1-32. However, while the nations are not related theologically to *Israel* in the Table, they are related to *Shem*, whose genealogy leads to Abraham (Gen. 11.10-26). As has been noted, the reversal of primogeniture places Shem in the position of the main line and Japheth and Ham as secondary lines. Tengström argues, in fact, that Israel has a central position in Gen. 10.1-32. He suggests that the genealogy moves spatially from the periphery (Japheth's descendants, then to Ham's descendants) to the centre which has its focus on Israel (Shem's descendants). He thus concludes that Israel dominates the Table.[36] It could be argued, therefore, that the goal of the Table is not the nations as a whole, but Shem's genealogy in particular. This is intimated in the reversal of primogeniture in the Table and confirmed by the two *linear* genealogies (Gen. 5.1-32; 11.10-26), which establish a genealogical

---

34. Von Rad, *Genesis*, p. 144 (= *Das erste Buch Mose*, p. 110).
35. Von Rad, *Old Testament Theology*, Vol. 1, p. 162 (= *Theologie des Alten Testaments*, Bd. I, pp. 175–76).
36. Tengström, *Die Toledotformel*, p. 27; cf. Ross, *Creation and Blessing*, p. 230.

line from creation to Israel (through Abraham). Accordingly, Williamson points out that the Chronicler has shown that the line of God's election is traced directly from Adam to Israel.[37] We suggest that already in the Table of Nations there is a narrowing down of focus from Noah's three sons to Shem in particular. It is not surprising that von Rad maintains that the primaeval blessing is fulfilled through all *three* sons since he did not consider Shem's line to be important in the Table. He would conclude, therefore, that realization of the primaeval blessing progresses from Noah (9.1) to the nations (10.1-32). We have argued, however, that the reversal of primogeniture indicates that Japheth and Ham are secondary lines and that Shem's line is the main line. The theological significance of this is that it intimates that the primaeval blessing is being taken up in the Shemite genealogy.

As with von Rad, Clines argues that the primaeval blessing is fulfilled in Gen. 10.1-32,[38] yet he has not given attention to the reversal of primogeniture in the Table and the significance it may have in regard to the realization of the blessing. Weimar also maintains that the primaeval blessing is fulfilled in Gen. 10.1-32,[39] yet he does not consider how the placement of Shem's genealogy last in the Table may relate to it. This is especially notable, given that Weimar discusses the Toledot structure in detail.[40] Contrary to the aforementioned scholars, we have argued thus far that the primaeval blessing is not fulfilled in the Table, but is in the *process* of being realized. The placement of Shem's genealogy last in the Table seems to indicate that the blessing will be taken up by Shem's line in particular (Gen. 10.21-31). Given that the Shemite genealogy is primary in Gen. 10.1-32, this may even have implications for how the Table is identified.

6. *Identification of the Table*

Scharbert has observed that the new Toledot marks a turning point in salvation history and that one part of the family, that is, the secondary line, is mentioned first and then drops off. While this point has been noted previously, Scharbert develops this idea further in his identification of the two lines. He identifies the secondary line as the *Ausscheidungstoledot*, 'separated out Toledot' or 'left out Toledot',[41] which has the connotation of disqualification. The result of the *Ausscheidungstoledot* is that the promise and blessing are narrowed down to a smaller group of people and are taken up in the main line which Scharbert identifies as the *Verheißungstoledot*, 'promise Toledot'. Relevant for the present discussion is

---

37. Williamson, *1 and 2 Chronicles*, p. 25.
38. Clines, 'Theme in Genesis 1–11', pp. 483–507 (494); cf. Hamilton, *Genesis 1–17*, p. 347.
39. Weimar, 'Die Toledot-Formel', pp. 65–93 (72); cf. *idem*, 'Aufbau and Struktur', pp. 174–203 (193).
40. Weimar, 'Die Toledot-Formel', pp. 65–93 (68).
41. Scharbert, 'Der Sinn der Toledot-Formel', pp. 45–56 (45). Scharbert notes that even if a Toledot is left out, it still keeps the more general blessing of Gen. 9.1 (pp. 45–56 [56]); cf. J. Scharbert, 'ברך', *TDOT*, Vol. 2, pp. 279–308 (307).

Scharbert's view that the Table of Nations is an *Ausscheidungstoledot.*[42] He suggests that, while the nations keep a more general blessing in Gen. 10.1-32, the story then moves forward to the Shemite genealogy (Gen. 11.10-26). Scharbert has highlighted that the placement of Gen. 10.1-32 and 11.10-26 seems to conform to the Toledot pattern which would indicate that the Table of Nations is the secondary line and that the Shemite genealogy is the main line. A similar view is espoused by Childs who notes that the segmented genealogies (Gen. 10.1; 25.12; 36.1) remain 'tangential to the one chosen line which is pursued by means of narratives and vertical genealogies'.[43] In view of the reversal already present in the Table of Nations, however, a modification of Scharbert's view may be necessary. While we would agree that Japheth (Gen. 10.2-5), Ham (Gen. 10.6-20), Aram (Gen. 10.23) and Joktan (Gen. 10.26-29) are being portrayed as secondary lines and thus they could be identified as part of the *Ausscheidungstoledot*, that the genealogy of Shem (i.e. Shem-Arpachshad-Shelah-Eber-Peleg) is being presented as the main line in the Table precludes Shem's line from being included in the *Ausscheidungstoledot*. This would, therefore, prevent the Table as a whole from being identified as an *Ausscheidungstoledot*. A question may also be raised concerning Scharbert's terminology. Given that the divine promises begin with Abram (Gen. 12.1-3), it is preferable to restrict the designation *Verheißungstoledot* to the Toledots of Isaac and Jacob. Thus we prefer to identify the genealogy of Shem in the primaeval history as the main line rather than the 'promise' Toledot, while acknowledging that it will become the line of promise.

A similar point may be made with respect to Andersen's view. Andersen maintains that the Table of Nations is being presented as the rejected genealogy.[44] He notes that Gen. 10.1-32 follows the pattern of the enumerative schema which is the same as the pattern used in the genealogies of Ishmael (Gen. 25.12-18) and Esau (Gen. 36.10-30). Andersen concludes that Gen. 10.1-32, like the Toledots of Ishmael and Esau, is the rejected genealogy whereas Gen. 11.10-26 is the chosen genealogy.[45] Andersen's arrangement of the lines from Noah to Shem is shown in the following diagram.[46]

42. Scharbert, 'Der Sinn der Toledot-Formel', pp. 45–56 (47).

43. B.S. Childs, *Introduction to the Old Testament as Scripture* (Philadelphia: Fortress Press, 1979), p. 146.

44. Andersen, 'Genealogical Prominence', pp. 242–63 (254–55).

45. As was noted previously, we have preferred to use the terms 'main' and 'secondary' lines rather than categories such as 'chosen' and 'rejected' since the notion of being 'chosen' by God is explicit only in the patriarchal narratives. Furthermore, as Scharbert has pointed out, the secondary lines do keep a more general blessing (cf. Gen. 21.13). This is in accordance with our view that the blessing is in the process of being realized in the Table of Nations; thus it is preferable to identify Ham and Japheth as secondary lines, rather than rejected lines.

46. Andersen, 'Genealogical Prominence', pp. 242–63 (255).

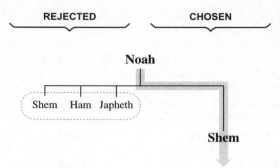

Andersen has not, however, discussed the reversal of order in the Table of Nations. If the reversal is taken into account, then it may be preferable to outline the genealogies in the following way:

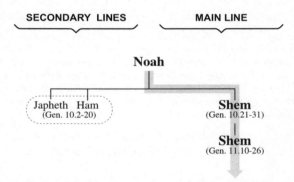

In sum, we have suggested that the Table of Nations shows that Japheth and Ham are secondary lines, and that Shem is the main line (Gen. 10.21-31). It is the main line that is then resumed in Gen. 11.10-26. Steinberg argues, however, that Shem's line is not the main line. Her view is worth closer examination.

7. *Steinberg's Assessment of Genesis 11.10-26*

Steinberg has considered the import of Gen. 11.10-26 for the book of Genesis and especially its function at the conclusion of the primaeval history. She rightly notes that current approaches to the Shemite genealogy are inadequate and that the 'problem of evaluating the genealogy of Shem, Gen. 11.10-26, in its present position in the text remains'.[47] Steinberg draws on the work of Tzvetan Todorov, a French literary critic, and applies his theory of narrative plot to the book of Genesis. Todorov proposes five stages in the movement of a narrative, moving

47. N. Steinberg, 'The Genealogical Framework of the Family Stories in Genesis', *Semeia* 46 (1989), pp. 41–50 (46).

from a stable situation (equilibrium) to an unstable situation (disequilibrium). Steinberg has applied this approach to Genesis, suggesting that the state of equilibrium is represented in the genealogies of Shem (Gen. 11.10-26), Ishmael (Gen. 25.12-18) and Esau (Gen. 36.1-43), whereas the state of disequilibrium is represented in the cycles of Terah (Gen. 11.27–25.11), Isaac (25.19–35.29) and Jacob (Gen. 37.1–50.26). Steinberg suggests that the genealogical material in Genesis has been organized into three cycles which are structurally parallel. Shem's genealogy (Gen. 11.10-26) is understood to be a genealogical superscription which introduces the first cycle of Terah's sons and their wives (Gen. 11.27–25.11). The second genealogical superscription is the genealogy of Ishmael (Gen. 25.12-18), which introduces the story of Isaac and his sons and their wives (25.19–35.29). The third cycle begins with Esau's genealogy (Gen. 36.1–37.1), which introduces the stories of Jacob's family (37.2–50.26). Steinberg suggests that the three genealogical superscriptions of Shem, Ishmael and Esau are structurally parallel, noting that no further information is given about their fates in the following narratives. Her conclusion about Gen. 11.10-26 is relevant to the present discussion. She suggests that

> the distinction made between the three genealogical superscriptions and the three genealogical units interrelated with the narratives casts a shadow on the three individuals mentioned as the leading figures in the former genealogies. Shem, Ishmael, and Esau are not distinguished as individuals chosen to be figures in the transmission of the primary Israelite family line. Rather, theirs is a secondary line of descent. They are placed outside the limelight given to the characters who are named in the genealogical narratives associated with the chosen Israelite lineage.[48]

While we would agree with Steinberg's assessment, that the lines of Ishmael and Esau are secondary, her view that Shem is also secondary is problematic for a number of reasons.

First, Steinberg maintains that Shem, Ishmael and Esau are parallel units and that 'in every respect, the generations of Ishmael recorded in Gen. 25.12-18 are the structural equivalent of the generations of Shem'.[49] It is important to recall, however, that these genealogies are not identical in form: the Shemite genealogy (Gen. 11.10-26) is linear whereas the genealogies of Ishmael (Gen. 25.12-18) and Esau (36.1-43) are segmented. If the form of a genealogy is related to its function, as Wilson has argued,[50] then one cannot assume that the linear Shemite genealogy has the same function as the segmented genealogies of Ishmael and Esau. Given that the Sethite (Gen. 5.1-32) and Shemite (Gen 11.10-26) genealogies are almost identical in form, it could be argued that the function of Gen. 11.10-26 should be compatible with the function of Gen. 5.1-32. Yet Steinberg does not discuss whether Gen. 11.10-26 is structurally related to 5.1-32 in any way. Instead, she assumes that Gen. 11.10-26 is structurally related only to what *follows*.

48. Steinberg, 'Genealogical Framework', pp. 41–50 (45).
49. Steinberg, 'Genealogical Framework', pp. 41–50 (46).
50. Wilson, 'Old Testament Genealogies', pp. 169–89 (179).

Secondly, Steinberg maintains that the genealogical superscriptions of Shem, Ishmael and Esau have 'no narratives to which they are later connected'.[51] While it may be true that the genealogies of Ishmael and Esau are not taken up in the following narratives, the same conclusion cannot be drawn regarding Shem's genealogy. Gen. 11.10-26 introduces Abram who is then the focus of the ensuing narrative. Even though Shem is not featured in the following chapters, it is evident that his genealogy is clearly connected to what follows. Thus there is a significant *difference* between the genealogies of Ishmael and Esau and Shem's genealogy: the former genealogies are followed by genealogical and narrative material concerning their *brothers*: Ishmael's Toledot is followed by *Isaac's* Toledot and Esau's Toledot is followed by *Jacob's* Toledot. In contrast, Shem's genealogy (Gen. 11.10-26) leads directly to narrative material about his descendants. His brothers have in fact already been mentioned in Gen. 10.1-32. It is evident, therefore, that Shem's genealogy *is* connected to the ensuing narrative since Terah and Abraham are his direct descendants.

Thirdly, Steinberg has not taken into account the reversal of primogeniture in Gen. 10.1-32, which places Shem's line as the primary line. As has been noted, special focus has been given to Shem in the Table of Nations; thus we may conclude, contrary to Steinberg, that Shem *has* been given the place of prominence. If the genealogies cast a 'shadow' on any individuals, as Steinberg suggests, it is Japheth and Ham who are in the shadow, not Shem. Rather than viewing Shem's line as the secondary line, we have argued that the lines of Japheth and Ham are being presented as secondary lines and that Shem's line is the main line. If this is the case, we may then enquire whether the Shemite genealogy has any function with regard to the primaeval blessing. Is there further evidence to support the view that the blessing is being taken up in Shem's line? What is the function of the *linear* Shemite genealogy in Gen. 11.10-26?

8. *The Shemite Genealogy (Genesis 11.10-26) and the Primaeval Blessing*

The importance of genealogies for biblical studies has been highlighted by M.D. Johnson[52] and R.R. Wilson.[53] Since the publication of Wilson's monograph, interest in Old Testament and ancient Near Eastern genealogies appears to have increased (although Robinson observes that genealogies have not featured in literary studies).[54] Genealogies in the book of Genesis have been the focus of a number of studies.[55] With regard to the primaeval history, Clines notes that the

51. Steinberg, 'Genealogical Framework', pp. 41–50 (44).

52. Johnson, *The Purpose of Biblical Genealogies*.

53. Wilson, *Genealogy and History*; cf. *idem*, 'The Old Testament Genealogies in Recent Research', *JBL* 94 (1975), pp. 169–89.

54. Robinson notes, for example, that Robert Alter does not discuss genealogies in his book, *The Art of Biblical Narrative* (Robinson, 'Literary Functions', pp. 595–608 [596 n. 1]).

55. Andersen, 'Genealogical Prominence', pp. 242–63 (267–82); T.C. Hartman, 'Some Thoughts on the Sumerian King List and Genesis 5 and 11B', *JBL* 91 (1972), pp. 25–32; R.S. Hess, 'The Genealogies of Genesis 1–11 and Comparative Literature', *Bib* 70 (1989), pp. 241–54; Robinson,

genealogies are not usually thought to have a theological function. He suggests, however, that there are 'some clues in the narrative sections of Gen 1–11 which point to the validity of a theological interpretation of the genealogies; that is, to the likelihood that the final author of the primaeval history intended them to express some theological purpose'.[56] Clines maintains that the genealogies affirm that the multiplication of the human race is to be viewed as a sign of the divine blessing. Westermann has also highlighted the importance of genealogies for Genesis 1–11. He notes that, while commentators discuss in great detail names that occur in genealogies, there is hardly any discussion of the meaning of genealogies for the whole. He maintains that 'to devalue implicitly the genealogies or to leave them aside must have far-reaching effects on one's final understanding of and judgment on the primaeval history'.[57] As with Clines and Westermann, Robinson has also expressed concern over the lack of attention to genealogies. His discussion of the interplay between the genealogies and narratives in Genesis underscores the import of genealogies for interpreting the text as a whole.[58]

While there has been an increased awareness of the import of genealogies, it is important to underscore that scholars who discuss the primaeval blessing in relation to the Table of Nations and the Babel story give no attention to how the Shemite genealogy in Gen. 11.10-26 may relate to the blessing. Anderson, for instance, comments briefly on Gen. 11.10-26, noting that it is different in genre from the Babel story. He also argues that the Babel story needs to be examined in its broader narrative context,[59] yet he does not discuss Gen. 11.10-26 in any way. Similarly, Harland does not consider the Shemite genealogy in his discussion of the Babel story, even though he discusses how Gen. 11.1-9 relates to what precedes (Gen. 9.1, 7; 10.5, 18, 32, etc.) and follows.[60] Kikawada has also considered Gen. 11.1-9 in relation to the primaeval blessing and concludes that it provides a 'fitting transition between the primeval history and the patriarchal history'.[61] Yet Gen. 11.10-26 is not included in his analysis. It is worth bearing in mind that the omission of Gen. 11.10-26 from the aforementioned discussions is not based on source-critical grounds, since each writer has considered how the blessing of Gen. 9.1 is being realized in the primaeval history according to its

'Literary Functions', pp. 595–608; J.M. Sasson, 'A Genealogical "Convention" in Biblical Chronography?', *ZAW* 90 (1978), pp. 171–85; Smith, 'Structure and Purpose', pp. 307–19 (307–18); Steinberg, 'Genealogical Framework', pp. 41–50 (41–50).

56. Clines, 'Theme in Genesis 1–11', pp. 483–507 (491).

57. Westermann, *Genesis 1–11*, p. 3 (= *Genesis*, Bd. I, pp. 3–4). See also Robinson, 'Literary Functions', pp. 595–608.

58. Robinson, 'Literary Functions', pp. 595–608.

59. Anderson, 'The Tower of Babel', pp. 165–78 (168, 173).

60. Harland, 'The Sin of Babel', pp. 515–33 (527–33). Regarding what follows, Harland notes that the Babel story has been placed immediately prior to the patriarchal narratives and that 'God uses the covenant with Abraham to deal with mankind's sinfulness' (pp. 515–33 [532]).

61. Kikawada, 'The Shape of Genesis 11.1-9', pp. 18–32 (32). Van Wolde does not mention Gen. 11.10-26 in her chapter on the Babel story (*Words Become Worlds*, pp. 104–109).

final form.[62] Why, then, has the Shemite genealogy been omitted from discussions of the primaeval blessing? To be sure, there are differing opinions as to whether Gen. 11.10-26 is part of the primaeval history or not, but does not the relentless succession of 'begettings' in the Shemite genealogy raise the question whether it is in some way related to the injunction to 'be fruitful and multiply'?

Lack of attention to Gen. 11.10-26 is even more surprising given that it (a) immediately follows the Babel story, (b) is temporally located in the *preceding* narrative (i.e. 'after the flood', Gen. 11.10; cf. Gen. 9.28; 10.1, 32), (c) resumes the earlier Shemite genealogy of Gen. 10.21-31, and (d) is similar in form to the Sethite genealogy (Gen. 5.1-32); thus suggesting that 11.10-26 is structurally parallel to 5.1-32. The question might rightly be asked, therefore, whether the Shemite genealogy has any theological function with respect to the realization of primaeval blessing after the flood.

9. *Structural Analysis: the Relationship of Genesis 5.1-32 and 11.10-26*

Westermann has considered the function of genealogies in relation to the primaeval blessing. He maintains that, just as Gen. 5.1-32 traces God's blessing from 1.28, Gen. 10.1-32 traces it from 9.1.[63] According to Westermann, the blessing is advancing through the succession of generations in Gen. 5.1-32, but through geographical dispersion in Gen. 10.1-32. This accords with the view espoused by a number of scholars, that the 'spreading out' of Noah's descendants marks the fulfilment of the blessing. It is important to examine the *structure* of the genealogies at this point, however.

Smith has evaluated Westermann's view by considering the structure of Genesis 1–11 and has made an important observation.[64] He affirms that Westermann's approach provides balance to the composition of the primaeval history since the blessing is traced in two genealogies – before the flood in the Sethite genealogy (Gen. 5.1-32) and after the flood in the Table of Nations (Gen. 10.1-32). Smith observes, however, that the Table of Nations is different in style from the linear genealogy in Gen. 5.1-32. The difference between the two genealogies has been noted by a number of scholars.[65] The Table of Nations is usually identified as a 'segmented' or 'enumerative' genealogy ('die namenaufzählende Genealogie' or 'Stammtafel'), whereas Gen. 5.1-32 and 11.10-26 are identified as 'linear'[66] or 'narrative' genealogies ('die erzählerische Genealogie').[67]

62. Harland first discusses the Babel story according to J and P sources; however, he does consider the story in its final form as well.

63. Westermann, *Genesis 1–11*, p. 528 (= *Genesis*, Bd. I, p. 705).

64. Smith, 'Structure and Purpose', pp. 307–19.

65. On the differences between Gen. 10.1-32 and the linear genealogies (Gen. 5.1-32; 11.10-26), see Tengström, *Die Toledotformel*, pp. 25–27; Wenham, *Genesis 1–15*, p. 215; Westermann, *Genesis 1–11*, p. 14 (= *Genesis*, Bd. I, p. 19).

66. Wilson, *Genealogy and History*, p. 9.

67. Tengström, *Die Toledotformel*, pp. 19–26; cf. Westermann, *Genesis 1–11*, p. 3 (= *Genesis*, Bd. I, p. 4).

Scholars have rightly observed that Gen. 5.1-32 is similar in form to Gen. 11.10-26.[68] Some have even argued that Gen. 5.1-32 and 11.10-26 originally comprised one continuous genealogy.[69] Furthermore, both genealogies conclude with segmentation: Gen. 5.32b concludes with the statement: ויולד נח את־שם את־חם ואת־יפת. This may be compared to the statement found at the conclusion of the Shemite genealogy where the names of Terah's three sons are given: ויולד את־אברם את־נחור ואת־הרן (Gen. 11.26b). The similarity between Gen. 5.1-32 and 11.10-26 is underscored by the fact that they both resume earlier genealogies (Gen. 4.25-26; 10.21-31). The genealogies mentioned first also have similar introductions. As has been noted, Shem's genealogy in Gen. 10.21 begins with the statement: ולשם ילד גם־הוא (Gen. 10.21). This resembles the statement made about Seth in Gen. 4.26: ולשת גם־הוא ילד־בן. Smith has rightly concluded that Gen. 10.1-32 is not the parallel genealogy to Gen. 5.1-32. Rather, the linear Shemite genealogy in 11.10-26 is the corresponding genealogy since it is almost identical in form.[70]

The importance of *form* in relation to genealogies has been underscored by Wilson, who has concluded from his analysis of anthropological data and Near Eastern texts that there is a close connection between the form and function of a genealogy. He maintains that the *function* of a genealogy is directly related to its form[71] and that 'future research must recognize the relationship between genealogical form and function'.[72] He concludes, therefore, that scholars who examine Old Testament genealogies 'must consider the influence of function on form and the limitations which form sometimes imposes on function'.[73] Given that the form of the linear Shemite genealogy (Gen. 11.10-26) is almost identical in form to the linear Sethite genealogy (Gen. 5.1-32), the question may well be raised whether these two genealogies have a similar *function*.

Wilson has analysed the function of the linear genealogy in Gen. 5.1-32. He notes, as other scholars have done, that the introduction echoes Gen. 1.27-28. He observes that 'man's fulfillment of the command to be fruitful is related by P in the genealogical narrative in 5.3' and suggests that 'the entire linear genealogy thus deals with the transmission of the divine image and the blessing through a

---

68. The similarity between Gen. 5.1-32 and 11.10-26 has been noted by a number of scholars: Brueggemann, *Genesis*, p. 94; Hess, 'Genealogies of Genesis 1–11', pp. 241–54 (243–44); Mathews, *Genesis 1–11.26*, p. 297; G.A. Rendsburg, *The Redaction of Genesis* (Winona Lake: Eisenbrauns, 1986), p. 19; Sailhamer, *The Pentateuch as Narrative*, p. 136; Sarna, *Genesis*, p. 85; Tengström, *Die Toledotformel*, pp. 19–21; Vawter, *On Genesis*, p. 159; Waltke, *Genesis*, p. 186; Weimar, 'Die Toledot-Formel', pp. 65–93 (76); Wenham, *Genesis 1–15*, p. 249; *idem*, 'The Priority of P', pp. 240–58 (242).

69. F.M. Cross, *Canaanite Myth and Hebrew Epic: Essays in the History of the Religion of Israel* (Cambridge, MA: Harvard University Press, 1973), p. 301; Hartman, 'Genesis 5 and 11B', pp. 25–32 (32); Speiser, *Genesis*, p. 79; Wenham, *Genesis 1–15*, p. 249.

70. Smith, 'Structure and Purpose', pp. 307–19 (311–12).

71. Wilson, 'Old Testament Genealogies', pp. 169–89 (179).

72. Wilson, 'Old Testament Genealogies', pp. 169–89 (189).

73. Wilson, 'Old Testament Genealogies', pp. 169–89 (189).

series of firstborn sons'.[74] He concludes, therefore, that the linear genealogy in Gen. 5.1-32 has a *theological* function. That the blessing of Gen. 1.28 is being realized through the Sethite genealogy has been noted by a number of scholars.[75] Given the frequency with which the verb ילד occurs in Gen. 5.1-32, it is not so surprising that the blessing has been linked to this genealogy. The focus of the genealogy is clearly on the multiplication of humankind, with only a few narrative comments (Gen. 5.1-2, 22, 24, 29). Genesis 5.2 testifies that genealogical succession is the result of the divine blessing. Accordingly, Robinson suggests that 'the genealogy of Seth in Genesis 5 is thus intended to take up the creation story' and concludes, therefore, that the genealogies become 'bearers of the creation theme'.[76] Smith reasons that if the Sethite genealogy traces the blessing from Gen. 1.28 *before* the flood and if the Shemite genealogy in Gen. 11.10-26 is its corresponding genealogy *after* the flood, then the commands, 'Be fruitful and multiply' are being realized in Gen. 11.10-26.[77] If this is the case, then Gen. 11.10-26 has a theological function comparable to the function of Gen. 5.1-32. Thus we may conclude that, just as the primaeval blessing is being realized *before* the flood in Gen. 5.1-32, it is being realized *after* the flood in 11.10-26. That these two linear genealogies have a similar function accords with Wilson's view that the function of a genealogy is directly related to its form.

It is noteworthy that Westermann agrees with Smith and others, that the genealogies of Gen. 5.1-32 and 11.10-26 are similar in form. He maintains that the Shemite genealogy is linked directly to the Sethite genealogy and that both genealogies form a steady, monotonous succession of generations. Westermann not only agrees that Gen. 5.1-32 and 11.10-26 are similar in form, but also maintains that P's genealogy in Gen. 10.1-32 is a completely new schema which has almost nothing in common with the genealogy in Gen. 5.1-32.[78] If the form of

---

74. Wilson, *Genealogy and History*, p. 164 (cf. pp. 158–68).

75. J.P. Fokkelman, 'Genesis', in R. Alter and F. Kermode (eds.), *The Literary Guide to the Bible* (Cambridge, MA: Harvard University Press, 1987), pp. 36–55 (42); Gunkel, *Genesis*, p. 137; Hamilton, *Genesis 1–17*, p. 255; Mathews, *Genesis 1–11.26*, p. 308; Robinson, 'Literary Functions', pp. 595–608 (600); Sarna, *Genesis*, p. 40; Weimar, 'Die Toledot-Formel', pp. 65–93 (80); Wenham, *Genesis 1–15*, p. 126; Westermann, *Genesis 1–11*, pp. 160, 528 (= *Genesis*, Bd. I, pp. 221, 705); Wilson, *Genealogy and History*, p. 164.

76. Robinson, 'Literary Functions', pp. 595–608 (600–601).

77. We agree with Smith's view that the commands to 'be fruitful and multiply' are being realized in the two linear genealogies (Gen. 5.1-32; 11.10-26); however, we are not persuaded by his view that the Table of Nations marks the fulfilment of the command to 'fill the earth' (see our earlier discussion of פרה and פרד). Furthermore, given that Noah's sons are clearly multiplying in Gen. 10.1-32, it is difficult to sustain the view that the commands to 'be fruitful and multiply' are *not* being realized in some way in Gen. 10.1-32. Mathews similarly argues that the universal blessing is realized through the progeny of Seth and Shem (Gen. 5.1-32; 11.10-26). We disagree with Mathews, however, in his assumption that the blessing is *only* realized through these lines (Mathews, *Genesis 1–11.26*, p. 116). What we are proposing is that the blessing is being realized whenever humankind multiply (e.g. Gen. 4.1, 2, 17; 6.1; 10.1, etc.), yet it is also advancing in the Sethite and Shemite genealogies in particular.

78. Westermann, *Genesis 1–11*, p. 14 (= *Genesis*, Bd. I, p. 19). Westermann comments on the differences between the two genealogies, noting that the Table of Nations is nothing more than a list of names. He observes that no statements of birth or begetting are made in P's genealogy and that even the term 'son' in Gen. 10.1-32 is used in the sense of 'belonging to' rather than the usual sense.

Gen. 11.10-26 is linked directly to that of Gen. 5.1-32, as Westermann suggests, and Gen. 5.1-32 traces the blessing of Gen. 1.28 through the succession of generations, is it not plausible, therefore, that the Shemite genealogy similarly traces the blessing of Gen. 9.1 through its own steady, monotonous succession of generations? Yet Westermann argues that the primaeval blessing is being traced from Gen. 1.28 to the linear Sethite genealogy (Gen. 5.1-32), then from Gen. 9.1 to the Table of Nations (Gen. 10.1-32). What we are suggesting, however, is that the primaeval blessing is being traced through the primary lines of Seth and Shem, that is, from Gen. 1.28 to the linear Sethite genealogy (Gen. 5.1-32), and from Gen. 9.1 to the linear Shemite genealogy (Gen. 11.10-26). In the case of Shem, the blessing is already advancing through his line in the Table (10.21-31), as indicated by the reversal of primogeniture. Our view is outlined in the following diagram:

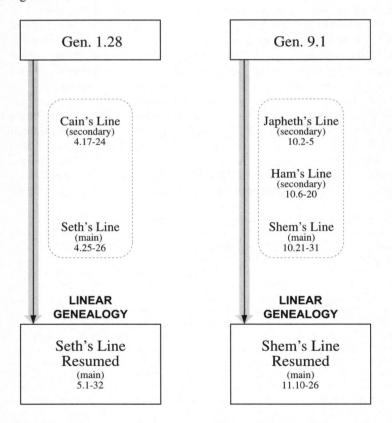

This is not to deny that the blessing is in the process of being realized in the secondary genealogies of Cain (4.17-24), Japheth (10.2-5) and Ham (10.6-20),[79]

---

79. The outworking of the blessing through the secondary lines will be discussed in the following chapter.

but is to suggest that the primaeval blessing is advancing in the Sethite (5.1-32) and Shemite (10.21-31; 11.10-26) genealogies in particular.

10. *Conclusion*

We observed at the outset of our discussion that the genealogies of Shem, Ham and Japheth in the Table are presented in the reverse order. It was noted that the literary feature of presenting the main line last is found in the patriarchal narratives. The reversal of primogeniture, which places Shem's genealogy last in the Table, seems to suggest that Shem's line is the main line. We noted that in the patriarchal narratives, the Abrahamic blessing advances in the main line. That Shem is being presented as the main line intimates that, already in the Table of Nations, the primaeval blessing is being taken up in his genealogy (10.21-31). Since Shem's genealogy is resumed in 11.10-26, the question was raised whether this genealogy has a similar theological function. This was confirmed by considering the *form* of the genealogy in 11.10-26. It was noted that the linear Shemite genealogy is similar in form to the linear Sethite genealogy (Gen. 5.1-32) and that the primaeval blessing is clearly being taken up in Gen. 5.1-32 (cf. 5.1-2). Since Gen. 11.10-26 is the parallel genealogy after the flood, it may well be the case that the primaeval blessing is progressing in Gen. 11.10-26 through the succession of generations. The linear Shemite genealogy may be seen, therefore, as a positive affirmation that God's creational purposes are advancing.[80]

---

80. Scholars have rightly noted that the statement, 'and he died', which is prominent in Gen. 5.1-32, is absent in 11.10-26. This may even suggest that there is a more optimistic outlook with regard to Shem's genealogy. Accordingly, Sarna writes that the 'air of pessimism about the seemingly incorrigible nature of man that rises from the preceding narratives is now relieved by the emphasis on life, on a new birth, on the orderly sequence of the generations, on the possibility of a fresh start for humanity' (*Genesis*, p. 85).

Chapter 6

DOES THE PRIMAEVAL HISTORY END ON A NOTE OF JUDGMENT?

1. *Introduction*

It has been argued thus far that the primaeval blessing is being taken up in Shem's line in particular (10.21-31; 11.10-26). Genesis 11.10-26 thus testifies to the advancement of the primaeval blessing in spite of YHWH's judgment at Babel. A number of scholars argue, however, that the primaeval history concludes on a sombre note of judgment with no hope for the future. This interpretation is based primarily on von Rad's analysis of the judgment-grace schema in the Yahwistic primaeval history. He observes that YHWH responds to human sin with increasingly severe judgments, culminating in the dispersion and dissolution of humankind's unity. He also notes, however, that in and after the judgment there is YHWH's saving and sustaining activity: Adam and Eve are banished from the garden, but YHWH clothes them and allows them to remain alive; Cain is to live a life wandering aimlessly, but YHWH provides a protective mark for him; the world is destroyed through the flood, but Noah and his family are preserved through divine intervention.[1] Von Rad has persuasively shown that alongside the divine judgment there is usually an act of mitigation or grace. Westermann similarly notes in his discussion of the crime-punishment schema in Genesis 1–11 that with each punishment there is some type of pardon or amnesty.[2]

Especially relevant to the present discussion is von Rad's observation, that there is no word of grace after YHWH's judgment at Babel. He concludes that the primaeval history breaks off in 'shrill dissonance' and that the question regarding God's relationship to the nations is an urgent concern.[3] Are the nations rejected under God's wrath forever? According to von Rad, the primaeval history gives no answer to the question whether God's grace is finally exhausted. He maintains, however, that the 'missing' element of grace or mitigation is to be found in Gen. 12.1-3 in YHWH's promise to Abram.[4] He notes that YHWH's plan is to bless the

---

1. Von Rad, *Genesis*, p. 152 (= *Das erste Buch Mose*, p. 116); cf. von Rad, *Old Testament Theology*, Vol. 1, p. 163 (= *Theologie des Alten Testaments*, Bd. I, p. 177).
2. Westermann, *The Promises to the Fathers*, p. 54 (= *Die Verheißungen an die Väter*, p. 56).
3. Von Rad, *Genesis*, p. 153 (= *Das erste Buch Mose*, p. 117).
4. Von Rad, *Old Testament Theology*, Vol. 1, pp. 163–65 (= *Theologie des Alten Testaments*, Bd. I, pp. 176–78); cf. *idem*, *Genesis*, pp. 153–34 (= *Das erste Buch Mose*, pp. 117–18).

nations through Abram (Gen. 12.3).[5] Von Rad is of the opinion, therefore, that Gen. 12.1-3 is the real key to the primaeval history and indeed its conclusion.

Von Rad's view, that God's gracious action is missing in and after the Babel judgment, is espoused by a number of scholars. Ross, for instance, states that the history of all mankind

> comes to an abrupt end, which leaves the human race hopelessly scattered across the face of the earth. It is this that makes the present narrative so different from those preceding it: In each judgment there was a gracious provision for hope but in this judgment there is none. It does not offer a token of grace, a promise of a blessing, a hope of salvation, or a way of escape… There is no ray of hope…The blessing is not here…[6]

A similar view is expressed by Muilenburg who observes that there is no element of grace after the Babel judgment. He concludes, therefore, that the scattering of the nations 'is, to all intents and purposes, the end'[7] and that 'at Babel's tower and the nations' scattering, the gates to the future seemed closed once for all…'.[8] It is evident that these scholars agree with von Rad, that God's gracious action is absent in and after the Babel judgment and that the primaeval history concludes on a note of exile. The 'missing' element of grace is thus located in the call of Abram in Gen. 12.1-3. Clines has developed von Rad's view further, arguing that the patriarchal narratives as a whole function as the mitigation element.[9]

These scholars have rightly drawn attention to the significance of YHWH's initiative with Abram, concluding that Gen. 12.1-3 is to be seen as an act of grace or mitigation and that God's blessing to the nations will come through him (Gen. 12.3). Is their view, however, that there is no word of God's 'preserving and succouring grace'[10] after the Babel judgment, an accurate assessment? Does YHWH's scattering the Babelites indicate that the 'gates to the future seemed closed once for all'? Before answering these questions, consideration needs to be given to the relationship of Gen. 11.1-9 to 10.1-32. Scholars have rightly observed that even though Gen. 10.1-32 has been placed *before* 11.1-9, the Table describes what took place *after* the Babel judgment. The question may well be asked, therefore, whether the 'missing' element of grace is in any way present in Gen. 10.1-32, since it 'chronologically' follows 11.1-9. It is first necessary, however, to discuss the literary relationship of Gen. 10.1-32 and 11.1-9 and consider whether it is valid to interpret these two texts in light of each other.

5.   Von Rad, *Old Testament Theology*, Vol. 1, p. 164 (= *Theologie des Alten Testaments*, Bd. I, p. 177).

6.   Ross, 'The Dispersion of the Nations', pp. 119–38 (127); cf. Bailey, 'Genealogies in Genesis', pp. 267–82 (269); Turner, *Genesis*, p. 60.

7.   J. Muilenburg, 'Abraham and the Nations', *Int* 19 (1965), pp. 387–98 (389).

8.   Muilenburg, 'Abraham and the Nations', pp. 387–98 (393); cf. Mathews, *Genesis 1–11.26*, p. 59; Nacpil, 'Between Promise and Fulfilment', pp. 166–81 (170).

9.   Clines, *The Theme of the Pentateuch*, p. 78; cf. Bailey, 'Genealogies in Genesis', pp. 267–82 (269).

10   Nacpil, 'Between Promise and Fulfilment', pp. 166–81 (170).

2. *Chronological Considerations: Genesis 10.1-32 and 11.1-9*

As has been noted, several scholars conclude that Gen. 10.1-32 and 11.1-9 present *different* views of the dispersion and division of languages.[11] They argue that the dispersion is viewed positively in Gen. 10.1-32, but negatively in 11.1-9. Furthermore, they note that the dispersion is presented as a natural phenomenon in 10.1-32, but the result of divine judgment in 11.1-9. Some scholars conclude, therefore, that the two texts are incompatible and irreconcilable. Driver suggests that the Babel story developed independently and has been rather imperfectly accommodated into its present literary context.[12] Similarly, von Rad maintains that these texts are only rather loosely connected.[13] In light of these views, the relationship between Genesis 10 and 11 is in need of closer examination. Is there any evidence to suggest that the Babel story is more closely connected to its literary context than is supposed by these scholars?

a. *Genesis 11.1-9 in Its Literary Context*

An examination of Gen. 11.1-9 shows that a number of key words and motifs employed in the Babel story also occur in the primaeval history. First, the dispersal motif, which is dominant in the Babel story (פוץ: Gen. 11.4, 8, 9), has already been introduced in Gen. 9.19 (נפץ) and appears in the Table as well (פוץ, Gen. 10.18).[14]

Secondly, the location of the Babelites' settlement מקדם, 'from the east' (NRSV, Gen. 11.2), is thematically related to the preceding narrative. The phrase מקדם in Gen. 11.2 has been translated in a variety of ways including 'from the east' (NRSV; KJV, NKJV),[15] 'eastward, east' (NIV; NASB),[16] or 'in the east'.[17] While English translations may differ, it is noteworthy that קדם occurs on several occasions (with the preposition מן and without it) in the preceding chapters: YHWH plants a garden in Eden מקדם (Gen. 2.8); he drives out Adam and Eve from the garden and places the cherubim מקדם לגן־עדן (Gen. 3.24); Cain went from the presence of the LORD, and settled in the land of Nod קדמת־עדן (Gen. 4.16) and Joktan's descendants dwelt הר הקדם (Gen. 10.30).[18] Some scholars have argued that the

---

11. See our Introduction, pp. 2–4.

12. Driver, *Genesis*, p. 133; cf. Skinner, *Genesis*, p. 224.

13. Von Rad, *Genesis*, p. 152 (= *Das erste Buch Mose*, p. 116).

14. As has been noted, the connection between Gen. 9.19 and the Babel story is also seen in the fact that כל־הארץ is the subject in 9.19 and 11.1.

15. Hamilton, *Genesis 1–17*, p. 349; von Rad, *Genesis*, p. 147 (= *Das erste Buch Mose*, p. 112); Sarna, *Genesis*, p. 81; Westermann, *Genesis 1–11*, p. 544 (= *Genesis*, Bd. I, p. 724). Skinner argues that נסע is essentially a verb of departure and thus it is more likely that מקדם would signify the point *from which* the Babelites travelled (*Genesis*, p. 225, n. 1).

16. BDB, p. 869; Mathews, *Genesis 1–11.26*, p. 478; cf. Gen. 13.11 where מקדם is used with נסע, as in Gen. 11.1, and means 'eastward'.

17. Gunkel, *Genesis*, p. 97; Wenham, *Genesis 1–15*, p. 238; cf. Gen. 2.8; 12.8; Isa. 9.12 [11].

18. See Sailhamer's discussion of the eastward movement in Genesis (*The Pentateuch as Narrative*, pp. 134–35).

'eastward' movement of the builders has negative connotations in this context.[19] The point to note is that מִקֶּדֶם in Gen. 11.2 is thematically related to the preceding narrative.

Thirdly, the Babelites are identified as בְּנֵי הָאָדָם in Gen. 11.5. Even though the identical construct phrase does not occur elsewhere in Genesis, הָאָדָם does appear throughout the primaeval history.[20] In fact, the term אָדָם (or הָאָדָם) occurs over fifty times in Genesis 1–11, but only once in Genesis 12–50 (Gen. 16.12). The construct expression בְּנוֹת הָאָדָם also occurs in Gen. 6.2, 4. The identification of the builders as בְּנֵי הָאָדָם thus accords well with the primaeval history which focuses on humankind.

Fourthly, there are a number of other features in the Babel story which are also found in the primaeval history: the divine plural (Gen. 11.7; cf. Gen. 1.26; 3.22); YHWH's investigating (i.e. 'seeing') a crime prior to his act of judgment (Gen. 11.5; cf. Gen. 6.5); YHWH's intervention against *potential* human behaviour (Gen. 11.6; cf. Gen. 3.22, 24); the act of building a city (Gen. 10.10-12; 11.4; cf. Gen. 4.17); reference to the city בָּבֶל (Gen. 10.10; 11.9); the place עַל־פְּנֵי כָּל־הָאָרֶץ (Gen. 11.4, 8, 9; cf. Gen. 1.29; 7.3; 8.9);[21] and the theme of language/ tongue (Gen. 10.5, 20, 31; 11.1, 7, 9). Mathews has outlined vocabulary present in the Babel story which also occurs in the garden of Eden story (Genesis 2–3).[22] He concludes that Gen. 11.1-9 must be understood against the background of the primaeval events collectively.[23]

Fifthly, Rendsburg has shown that the Babel story and the Nephilim episode share a number of motifs and words which underscore the interconnectedness of the two texts.[24] Other scholars have seen a connection between Gen. 6.1-8 and 11.1-9 at a structural level.[25] Clines has also pointed out that the name motif found in Gen. 6.1-4 (i.e. 'men of name') is related thematically to Cain's ambition of striving to perpetuate his family name (Gen. 4.17) and to the Babelites' striving to make a name for themselves (Gen. 11.4).[26] As has been noted, the name motif is even present in the proper name שֵׁם (Gen. 9.18; 10.1, 21; 11.10) and in the identification of his descendants as בְּנֵי שֵׁם (Gen. 10.22). Furthermore, YHWH's promise to make Abraham's שֵׁם great in Gen. 12.2 is in juxtaposition with the Babelites' striving for a שֵׁם *for themselves* (Gen. 11.4).[27] Och suggests

---

19. Cf. Mathews, *Genesis 1–11.26*, p. 478; Sailhamer, *The Pentateuch as Narrative*, p. 134.

20. E.g., Gen. 2.7, 8, 16, 18, 20, 25; 3.9, 20; 4.1, 25; 5.1.

21. Kikawada, 'The Shape of Genesis 11.1-9', pp. 18–32 (31).

22. Mathews, *Genesis 1–11.26*, p. 467, n. 134.

23. Mathews, *Genesis 1–11.26*, p. 465.

24. Rendsburg, *The Redaction of Genesis*, pp. 19–22.

25. Andersen, 'Genealogical Prominence', pp. 242–63 (260–61); Sasson, 'The "Tower of Babel"', pp. 211–19 (218–19).

26. Clines, 'The Significance of the "Sons of God" Episode', pp. 33-46 (37-38); cf. Jenkins, 'A Great Name', pp. 41–57 (46).

27. See Jenkins, 'A Great Name', pp. 41–57 (45); Ruppert, '"Machen wir uns einen Namen…" (Gen. 11,4)', pp. 28–45; O.H. Steck, 'Genesis 12,1-3 und die Urgeschichte des Jahwisten', in H.W. Wolff (ed.), *Probleme biblischer Theologie: G. von Rad FS* (Munich: Chr. Kaiser Verlag, 1971), pp. 525–54 (536); Turner, *Announcements of Plot*, p. 52; H.M. Wolff, 'The Kerygma of the Yahwist',

that YHWH's making Abram's name great is to be seen as a reversal of the disintegration seen in the Babel story: God freely grants to Abram what the generation at Babel sought to secure independently from God.[28] It seems to be the case, therefore, that the Babelites' striving to make a name for themselves is thematically related to what precedes (Gen. 4.17; 6.4; 10.1, 21, 22) and to what follows (Gen. 11.10; 12.2).

In sum, while the Babel story may have originally been an independent story, as it now stands, the presence of key words and motifs in Gen. 11.1-9, which are present in the broader literary context, suggests that the Babel story has been incorporated into the primaeval history.[29] We may conclude, therefore, that Gen. 11.1-9 is not as 'loosely connected' as von Rad suggests. As has been noted, the Babel story is not only thematically related to the primaeval history as a whole, but also to the Table of Nations which immediately precedes it. Thus it seems appropriate to interpret Gen. 10.1-32 and 11.1-9 together since the two stories share common themes. Accordingly, even von Rad acknowledged that Gen. 10.1-32 and 11.1-9 must be read together, because they have been placed 'intentionally next to each other in spite of their antagonism'.[30]

b. *Are the Two Texts Reconcilable?*
While some scholars have concluded that Gen. 10.1-32 and 11.1-9 are irreconcilable, a number of more recent scholars are of the opinion that the two accounts are complementary and mutually explanatory.[31] Wenham argues, for example, that the author of Genesis regarded the Table of Nations and the Babel story as complementary. He maintains that the two stories have been brought into 'mutual relationship' and that they 'shed light on each other'.[32] Similarly, Cassuto maintains that the two accounts are not only complementary, but necessary to each other. He notes that, while the Table of Nations assumes different languages, the Babel story *explains* how this occurred.[33] It may also be pointed out that, even though the dispersion is portrayed as a natural process of migration in Gen. 10.1-32, this does not necessarily mean that it contradicts Gen. 11.1-9, as some scholars assert.[34] To be sure, Gen. 10.1-32 does not mention that the dispersion and different languages are the result of divine judgment as the Babel story does, but its silence

---

Int 20 (1966), pp. 131–58 (141–42) (= 'Das Kerygma des Jahwisten', *Evangelische Theologie* 24 [1964]), pp. 73–98 [83]).

28. B. Och, 'The Garden of Eden: From Re-Creation to Reconciliation', *Judaism* 37 (1988), pp. 340–51 (343 n. 1).

29. See Kikawada, 'The Shape of Genesis 11.1-9', pp. 18–32 (31–32); Sailhamer, *The Pentateuch as Narrative*, pp. 134–36.

30. Von Rad, *Genesis*, p. 152 (= *Das erste Buch Mose*, p. 116).

31. Blenkinsopp, *The Pentateuch*, p. 90; Cassuto, *Genesis*, Vol. 2, p. 144; Mathews, *Genesis 1–11.26*, p. 473; J. Rogerson, *Genesis 1–11* (Old Testament Guides; Sheffield, JSOT Press, 1991), p. 75; Ross, *Creation and Blessing*, p. 243; Wenham, *Genesis 1–15*, p. 242.

32. Wenham, *Genesis 1–15*, p. 242; cf. Ross, *Creation and Blessing*, p. 243.

33. Cassuto, *Genesis*, Vol. 2, pp. 143–44; cf. Blenkinsopp, *The Pentateuch*, p. 90.

34. Driver, *Genesis*, p. 133; Skinner, *Genesis*, p. 224.

regarding the reason for this does not mean that it contradicts Gen. 11.1-9. That is, Gen. 10.1-32 does not give a *different* explanation for the dispersion and the variety of languages. Rather, it does not give *any* explanation. It simply describes the dispersion as a fact and assumes the presence of different languages (10.5, 20, 31). Von Rad's view, therefore, that the Babel story 'gives a quite different explanation of the division of mankind into a great number of peoples'[35] seems to lack evidence. It could even be argued that the absence of an explanation for the different languages in Gen. 10.1-32 actually points forward to Gen. 11.1-9 where the reason is given.

c. *Is the 'Dischronology' of Genesis 10.1-32 and 11.1-9 Problematic?*

Another problem inherent in Gen. 10.1-32 and 11.1-9 is the 'dischronology' of the two texts. Scholars have rightly observed that the circumstantial clause which introduces the Babel story, ויהי כל־הארץ שפה אחת ודברים אחדים, 'Now the whole earth had one language and the same words' (NRSV, Gen. 11.1), takes the reader back to a period *prior* to the Table. This indicates, therefore, that even though the Table of Nations has been placed *before* Gen. 11.1-9, it actually follows the Babel story *chronologically*. While the 'dischronology' of the two texts has been problematic for some scholars, this need not be the case. Martin has shown that 'dischronology' is found in Egyptian and Assyrian texts, as well as in a number of biblical texts.[36] Long has also observed that a writer can 'manipulate the chronology of events' for a number of reasons: 'the narrator could sharpen characterization, provide ironic perspective, or comment on the story with didactic intent – all in the rhetorical interest of shaping sympathies, attitudes and perceptions'.[37] It is also worth pointing out that there are several instances in the primaeval history where a genealogy or new episode is introduced by a statement that takes the reader back to an earlier time (Gen. 5.1-2; 6.1; 11.10). This literary feature has been observed by Anderson, who notes that in the editorial process of the primaeval history, the writers

> give primacy to Priestly material, but at appropriate places add the Old Epic tradition that harks back to an earlier point in the Priestly outline, and to a certain extent, is parallel… Similarly, after the flood story the writers continue with the (basically) Priestly Table of Nations, then add the Babel story, which resumptively reverts to an earlier time before the proliferation of Noah's sons into ethnic and linguistic groups.[38]

In the case of the Babel story, the 'dischronology' means that the *effect* (Gen. 10.1-32) has been told before the *cause* (Gen. 11.1-9). We may recall at this

---

35. Von Rad, *Old Testament Theology*, Vol. 1, p. 163 (= *Theologie des Alten Testaments*, Bd. I, p. 176).

36. W.J. Martin, ' "Dischronologized" Narrative in the Old Testament', in *Congress Volume, Rome 1968* (VTSup, 17; Leiden: E.J. Brill, 1969), pp. 179–86. He concludes that there are three possible reasons for 'dischronology': (a) poor memory of the events, (b) arrangement of events according to their geographical location, and (c) subordination of certain events to highlight more important events (pp. 179–86 [186]).

37. B.O. Long, 'Framing Repetitions in Biblical Historiography', *JBL* 10 (1987), pp. 385–99 (399).

38. Anderson, 'The Tower of Babel', pp. 165–78 (174).

point the view of Clines, who argues that the placement of Gen. 10.1-32 prior to 11.1-9 means that the dispersion is being presented as the fulfilment of the primaeval blessing. We have suggested, however, that the dispersion in Gen. 10.1-32 is not as 'positive' as is commonly assumed and that there is no indication in Gen. 10.1-32 that the primaeval blessing has been fulfilled. Is there an alternative solution to the placement of these two texts?

d. *Divine Providence*
When Gen. 10.1-32 and 11.1-9 are read in light of each other, the Babel story provides the *theological* explanation for events which are first presented as a 'natural' phenomenon (Gen. 10.1-32). It is worth noting, however, that while the theological explanation *follows* Gen. 10.1-32, there are hints of divine involvement already in the Table. To begin with, we have argued that the reversal of primogeniture indicates that Japheth and Ham are secondary lines and that Shem's line is primary. The emergence of Shem's line as the primary line seems to intimate that divine election is in process in the Table. Secondly, Cassuto suggests that the numerical symmetry in the Table shows that the dispersion of people did not occur haphazardly according to chance circumstances, but took place according to a preconceived divine plan – even though humankind were unaware of it. Cassuto thus concludes that the Table reveals divine providence at work.[39]

In terms of the placement of the two texts, that a theological explanation lies behind seemingly 'natural' events and that the explanation actually *follows* the events rather than preceding them invites comparison with the Joseph story. Genesis 37 relates how Joseph was sold into slavery by his brothers. The following chapters then describe the events that ensue. But it is not until Gen. 45.5, some eight chapters later, that a *theological* explanation for Joseph's being sold into slavery is revealed: God himself had caused it to take place (Gen. 45.5, 7-8; 50.20; cf. Ps. 105.17). Cohn has observed that, apart from one occasion (Gen. 46.2-4), God is silent in the Joseph narratives. He notes, however, that 'if God is not a visible presence, he is nonetheless credited with the invisible movement of events... Not above but within human actions God works, even if the actors are unaware of it'.[40] That the revelation of God's involvement is delayed in the Joseph story serves to underscore divine providence behind seemingly 'natural' events. The Table of Nations and the Babel story may be analogous to the Joseph story in that the dispersion of the nations is portrayed as a seemingly 'natural' event, but the *following* story reveals that God was the one who brought it to pass. As has been noted, there are already hints of this in the Table. The placement of the Babel story *after* the Table of Nations may well serve to underscore divine providence. If Gen. 10.1-32 and 11.1-9 are read together, then the Babel story indicates that a seemingly natural process of migration was brought about through divine intervention. This accords with Deut. 32.7-8, which attributes the division of humankind to God.[41]

---

39. Cassuto, *Genesis*, Vol. 2, p. 175.
40. Cohn, 'Narrative Structure', pp. 3–16 (12).
41. As has been noted, Deut. 32.8 marks the only occurrence of פרד in the Pentateuch outside

In sum, there is sufficient evidence to indicate that, while the Babel story may have been originally independent, as it now stands, it is an integral part of the primaeval history and is not irreconcilable with its immediate context. Thus it is appropriate to read Gen. 10.1-32 and 11.1-9 in light of each other. The 'dischronology' of the two texts may well serve to underscore divine providence at work. We may now return to the question posed earlier – whether the element of grace after the Babel judgment is in any way present in the Table of Nations.

3. *Does Genesis 10.1-32 Contribute to the Judgment-Grace Schema?*

Von Rad maintains that the element of grace, which is missing in and after the Babel story, is located in Gen. 12.1-3. Turner similarly suggests that the reader is to look for the 'missing' element of grace in the ensuing narrative (Gen. 12.1-3).[42] But if Gen. 10.1-32 chronologically *follows* Gen. 11.1-9, is it possible that the 'missing' element of grace is located in the *preceding* Table? Clines seems to have alluded to this possibility when examining the judgment-grace schema in the primaeval history. It is noteworthy that he locates Gen. 10.1-32 under the column entitled *Mitigation* – albeit with a question mark. His chart is outlined as follows.[43]

	I. *Sin*	II. *Speech*	III. *Mitigation*	IV. *Punishment*
1. Fall	3.6	3.14-19	3.21	3.22-24
2. Cain	4.8	4.11-12	4.15	4.16
3. Sons of God	6.2	6.3	? 6.8, 18ff.	? 7.6-24
4. Flood	6.5, 11f.	6.7, 13-21	6.8, 18ff.	7.6-24
5. Babel	11.4	11.6f.	? 10.1-32	11.8

Even though Clines concludes with von Rad, that the element of grace associated with YHWH's judgment in the Babel story is to be found in Gen. 12.1-3 and in the patriarchal narratives as a whole, his chart suggests that Gen. 10.1-32 could at least be a *potential* location in which God's gracious action is at work. The question may be asked, therefore, whether the element of grace is in any way present in the Table of Nations.

According to von Rad, the goal of the Table is the *nations*; thus he does not consider Shem's line to be particularly important. Rather, the line is drawn from Noah to the nations (Gen. 10.1-32).[44] Nacpil similarly concludes that the

---

Genesis. The hiphil form of פרד in Deut. 32.8 underscores the divine causation of the division. While the niphal form of פרד in the Table (10.5, 32) could have an active meaning (cf. Gen. 13.11), thus suggesting that the people are separating themselves, it could also have a passive sense (cf. Gen. 25.23). This would be in accordance with Gen. 11.1-9, which shows that YHWH caused the division. The niphal form of פוץ also occurs in Gen. 10.18; however, the hiphil form of פוץ occurs in the Babel story (11.8, 9), thus underscoring that YHWH brought about the scattering.

42. Turner, *Genesis*, p. 60.

43. Clines, *The Theme of the Pentateuch*, p. 63.

44. Von Rad, *Old Testament Theology*, Vol. 1, p. 162 (= *Theologie des Alten Testaments*, Bd. I, p. 175).

historical line of Israel's election is not a linear line from Noah to Abraham, but God – the nations – Israel.[45] No special importance is again ascribed to Shem's line in the Table. As with von Rad, Nacpil has not discussed the reversal of primogeniture in any way. We have argued thus far, however, that Noah's three sons are not presented in equal light. On the contrary, the reversal of primogeniture indicates that the lines of Japheth and Ham are secondary and Shem's line is the main line. This observation, along with the presence of the linear Shemite genealogy (Gen. 11.10-26), indicates that the line from primaeval time leads lineally, from Adam to Abraham (Gen. 5.1-32; 11.10-26; cf. 10.21-31). This linear genealogical line is confirmed in 1 Chron. 1.1-27 where the primaeval and patriarchal genealogies have been brought together. The Chronicler thus demonstrates that 'if Israel's election was realized in Jacob, it was implicit in Adam'.[46] Similarly, Japhet writes of the Chronicler's genealogy, that it 'expresses a unique concept of the election of Israel as beginning with Adam'.[47] Von Rad's view, that Israel did not draw a direct line from Noah to Abraham, is thus problematic. Israel is implicitly represented in the Table in the Shemite genealogy (Gen. 10.21-31).

In light of the views of von Rad and Nacpil, it is not surprising that they conclude that there is no hope for the future after the Babel judgment, since they have not taken note of the reversal of primogeniture in the Table. That there even *is* a primary line in Gen. 10.1-32 suggests that there is a ray of hope amidst the dispersion. If the primaeval blessing is advancing in the Shemite genealogy (Gen. 10.21-31), then YHWH's scattering the nations is not 'to all intents and purposes, the end'.[48] Rather, God's intention for his creation is advancing through Shem's line. Given that the Table of Nations describes what took place *after* the Babel story, we may conclude that God's relationship to the nations has not been finally broken off after his judgment in 11.1-9. Rather, the divine relationship with the nations continues through the line of *Shem*. Given that YHWH is identified as the 'God of Shem' in Gen. 9.26 (NIV, NASB), this may even indicate that Shem is in a special relationship with YHWH, analogous to YHWH's unique relationship with Abraham, Isaac and Jacob in Genesis,[49] and with Israel in Exodus.[50] We may conclude, therefore, that the 'gates to the future' are not 'closed once for all' after the Babel judgment.[51] Neither has God's grace been finally exhausted: amidst divine judgment there is once again evidence of divine grace, demonstrated by the emergence of Shem's line as the primary line. This is congruent with Williamson's view, that the genealogies in 1 Chronicles 1 emphasise 'the element of divine election and grace inherent in this material'.[52] Just as divine election and grace

45. Nacpil, 'Between Promise and Fulfilment', pp. 166–81 (168).

46. Williamson, *1 and 2 Chronicles*, p. 41.

47. Japhet, *I & II Chronicles*, p. 56.

48. Muilenburg, 'Abraham and the Nations', p. 389.

49. YHWH is identified as the God of Abraham (e.g. Gen. 24.12, 27, 42, 48; 26.24; 28.13; 31.42, 53; 32.9) and Isaac (Gen. 28.13; 32.9) in Genesis, and the God of Abraham, Isaac and Jacob in the book of Exodus (e.g. Exod. 3.15, 16).

50. E.g. Exod. 5.1; 34.23.

51. Muilenburg, 'Abraham and the Nations', p. 393.

52. Williamson, *1 and 2 Chronicles*, p. 40.

are inherent in the structuring of the genealogies in 1 Chronicles 1, we suggest that they are inherent in the structuring of the genealogies in Gen. 10.1-32 which places Shem's line as the primary line. We conclude, therefore, that God's preserving and succouring grace is not 'oddly absent' after the judgment of Babel, as Nacpil suggests.[53] Rather, divine grace is effective in the primary line of Shem (Gen. 10.21-31; 11.10-26). Herein lies the hope after the Babel judgment.

One final observation may be made. Clines has noted that God's grace is not only present in and after the judgment, as von Rad proposes, but even *before* the execution of punishment. Clines observes, for example, that YHWH clothes Adam and Eve (Gen. 3.21) *before* they are banished from the garden (Gen. 3.22-24). Similarly, YHWH places a mark on Cain (Gen. 4.15) *before* he leaves for the land of Nod (Gen. 4.16). We noted that Clines locates Gen. 10.1-32 under the *Mitigation* column, which *precedes* column IV entitled *Punishment*. It is helpful to recall line five of Clines' chart.[54]

	I. *Sin*	II. *Speech*	III. *Mitigation*	IV. *Punishment*
5. Babel	11.4	11.6f.	? 10.1-32	11.8

If the element of grace is present in the Table of Nations in the Shemite genealogy (Gen. 10.21-31), then the placement of the Table *prior* to the Babel judgment locates the element of mitigation *before* the execution of the judgment – not chronologically but thematically. The 'dischronology' of the two texts shows, therefore, that even before the judgment at Babel, God's gracious action is effective in the line of Shem. Since Shem's genealogy is resumed *after* the Babel story in Gen. 11.10-26, we may also conclude that God's gracious action continues to be effective after the divine judgment at Babel as well.

4. *How Does the Primaeval History Conclude?*

Von Rad argues, however, that God's gracious action *is* missing after the Babel judgment. It is important to note at this point that von Rad's analysis of the judgment-grace schema lacks a discussion not only of the reversal of primogeniture in the Table, but also of the linear Shemite genealogy in Gen. 11.10-26. When von Rad asserts that the primaeval history concludes with God's judgment, it is evident that he is referring to Gen. 11.1-9. As has been noted, von Rad then argues that God's gracious action missing after the Babel judgment is to be located in Gen. 12.1-3 with the call of Abram. A discussion of the linear Shemite genealogy in Gen. 11.10-26 is conspicuously absent, however, from his analysis. Rather, he seems to assume that *Gen. 12.1-3* immediately follows the Babel story. Similarly, Nacpil, who affirms von Rad's view, concludes that

> with sudden abruptness the text under consideration marks off the *end* of primordial history and at the same time *begins* a new history in the call of Abraham. The field of action suddenly narrows from universal history to the life of one man and the history

53. Nacpil, 'Between Promise and Fulfilment', pp. 166–81 (170).
54. Clines, *The Theme of the Pentateuch*, p. 63.

of one people. Between the one and the other, there is marked off unmistakable a radical break, a revolutionary change.[55]

As with von Rad, Nacpil does not discuss Gen. 11.10-26 in any way. He seems to assume that the call of Abram in Gen. 12.1-3 follows immediately after the Babel story. Wenham also suggests that the primaeval history ends on a gloomy note in Gen. 11.1-9, yet he does not mention the Shemite genealogy in 11.10-26. Rather, he proceeds to the patriarchal stories beginning in ch. 12.[56] An examination of von Rad's work shows that his omission of the Shemite genealogy is based on source-critical grounds – he is simply dealing with the Yahwistic narrative.[57] But von Rad is inconsistent in his omission of Gen. 11.10-26 from the discussion since he argues that the Table of Nations and Babel story 'must be read together, because they are intentionally placed next to each other in spite of their antagonism'.[58] If Gen. 10.1-32 and 11.1-9 *must* be read together, could it not be argued that Gen. 11.1-9 and 11.10-26 must also be read together, since they have been intentionally placed next to each other? To be sure, von Rad assigns Gen. 11.1-9 to J and 11.10-26 to P. Yet his omission of 11.10-26 on source-critical grounds cannot be defended, since he argues that Gen. 10.1-32 and 11.1-9 – texts which von Rad himself ascribes to two different sources – must be read together.[59] We suggest, therefore, that the Babel story (Gen. 11.1-9) and the Shemite genealogy (Gen. 11.10-26) should also be read together, since they have been intentionally placed next to each other.

This view is confirmed by observing that Gen. 11.10-26 is clearly connected to the preceding context. First, Gen. 5.1-32 and 11.10-26 are structurally parallel, thus suggesting that 11.10-26 is an integral part of the primaeval history. Secondly, the temporal marker in 11.10, which states that Arpachshad was born 'two years after the flood' (Gen. 11.10), locates the genealogy in the preceding narrative (cf. Gen. 10.1, 32). Thirdly, Gen. 11.10-26 is also connected to 10.1-32 in its resumption of the Shemite genealogy already mentioned in 10.21-31. Moreover, we have noted that special attention has been given in the Shemite genealogy to Eber's *two* sons, Peleg and Joktan (Gen. 10.25), yet only Joktan's descendants are listed in the Table (Gen. 10.26-29). That Peleg's descendants are not listed in the Table seems to point forward to Gen. 11.10-26 where his genealogy is resumed. The omission of Peleg's sons from the Table makes sense only when it is read in connection with Gen. 11.10-26. Fourthly, Clines has rightly noted that the identity of Shem as the first member of the genealogy (Gen. 11.10-26) can only properly be understood when read in connection with the preceding narrative

55. Nacpil, 'Between Promise and Fulfilment', pp. 166–81 (170).

56. Wenham, *Story as Torah*, pp. 36–37.

57. Von Rad notes briefly at the end of his discussion that the link between the primaeval history and the sacred history exists only in the Priestly version (11.10-26). No theological significance, however, is drawn from the placement of the Shemite genealogy after the Babel story and prior to the call of Abram (von Rad, *Genesis*, p. 155 [= *Das erste Buch Mose*, p. 118]).

58. Von Rad, *Genesis*, p. 152 (= *Das erste Buch Mose*, p. 116).

59. P = 10.1a, 2-7, 20, 22-23, 31-32; J = 10.1b, 8-19, 21, 24-30; 11.1-9 (von Rad, *Genesis*, pp. 139, 145, 147 [= *Das erste Buch Mose*, pp. 105, 110, 112]).

where he is identified as: (a) one of the three sons of Noah (Gen. 5.32; 9.18; 10.1); (b) the son blessed by his father (Gen. 9.26) and (c) one of three families who separated after the flood (Gen. 10.21-31).[60] In sum, while the linear Shemite genealogy may have originally been an independent genealogy, as it now stands, it is an important part of the primaeval history. We suggest, therefore, that the Shemite genealogy in Gen. 11.10-26 should not be precluded from the discussion of the judgment-grace schema in the primaeval history. Its placement immediately after the Babel story and prior to the call of Abram in Gen. 12.1-3 needs to be taken seriously.

If Gen. 11.10-26 is included in the discussion, then the assertion of von Rad and other scholars, that the primaeval history ends on a note of judgment, may need some modification. To be sure, the Babel story does end with YHWH's judgment, but already in the Table of Nations, God's gracious action is effective in the primary line of Shem. The linear Shemite genealogy, which immediately *follows* the Babel story, resounds with the affirmation that, in spite of divine judgment, divine grace is at work ensuring that God's intention for his creation advances. Thus God's grace or forgiving will to save is revealed both *before* the execution of judgment (Gen. 10.21-31) and *after* it (Gen. 11.10-26). The primaeval history does not, therefore, come to an abrupt end, leaving the human race hopelessly scattered over the earth.[61] Amidst the context of divine judgment, the primaeval blessing continues to advance in the Shemite genealogy. Therefore, the gates to the future are not closed once for all. Divine grace ensures that God's intention for his creation continues to advance.

5. Conclusion

The question was raised at the outset of the discussion whether von Rad's view, that the element of grace is absent after the Babel judgment, is an accurate assessment. Having argued that Gen. 10.1-32 and 11.1-9 should be read together, we suggested that the 'missing' element of grace may well be located in the Table of Nations, which describes what took place *after* the Babel judgment. The reversal of primogeniture in the Table, which presents Shem's line as the main line, points to divine grace at work. Since the primaeval blessing is being taken up in the Shemite genealogy, this intimates that there is hope amidst the dispersion. Thus we maintain that the primaeval history does not end on a note of judgment. On the contrary, the Shemite genealogy affirms that, in spite of the divine judgment, God's preserving and succouring grace has not been finally exhausted. Given that Shem's genealogy leads to Abraham, we may raise the question whether God's gracious action continues to be effective in the lives of the patriarchs. If so, in what way? Moreover, does the divine promise of increase given to Abraham and his seed contribute in any way to the realization of the primaeval blessing after the flood?

60. Clines, *The Theme of the Pentateuch*, p. 78.
61. Ross, 'The Dispersion of the Nations', pp. 119–38 (127); cf. Bailey, 'Genealogies in Genesis', pp. 267–82 (269); Turner, *Genesis*, p. 60.

Chapter 7

DOES THE PROMISE OF INCREASE TO THE PATRIARCHS CONTRIBUTE TO THE REALIZATION OF THE PRIMAEVAL BLESSING AFTER THE FLOOD?

1. *Abram as the Goal of the Shemite Genealogy (Genesis 11.10-26)*

We have argued thus far that the primaeval blessing is advancing in the Shemite genealogy (Gen. 10.21-31; 11.10-26). The linear Shemite genealogy in Gen. 11.10-26 moves swiftly forward, without interruption, until it reaches Terah and his three sons (Gen. 11.26). It is noteworthy, however, that Terah, who occupies the ninth position in the genealogy,[1] is not its goal. In the parallel Sethite genealogy (Gen. 5.1-32), it is the tenth position occupied by Noah which is of prime importance. That Terah is not the central figure may even be confirmed by the fact that his death notice is given in v. 32, only five verses after his Toledot has been introduced. The linear genealogy seems to point forward to the tenth position, which is occupied, in fact, by Terah's *three* sons: Abram, Nahor and Haran (Gen. 11.26). Gen. 11.26-28 reads as follows:

> When Terah had lived for seventy years, he became the father of Abram, Nahor, and Haran. Now these are the descendants of Terah. Terah was the father of Abram, Nahor, and Haran; and Haran was the father of Lot. Haran died before his father Terah in the land of his birth, in Ur of the Chaldeans (NRSV, Gen. 11.26-28).

Even though Terah's three sons are listed at the conclusion of the genealogy (Gen. 11.26), the linear form seems to indicate that, in the final analysis, only one member will occupy the tenth position. Analogously, the linear Sethite genealogy concludes with Noah's three sons, Shem, Ham and Japheth (Gen. 5.32), yet only Shem is mentioned in 11.10-26. We may well ask the question: who will occupy the important tenth position in the linear Shemite genealogy?

If the literary feature of presenting the secondary line first is taken into consideration, the presentation of Haran's genealogy *first* in v. 27, 'Haran was the father of Lot', even though he is mentioned *last* in the preceding verse (i.e. Abram, Nahor, Haran), intimates that Haran's line is a secondary line.[2] That details of

---

1.   While Terah occupies the ninth position in the MT, the LXX has inserted the name Cainan (Καϊνάν) after Arpachshad (11.12), making Terah the tenth member of the genealogy. See G. Larsson, 'The Chronology of the Pentateuch: A Comparison of the MT and the LXX', *JBL* 102 (1983), pp. 401–409.

2.   The same feature is found in Gen. 9.18 where the three sons of Noah are given. This is

Haran's death are given in v. 28 confirms this, leaving either Abram or Nahor as the potential tenth member. Given that Abram is the focus of the ensuing narrative and that YHWH speaks to him alone (Gen. 12.1-3), we can conclude that he is the main figure; thus he could be identified as the tenth member of the genealogy.[3] This is the position assigned to Abram by the Chronicler in 1 Chron. 1.24-27. Instead of concluding the linear genealogy with Terah's *three* sons, Abram, Nahor and Haran (Gen. 11.26), the genealogy in 1 Chron. 1.24-27 mentions only Abram: 'Shem, Arpachshad, Shelah; Eber, Peleg, Reu; Serug, Nahor, Terah; Abram, that is, Abraham' (NRSV, 1 Chron. 1.24-27). The Chronicler's omission of Terah's two sons, Nahor and Haran (cf. Gen. 11.27), from the genealogy clearly places Abraham in the tenth position. It appears, therefore, that a direct line has been drawn from Shem to Abraham.[4]

We have argued thus far that the primaeval blessing is in the process of being realized in the Table of Nations, but is not *fulfilled* there. Rather, it is advancing in the Shemite genealogy in particular. It would not be surprising, therefore, if language from the primaeval blessing were to reappear in connection with Abraham's progeny, since Shem's genealogy leads to Abraham. Moreover, given that the element of grace after the judgment at Babel seems to be effective in Shem's line, the question may be raised whether God's gracious action is in any way effective in the patriarchal narratives. If this is the case, it would further support Clines' view that the patriarchal narratives as a whole function as the mitigation element.

2. *The Primaeval Blessing Is Reaffirmed to Abraham's Progeny*

We noted earlier that the verbs פרה, 'be fruitful' and רבה, 'multiply', which are employed in the primaeval blessing, are frequently used in connection with Abraham and his seed.[5] The occurrences of these two verbs in Genesis are outlined as follows.[6]

---

immediately followed by the statement that 'Ham was the father of Canaan' (Gen. 9.18b). While this information anticipates the ensuing story, Ham is again identified as the father of Canaan in v. 22. The brief genealogical notice in Gen. 9.18b may well alert the reader to the fact that Ham's line (Ham-Canaan) will not be the main line. Noah's cursing of Canaan in Gen. 9.25 would then confirm what is already intimated in Gen. 9.18. Analogously, we suggest that the brief genealogy of Haran (Haran-Lot) intimates that Haran's line, which includes Lot, will not be the main line. The separation of Lot from Abram in Genesis 13 would then confirm that Lot is not part of the main line.

3. G.W. Coats, *Genesis, with an Introduction to Narrative Literature* (Forms of the Old Testament Literature, 1; Grand Rapids: Eerdmans, 1983), p. 105; Vawter, *On Genesis*, p. 159.

4. Hereafter we will not distinguish between Abram or Abraham, but simply use the name Abraham.

5. Citations are from the NRSV. The verbs פרה and רבה (Gen. 1.28; 9.1) occur together a further five times in Genesis 12–50 (Gen. 17.20; 28.3; 35.11; 47.27; 48.4) and together only another five times in the remaining books of the Old Testament (Exod. 1.7; Lev. 26.9; Jer. 3.16; 23.3; Ezek. 36.11).

6. Our emphasis is not on the *origin* of the promises, but on how they are related to the primaeval blessing according to the final form of the text. As has been noted previously, the view that the primaeval blessing is fulfilled through YHWH's scattering the Babelites requires that J and P texts be read together.

Humankind:	God blessed them, and God said to them, 'Be *fruitful* and *multiply*, and fill the earth' (Gen. 1.28a).
Noah:	God blessed Noah and his sons, and said to them, 'Be *fruitful* and *multiply*, and fill the earth' (Gen. 9.1).
	'And you, be *fruitful* and *multiply*, abound on the earth and *multiply* in it' (Gen. 9.7).
Abraham:	...the LORD appeared to Abram, and said to him, '...and [I] will make you exceedingly *numerous*... I will make you exceedingly *fruitful*' (Gen. 17.1-2, 6).
	The angel of the LORD called to Abraham a second time from heaven, and said, '... I will indeed bless you, and I will make your offspring as *numerous* as the stars of heaven and as the sand that is on the sea-shore' (Gen. 22.15-17).
Isaac:	The LORD appeared to Isaac and said, '... I will make your offspring as *numerous* as the stars of heaven' (Gen. 26.2, 4).
	[Isaac said] 'Now the LORD has made room for us, and we shall be *fruitful* in the land' (Gen. 26.22).
	And that very night the LORD appeared to him and said, '... [I] will bless you and make your offspring *numerous* for my servant Abraham's sake' (Gen. 26.24).
Ishmael:	The angel of the LORD also said to her, 'I will so greatly *multiply* your offspring that they cannot be counted for multitude' (Gen. 16.10).
	[God said to Abraham] 'As for Ishmael, I have heard you; I will bless him and make him *fruitful* and exceedingly *numerous*' (Gen. 17.20a).
Jacob:	Then Isaac called Jacob and blessed him, ... 'May God Almighty bless you and make you *fruitful* and *numerous*, ...' (Gen. 28.1, 3).
Jacob/Israel:	God said to him, 'I am God Almighty: be *fruitful* and *multiply*' (Gen. 35.11). And Jacob said to Joseph, 'God Almighty appeared to me . . . and he blessed me, and said to me, "I am going to make you *fruitful* and *increase* your numbers; ..."' (Gen. 48.3-4).
Israel:	Thus Israel settled in the land of Egypt, ...and they gained possessions in it, and were *fruitful* and *multiplied* exceedingly (Gen. 47.27).

It is noteworthy that פרה and רבה have not been used in reference to the nations in general. In other words, we do not read that God promises to 'make fruitful and multiply' someone other than Abraham's progeny. Instead, the promise of increase proceeds along the genealogical line of Abraham, Isaac and Jacob (and Ishmael who is blessed by God on account of his being Abraham's offspring;[7] cf. Gen. 21.13). In view of the above texts, Clines has rightly concluded that the primaeval blessing has been *reaffirmed* or *reapplied* to Abraham's progeny.[8] The blessing given to humankind in Gen. 1.28 and 9.1 thus advances in one family in particular. Accordingly, Wenham rightly notes that the Abrahamic promises mean 'that at least one nation is going to achieve that goal'.[9] Clines has further observed that, since the primaeval commands are confined primarily to the Abrahamic family, the outworking of them 'proceeds in a significantly different way from

---

7.   Robinson, 'Literary Functions', pp. 595–608 (604).

8.   Clines, *The Theme of the Pentateuch*, p. 79; cf. Bailey, 'Genealogies in Genesis', pp. 267–82 (269); Clines, *What Does Eve Do to Help?*, pp. 55–56; W.J. Dumbrell, *Covenant and Creation* (Grand Rapids: Baker Book House, 1984), pp. 63, 71.

9.   Wenham, *Genesis 1–15*, p. li.

that envisaged in ch. 1'.[10] Clines appears to be referring to the *particular* outworking of the blessing, which is different from Gen. 1.28 and 9.1 where the blessing is given to humanity as a whole. If, however, the primaeval blessing is advancing in Shem's line already in the Table, then this *different* way, namely, the *particular* outworking of the primaeval blessing, is already suggested in Gen. 10.1-32. It is also intimated prior to the flood in the Sethite genealogy (Gen. 4.25-26; 5.1-32). The promise of increase given to Abraham could be construed, therefore, as the continuation and elaboration of what has already begun in the Table. Similarly, if the element of grace after the Babel judgment is effective in the Shemite genealogy (Gen. 10.21-31; 11.10-26), then God's promises to Abraham may be seen as a further development of the grace motif which is already intimated in Gen. 10.1-32. Our interpretation of the Shemite genealogy does not deny, therefore, that the element of grace is effective in Gen. 12.1-3 and indeed in the patriarchal narratives as a whole, as Clines proposes. What we are suggesting, however, is that the element of grace after the Babel judgment is already present in the primaeval history in Shem's genealogy (Gen. 10.21-31; 11.10-26).

The implication of these two observations, that the particular blessing is already in progress in the Table and that the element of grace is effective in Shem's line, is that a clear break between the primaeval history (Genesis 1–11) and salvation history (Genesis 12–50) is not so easily discerned. Clines has already drawn this conclusion by observing that there is no textual break at the end of the Babel story. He notes that the Abrahamic material does begin a new section, yet also observes that one cannot determine where the pre-Abrahamic material actually concludes.[11] He notes that Shem's genealogy in Gen. 11.10-26 is clearly connected to both what precedes and what follows. He draws the conclusion, therefore, that it is unlikely that the primaeval history and patriarchal history are opposed to each other thematically.[12] We have come to a similar conclusion, suggesting that salvation history is already in progress in the Table,[13] with the emergence of Shem's line as the primary line, and that the promise of increase given to Abraham is a continuation of the primaeval blessing in Gen. 9.1. It is not surprising, therefore, to find that the Chronicler has drawn a genealogical line from Adam (1 Chron. 1.1) to Israel (1 Chron. 2.1) and that 'no particular attention is drawn to Abraham. Rather, the break comes only with Israel (2.1), after whom the genealogies are arranged on a quite different principle'.[14] According to the Chronicler's presentation of the primaeval and patriarchal genealogies, Israel's election does not begin with Abraham. Rather, it is already in progress in the primaeval history, beginning

10. Clines, *The Theme of the Pentateuch*, p. 79.

11. See the discussion of Clines on this topic (*The Theme of the Pentateuch*, p. 77); cf. Steinberg, 'Genealogical Framework', pp. 41–50 (48).

12. Clines, *The Theme of the Pentateuch*, p. 78.

13. Steinberg has come to a similar conclusion, arguing that the special history of Israel begins as early as Gen. 11.10 ('Genealogical Framework', pp. 41–50 [47]). While we agree with Steinberg's conclusion, we are not persuaded by her reason for it, namely that Gen. 11.10-26 is a genealogical subscription parallel to the Toledots of Esau and Ishmael.

14. Williamson, *1 and 2 Chronicles*, p. 40.

with Adam.[15] A similar point has been made by Luyten. He notes that in Deut. 32.8-9, the 'history of Israel itself starts in primeval times, before the patriarchs'[16] and suggests that the main theme of Deuteronomy 32 is that YHWH elected Israel as his people already in primaeval times. This is in accordance with our observation, that the *particular* outworking of the divine blessing is already in progress prior to the call of Abraham. What, then, is the import of the Abrahamic cycle in relation to the primaeval blessing? Is there any difference between the out-working of the blessing in the primaeval history and in the patriarchal narratives?

3. *What Is the Significance of the* Promise *of Increase Given to the Patriarchs?*

It is not insignificant that the reapplication of the primaeval blessing in Genesis 12–50 is in the form of a *promise*, being one of three main promises given to the patriarchs.[17] The promise of increase given to Abraham is articulated in Genesis 17, for example, when YHWH promised him: 'I will make you exceedingly numerous' (Gen. 17.2) and 'I will make you exceedingly fruitful' (Gen. 17.6).[18] Clines rightly notes that the first divine announcement in Gen. 1.28 is not 'set on one side but, apparently, added to. The reproduction element is turned from a command (1.28) into a prediction (12.2) and two further expectations are intro-duced'.[19] Scholars have noted that the reproduction element, which can also be identified as the *promise of increase*, is central to Genesis, whereas the promises of relationship and land have a subsidiary role.[20] Given the centrality of the reproduction element in Genesis, it is worth examining whether it relates to the primaeval blessing in Gen. 9.1 and whether there is further significance to the fact that the primaeval commands have been changed into a *promise*.

It has been argued thus far that the nations are under the blessing of Gen. 9.1. Since Abraham's progeny are included under the general blessing of fertility (Gen. 9.1), why, then, does God *promise* to multiply Abraham, Isaac and Jacob? Is not the multiplication of Abraham's offspring already assumed in light of Gen. 9.1? Why is there even the need for a divine promise? This raises the question whether the promise of increase given to the patriarchs is in any way different from the primaeval blessing.

15. Japhet, *I & II Chronicles*, p. 56; Williamson, *1 and 2 Chronicles*, p. 41.

16. J. Luyten, 'Primeval and Eschatological Overtones in the Song of Moses (DT 32,1-43)', in N. Lohfink (ed.), *Das Deuteronomium* (Leuven: Leuven University Press, 1985), pp. 341–47 (342).

17. For a comprehensive list of biblical texts relating to each of these promises, see Clines, *The Theme of the Pentateuch*, pp. 31–43.

18. The promissory nature of the blessing of increase is reflected in the verbal form used in the promises. Instead of the qal imperatives employed in Gen. 1.28, 9.1 and 9.7 (cf. Gen. 35.11), the verbs פרה and רבה commonly occur in the hiphil verbal form with the divine subject (e.g. Gen. 17.6, 20; 22.17; 26.4, 24; cf. Gen. 28.3; 41.52; 48.4; Ps. 105.24). The hiphil form underscores the causative action of God in bringing to fruition his promise.

19. Clines, *What Does Eve Do to Help?*, p. 55.

20. Clines, *The Theme of the Pentateuch*, pp. 45–46; cf. Wolff, 'The Kerygma of the Yahwist', pp. 131–58 (140–41) (= 'Das Kerygma des Jahwisten', pp. 73–98 [81–83]).

a. *Weimar's Approach*

Weimar has observed that the primaeval blessing, represented in stereotypical language by the three verbs ברך, פרה and רבה, continues throughout the patriarchal narratives. He concludes that the blessing means nothing more than fertility and increase and that it is always fulfilled with the birth of children. Weimar suggests that the insertion of the Toledot formula emphasizes this central idea of the narratives and that there is a narrowing down of the blessing to the patriarchs.[21] He further argues that there is no Toledot of Abraham because the guiding thought of Abraham is covenant rather than blessing. While Weimar has rightly highlighted the importance of fertility in the book of Genesis, his view that Abraham does not have a Toledot because the predominant idea is covenant rather than blessing is difficult to sustain in view of Gen. 12.1-3 where the verb ברך occurs five times, and in other texts where Abraham and his progeny are clearly blessed.[22] It could even be argued that the predominant idea *is* blessing. Wolff has concluded, in fact, that *blessing* becomes the interpretative word (*Deutewort*) of Israel from Abraham to David.[23]

Moreover, an examination of the promises to the patriarchs shows that, while a distinction can be made between the blessing of increase on Ishmael (Gen. 17.20) and the covenant with Isaac (Gen. 17.21), this is not always the case. For example, in Genesis 17 we read that YHWH said to Abraham,

> 'And I will make my covenant between me and you, and will make you exceedingly numerous'. Then Abram fell on his face; and God said to him, 'As for me, this is my covenant with you: You shall be the ancestor of a multitude of nations… I will make you exceedingly fruitful…' (NRSV, Gen. 17.2-4, 6a).

In this text, the promise of fertility is clearly associated with the covenant. We cannot easily separate, therefore, the blessing of increase from the notion of covenant, as Weimar has done. This point has been noted by Clines who observes that the promise of many descendants is one of three promises which are interrelated: 'For here in the Pentateuch the triple elements are unintelligible one without the other, never strongly differentiated one from another in their manifestation in the text, and each, in the accumulative effect, with the implication of the others'.[24] That the promise of increase is closely related to the promises of relationship and land, which are associated with the covenant, suggests that Weimar's view is unlikely.

Secondly, Weimar's proposal, that the promise of increase is nothing more than fertility, does not explain why the blessing of Gen. 9.1 has been changed into a *promise* and why the promise of increase is limited to Abraham's progeny.

21. Weimar, 'Die Toledot-Formel', pp. 65–93 (89–90).
22. Cf. Gen. 22.17, 18; 24.1; 24.35. God also blesses Sarah (Gen. 17.16), Ishmael (Gen. 17.20), Isaac (Gen. 25.11; 26.3, 12, 24, 29) and Jacob/Israel (Gen. 28.14; 32.29; 35.9, etc.). Wolff argues that the five-fold occurrence of ברך in Gen. 12.1-3 is parallel to the five-fold occurrence of ארר in Genesis 1–11 ('The Kerygma of the Yahwist', pp. 131–58 [145] [= 'Das Kerygma des Jahwisten', pp. 73–98 (86)]).
23. Wolff, 'The Kerygma of the Yahwist', p. 141 (= 'Das Kerygma des Jahwisten', p. 83).
24. Clines, *The Theme of the Pentateuch*, p. 31.

That the verbs פרה and רבה have been changed from commands into a divine promise may even indicate that there is further significance to them beyond the more general blessing articulated in Gen. 9.1. While Weimar does not differentiate between the primaeval blessing and the promise of increase to the patriarchs, Scharbert and Harland have made such a distinction. Their approach to this issue is worth closer examination.

b. *Approaches of Scharbert and Harland*
Scharbert suggests that there is both a *general* blessing at work in the nations and a *special* blessing at work in Israel. He maintains that the nations in Gen. 10.1-32 keep a more general blessing, whereas God is doing something new in Shem's line.[25] According to Scharbert, all living creatures and humankind are under the blessing of the creator (cf. Gen. 1.22, 28; 5.2; 9.1), whereas Israel is under a special blessing that depends on obedience to the law and is bestowed on Israel by the priests (Num. 6.23-24).[26] Harland has similarly suggested that two concentric circles are operating: an outer one which includes the whole world through Noah and his sons (Gen. 9.1), and a smaller circle which concerns the specific blessing and promise to Israel through Abraham.[27] The distinction made by Scharbert and Harland between a more general blessing on the nations and a particular blessing that is at work in Israel through Abraham is helpful for analysing the outworking of the primaeval blessing in Genesis.

c. *God's Blessing on the Nations and His Blessing on Israel through Abraham*
We have suggested that a more general blessing of increase applies to the nations, while at the same time there is a particular blessing at work in the line of Shem which leads to Abraham. Although the covenant relationship is not formally established with Shem, that his line is primary seems to indicate that the special blessing is already in process in the Table of Nations in Shem's line (Gen. 10.21-31). This is already intimated in Gen. 9.26 which identifies YHWH as the God of Shem. Scharbert and Harland have rightly differentiated between a more general blessing on the nations and a special blessing at work in Israel through God's promise to Abraham. However, an important question remains: if all the nations – including Shem's line which leads to Abraham – are under the general blessing of Gen. 9.1, why is there even the need for a divine *promise* of increase? In other words, why have a 'reproductive element' included in the promises to the patriarchs when humankind are already reproducing? What is the difference between the more general blessing of Gen. 9.1 and the special blessing at work in Israel through Abraham? Before answering these questions, it is first necessary to examine briefly the outworking of the primaeval blessing in Genesis 1–11.

---

25. Scharbert, 'Der Sinn der Toledot-Formel', pp. 45–56 (47, 57).
26. Scharbert, 'ברך', *TDOT*, Vol. 2, pp. 279–308 (307).
27. Harland, *The Value of Human Life*, p. 148.

d. *The Outworking of the Primaeval Blessing in Genesis 1–11*
As has been noted, the blessing of Gen. 1.28 is being realized in the first few chapters of Genesis whenever humans multiply. Thus the births of Cain (Gen. 4.1), Abel (Gen. 4.2) and Seth (Gen. 4.25) are the result of God's blessing given in Gen. 1.28. The genealogies also witness to the realization of the blessing (e.g. Gen. 4.17-24; 5.1-32). We may conclude, therefore, that both Cain's descendants (Gen. 4.17-24) and Seth's descendants (Gen. 5.1-32) are under the creation blessing. Yet not every individual contributes to the multiplication theme. For example, although Abel was under the blessing of Gen. 1.28, he did not 'multiply' since he was murdered by Cain. Thus murder is contrary to the primaeval blessing and adversely affects its realization. Turner similarly suggests that the 'lust for murder could make the ultimate goal of filling the earth a more difficult task than it should be'.[28] Robinson has discussed murder in relation to the genealogies, commenting especially on the two murders in Genesis 4:

> the use of the genealogy to link two murderers is highly ironic. Their actions in bringing life to an end contradict the whole logic of the genealogies, which normally record the orderly continuation of life from generation to the next. The irony, in turn, highlights a fundamental theme in Genesis, that human sin stands in profound contradiction to the created order of God. Cain's and Lamech's acts subvert the very nature of genealogical succession, which rests on the command to be fruitful and multiply in Genesis 1.28.[29]

Robinson has rightly pointed out that genealogies are based on God's commands to be fruitful and multiply, and that murder is antithetical to these commands. The genealogies testify to the continuation of life, whereas murder concerns the cessation of life.[30] Robinson has drawn attention to the fact that sin works in opposition to the created order. Rendtorff similarly concludes that Genesis begins with creation, 'but there follows immediately the endangering of the original intention of the creator by human sin (Genesis 3–4)'.[31]

That sin is contrary to the created order may even be suggested in the flood narrative. On two occasions we are told that 'the earth was filled with violence' (Gen. 6.11, 13). While the term חמס can refer to a violent act such as murder,[32] it has a wider range of meanings including acts of injustice, falsehood and oppression.[33] It is noteworthy that Gen. 6.11 and 6.13 mark the next occurrences of the

28. Turner, *Announcements of Plot*, p. 26. Turner has discussed the commands to subjugate the earth and rule over the living creatures (Gen. 1.28). He concludes that the commands are not to be taken as absolutes, but are 'malleable, subject to change or negation by various outside forces' (p. 49).

29. Robinson, 'Literary Functions', pp. 595–608 (600 n. 8).

30. Turner has come to a similar conclusion, noting that the commands to 'be fruitful, multiply, and fill the earth', are 'threatened by several factors: the pain of childbirth (cf. 3.16); murder (ch. 4); death (cf. chs 5, 10); human desire to settle in the one place (11.1-9); infertility (11.30)' (*Announcements of Plot*, p. 48).

31. R. Rendtorff, '"Covenant" as a Structuring Concept in Genesis and Exodus', *JBL* 108 (1989), pp. 385–93 (386).

32. E.g. Gen. 49.5; Judg. 9.24; cf. texts where חמס is used in parallel with דם (e.g. Ps. 72.14; Ezek. 7.23; Hab. 2.8, 17).

33. H. Haag, 'חמס', *TDOT*, Vol. 4, pp. 478–87 (480–87). See also the discussion by Harland, *The Value of Human Life*, pp. 32–44.

verb מלא after Gen. 1.28. There may well be an ironic allusion to the command of Gen. 1.28 in these two texts.[34] Humankind were to fill the earth with *themselves*, yet we read in Genesis 6 that the earth was filled with *violence* because of them (Gen. 6.11, 13). Thus the earth, which is deemed as being 'good' in Gen. 1.12, has been corrupted by humankind (Gen. 6.11).

That *sin* adversely affects the realization of the primaeval blessing is also seen in God's judgment against humanity through the flood. Humankind had been multiplying prior to the flood (Gen. 5.1-32; 6.1, etc.), although not to the point that the earth was filled with them. God's wiping out humankind on account of their wickedness (Gen. 6.5), however, clearly has an adverse effect on his intention expressed in Gen. 1.28. Instead of humans *filling* the earth, God *empties* the earth of humankind, save Noah and his family. Harland suggests, in fact, that God's renewal of the blessing after the flood in Gen. 9.1 seems to indicate that the flood is being portrayed as a reversal of the blessings given at creation.[35] Similarly, other scholars have argued that the flood is being presented as 'uncreation', that is, a reversal or undoing of the order of creation.[36] Accordingly, the reissuing of the commands after the flood in Gen. 9.1 may be seen as the re-establishment or renewal of the created order. It seems to be the case, therefore, that the realization of the primaeval blessing is adversely affected not only by murder, but by God himself when he judges humans on account of their wickedness (Gen. 6.5). Mathews thus concludes that the realization of the primaeval blessing 'is postponed (though not completely) by human disobedience'.[37] Given that it is human wickedness that invokes God's judgment, it could be concluded, therefore, that the real threat to the realization of Gen. 1.28 is sin.

Although the primaeval blessing is renewed after the flood (Gen. 9.1) and thus the creation mandate is re-established, there is the potential that the blessing will not be fully realized. This is due to the fact that human wickedness, which invoked YHWH's judgment before the flood (Gen. 6.5), continues after the flood (Gen. 8.21). To be sure, the covenant with Noah and his offspring (Gen. 9.8-17) does ensure that the creation will continue in spite of human sin. Rendtorff has compared the sin of humanity in the flood narrative with the sin of Israel in the golden calf incident (Exodus 32–34) and concludes that

> Both humanity and Israel are sinful, and remain sinful. Humanity's sin severely endangered the existence of the creation; Israel's sin endangered God's covenant with Israel. Both times God decides not to annihilate humanity or Israel but to grant them a continued existence guaranteed by his covenant. In other words, humanity's or Israel's

34. Cf. Cassuto, *Genesis*, Vol. 2, p. 52; Mathews, *Genesis 1–11.26*, p. 359; Turner, *Genesis*, p. 46; Wenham, *Genesis 1–15*, p. 171.

35. Harland, *The Value of Human Life*, p. 103.

36. Blenkinsopp, *The Pentateuch*, pp. 46–47; D.J.A. Clines, 'Noah's Flood: The Theology of the Flood Narrative', *Faith and Thought* 100 (1972–73), pp. 128–42 (136–38); *idem*, *The Theme of the Pentateuch*, pp. 73–76; Och, 'The Garden of Eden', pp. 340–51 (341).

37. Mathews suggests that God resolves to continue the hope of blessing through the lines of Seth and Noah (*Genesis 1–11.26*, p. 51).

> sin no longer can endanger the very existence of the creation or the covenant because
> God himself guarantees its continuation, despite human sin, because of his grace.[38]

Rendtorff has rightly noted that God's covenant in Genesis 9 guarantees the survival of the creation in spite of humanity's sin, and that creation exists by God's grace. It is worth pointing out, however, that the covenant in Genesis 9 does not guarantee that the primaeval blessing will be fully realized as envisaged in Gen. 1.28. God does not promise that he will refrain from *other* forms of judgment. What he does guarantee in Genesis 9 is that he will not wipe out his creation again as he did in the flood. Accordingly, while there are no floods in the post-diluvial world that wipe out humanity, God does judge individuals, people and nations: he scatters the Babelites (Gen. 11.1-9); he will judge the nation whom Abraham's descendants serve (Gen. 15.14); he destroys the inhabitants of Sodom and Gomorrah on account of their sin (Gen. 18.16-33; 19.1-29); and he takes the lives of Er and Onan who are evil in his sight (Gen. 38.7, 10). God's destroying the inhabitants of Sodom and Gomorrah, for instance, is thus contrary to the creational commands in Gen. 9.1 in the same way that the flood judgment is contrary to Gen. 1.28. While the destruction is not on the scale brought about by the flood, nevertheless, God's actions are still contrary to his intention for his creation expressed in Gen. 9.1. It seems to be the case, therefore, that God's judgment *after* the flood adversely affects the realization of the primaeval blessing. Clines has observed that the only obstacles in the path of fulfilling Gen. 9.1 are put there by God himself.[39] It needs to be pointed out, however, that on each occasion, God's 'obstacles' are his judgment against humans. Thus the real obstacle to the realization of Gen. 9.1 is human sin.

It may be concluded, therefore, that even though the primaeval blessing is given to humankind as a whole in Gen. 9.1, sin can endanger its realization at an individual level (e.g. Gen. 38.7, 10), as well as at the broader level of people and nation (e.g. Gen. 15.14; 19.1-29), as it did before the flood. We suggest, therefore, that while the primaeval blessing in Gen. 9.1 and the promise of increase to the patriarchs both speak of fertility, the reissuing of the primaeval commands by God in Gen. 9.1 does not guarantee that they will be fully realized. This provides the essential background against which to understand the divine promise of increase given to the patriarchs, and indeed, the *necessity* for the divine promise.

4. *The Promise of Increase to the Patriarchs Has the Divine Guarantee*

It is not coincidental that prior to the call of Abraham we are told that Sarah was barren (Gen. 11.30). Westermann suggests that this actually marks the beginning of the Abrahamic cycle.[40] Turner has noted that regardless of whether Gen. 11.30 is part of the conclusion to the primaeval history or whether it introduces the patriarchal narratives, the statement in Gen. 11.30 'announces that the fulfilment

---

38. Rendtorff, '"Covenant" as a Structuring Concept', pp. 385–93 (390).
39. Clines, *What Does Eve Do to Help?*, p. 52.
40. Westermann, *The Promises to the Fathers*, p. 133 (= *Die Verheißungen an die Väter*, p. 123).

of the command to multiply is under threat'.[41] We read further that Sarah is not only barren, but past the age of child-bearing (Gen. 18.11). This is striking in view of YHWH's promise to multiply Abraham's descendants. Moreover, it is not coincidental that Isaac's wife, Rebekah, is also barren (Gen. 25.21). This seems even more ironic, given that Rebekah is chosen as a wife for Isaac through divine guidance (Gen. 24.27, 48). Why would Abraham's servant be guided to a barren woman? To be sure, he was not aware of this, and Rebekah's family seem unknowingly to bless her with the hope that she would 'become thousands of myriads' (Gen. 24.60). Since Rebekah was chosen through divine guidance, however, there is the suggestion that even Rebekah's barrenness is within the divine plan. Finally, we read that Rachel, the beloved wife of Jacob, is barren (Gen. 29.31). In this case, Jacob clearly understood that it was God who had withheld the fruit of the womb from Rachel (Gen. 30.2; cf. Gen. 16.2). The patriarchal narratives thus underscore that God miraculously enables the patriarchs to multiply: God provides a son for Sarah in spite of her barrenness and old age (Gen. 18.10-14;[42] 21.1-2; 24.36). Sarah recalls these unusual circumstances when stating after the birth of Isaac, 'Who would ever have said to Abraham that Sarah would nurse children? Yet I have borne him a son in his old age' (Gen. 21.7). We read further that Rebekah gives birth to twins in answer to the prayer of Isaac (Gen. 25.24-26). God also opens Rachel's womb (Gen. 30.22), enabling her to bear Joseph (Gen. 30.23-24) and Benjamin (Gen. 35.16-18). Even Joseph, who was sold into slavery in Egypt, acknowledges when Ephraim was born that God had made him fruitful in the land of his *misfortunes* (Gen. 41.52). These stories testify to the realization of God's promise of increase to the patriarchs in spite of circumstances which would – without divine intervention – threaten its fulfilment. Fertility and increase, it seems, are guaranteed to Abraham's progeny because they have been promised by God himself.

a. *The Promise of Increase under Threat*
It is evident that an important motif that runs through the patriarchal narratives is that the patriarchs increase amidst humanly impossible circumstances. Helyer observes eight crises in the Abrahamic cycle alone (Gen. 11.27–25.11) which threaten the promise of an heir.[43] Similarly, Robinson notes that the promise proceeds along a linear genealogical line, while also observing that

41. Turner, *Announcements of Plot*, p. 33.
42. Westermann differentiates between the promise of a son and the promise of many descendants (*The Promises to the Fathers*, pp. 11–18 [= *Die Verheißungen an die Väter*, pp. 19–24]). Hamilton has also noted that in Genesis 15 the promise of a son (15.4) precedes the promise of many descendants (15.5), whereas in Genesis 17 the order is reversed (many descendants: 17.2, 16; a son: 17.16). Given the close relationship between the promise of a son and many descendants, we have included the promise of a son in the discussion of the promise of increase.
43. Helyer suggests the following crises: (1) Sarai's barrenness (Gen. 11.30); (2) the separation of Lot from Abraham which eliminates Lot as a potential heir (Genesis 13); (3) the war between several kings involving Lot and Abraham (Genesis 14); (4) the setting aside of Eliezer as a potential heir and the rejection of Ishmael as heir (Genesis 15–17); (5) Sarah's being taken by Abimelech (Genesis 20); (6) the emergence of Ishmael as a rival heir (Genesis 21); (7) Abraham's offering up his heir, Isaac

Genesis pursues virtually every imaginable threat to a linear genealogy. Sarai remains barren for eight full chapters until all hope of bearing children ceases. Then Isaac is born. Almost incomprehensibly, Abraham is shortly ordered to sacrifice his son. The God who up until this point has diligently protected the promise now appears its mortal enemy. But God spares Isaac; the reader has not been misled about divine intentions. Isaac takes a wife and the promise seems back on its genealogical track, but Rebecca and Isaac long remain childless.[44]

These threatening circumstances underscore that the increase of the patriarchs will be realized only through divine intervention. God's promise of increase thus comes with divine protection of the patriarchs and their wives. For example, God intervened to ensure Sarah's protection from Pharaoh (Gen. 12.10-20) and from Abimelech (Gen. 20.1-18). Jacob's life was also under threat because he had deceived Esau (Gen. 27.41). It is noteworthy that when Jacob asked God for protection from Esau (Gen. 32.11), he recalled the divine promise of increase: 'Yet you have said, "I will surely do you good, and make your offspring as the sand of the sea, which cannot be counted because of their number"' (NRSV, Gen. 32.12). It is not insignificant that Jacob did not appeal to the primaeval blessing (Gen. 9.1) as the basis for divine protection and deliverance. Rather, it was God's *promise* of increase that provided the guarantee that Jacob would be preserved. Harland draws a similar conclusion regarding the promise of increase to the patriarchs, noting that the 'blessing was a guarantee that despite the weakness of their present position as wanderers, God would grant to them not just their own survival but growth for their descendants'.[45] The patriarchal narratives seem to highlight that the increase of Abraham's progeny is guaranteed because God promised he would multiply them. These threatening circumstances continue beyond the book of Genesis in the opening verses of Exodus. Egypt was the place where the Israelites were fruitful and multiplied (Exod. 1.7), yet this took place amidst the context of Egyptian oppression. These threatening circumstances parallel the patriarchal narratives in that they underscore that God himself will bring about his promise to the patriarchs. Thus Israel's increase is not attributed to themselves, but to God (Deut. 10.22; Ps. 105.23-24). Mathews rightly concludes that the blessing of procreation is a significant motif that runs through the patriarchal narratives and that even though child-bearing is improbable (Gen. 18.10-15; 21.1-7), God's intervention ensures that the blessing is realized.[46] Having observed that God himself is bringing about his promise of increase to the patriarchs, we are now in a position to compare the promise with the primaeval blessing. We suggest that the essential difference between the primaeval blessing and the

(Genesis 22); and (8) the need to secure a wife for Isaac (Genesis 24). See L.R. Helyer, 'The Separation of Abram and Lot: Its Significance in the Patriarchal Narratives', *JSOT* 26 (1983), pp. 77–88 (82–85).

44. Robinson, 'Literary Functions', pp. 595–608 (605); cf. J. Goldingay, 'The Patriarchs in Scripture and History', in A.R. Millard and D.J. Wiseman (eds.), *Essays on the Patriarchal Narratives* (Leicester: InterVarsity Press, 1980), pp. 11–42 (13).

45. Harland, *The Value of Human Life*, p. 148.

46. Mathews, *Genesis 1–11.26*, p. 174.

promise of increase is that Gen. 9.1 does not guarantee that the blessing will be fully realized whereas the divine *promise* of increase to the patriarchs does.

It is worth recalling Brueggemann's view of the primaeval blessing at this point. He argues that the five verbs used in Gen. 1.28 show that God's intent 'cannot be frustrated by any circumstance, even those circumstances of the traditionalist's context of exile'.[47] The question was raised in our introduction, however, whether God's creational purposes are in any way thwarted by humankind.[48] What we are suggesting is that the five verbs in Gen. 1.28 and 9.1 do not in themselves provide such a guarantee. Genesis 1.28 and 9.1 can be frustrated by human sin and God's judgment. It is only when the verbs פרה, 'be fruitful', and רבה, 'multiply', have been changed to a divine *promise* that their fulfilment is guaranteed.[49] As with Brueggemann, Wenham maintains that the

> word of blessing, whether pronounced by God or man, guarantees and effects the hoped-for success. So here the words of command 'be fruitful and multiply' carry with them the divine promise that they can be carried out. Once uttered, the word carries its own life-giving power and cannot be revoked by man (cf. Gen. 27.17-40).[50]

Gilbert similarly concludes that God's blessing in Gen. 1.28 gives the man and the woman the *assurance* of fruitfulness.[51] We maintain, however, that while the intent of the human heart remains evil (Gen. 8.21), there is the possibility that the blessing will not be fully realized. Thus we have argued that God's intention for creation, expressed in the commands, 'Be fruitful and multiply, and fill the earth' (Gen. 1.28; 9.1), can be frustrated by human sin. It seems to be the case, therefore, that the word of blessing in Gen. 9.1 does not guarantee and effect the hoped-for success. However, the primaeval blessing is guaranteed when it is in the form of a divine *promise*.

b. *Does Sin Pose a Threat to the Realization of the Promise of Increase?*
One further threat remains, however. If God's promise of increase guarantees that Abraham's progeny will multiply in spite of threatening circumstances, we may well enquire whether sin poses a potential threat to their increase as it did in Genesis 1–11 with respect to the realization of the primaeval blessing. Could YHWH's judgment against sin endanger the realization of his promise to the patriarchs?

Hamilton has made some insightful observations with regard to this issue.[52] He notes, as other scholars have done, that in the primaeval history humans are

47. Brueggemann, 'The Kerygma of the Priestly Writers', pp. 397–414 (401).
48. Cf. our Introduction.
49. This idea may even be present in YHWH's promise to multiply Hagar's seed (Gen. 16.10). One observes that the *promise* of increase is given to Hagar while she is fleeing from Sarah. While Ishmael would be under the more general blessing of Gen. 9.1, his life-threatening circumstances pose a potential threat to the realization of the blessing. The promise of increase gives Hagar (Gen. 16.10) and Abraham (Gen. 17.20; cf. 21.13) the *guarantee* that Ishmael will increase, which the more general blessing of Gen. 9.1 does not.
50. Wenham, *Genesis 1–15*, p. 24.
51. Gilbert, '"Soyez féconds et multipliez"', pp. 729–42 (742).
52. See Hamilton for a thought-provoking discussion of this topic (*Genesis 1–17*, pp. 43–52).

held accountable for their actions. Adam and Eve, for example, are banished from the garden (Gen. 3.24) and Cain is assigned the life of a wanderer (Gen. 4.12). Hamilton concludes that 'Gen. 3–11 is quite clear in its message that one cannot sin with impunity or immunity'.[53] A similar idea is suggested in Westermann's crime and punishment schema in the primaeval history.[54] His analysis of Genesis 1–11 is outlined as follows.[55]

	2–3	4.1-16	6.1-4	6–9	11.1-9	(9.20-27)
Transgression	3.6	4.8b	6.1-2	6.5-7	11.4	9.22
Verbal Expression	3.14-19	4.11-12	6.3	6.5-7	11.6-7	9.24-25
Act of Punishment	3.22-24	4.16		7.6-24	11.8-9	

Relevant to the present discussion is the observation of Westermann and other scholars, that throughout the primaeval history humans are held accountable for their actions. There is, therefore, a crime and a punishment.

Westermann observes, however, that the crime and punishment schema is not found in the patriarchal cycle, even though he concedes that 'Sodom and Gomorrah has something of crime and punishment about it'.[56] He notes that there is hardly a word in the patriarchal stories about the sins of the patriarchs and their being punished by God.[57] Why, then, is the crime and punishment schema that is so prominent in the primaeval history absent in the patriarchal narratives?

Hamilton has shown that the schema is not entirely absent in Genesis 12–50. *Some* people are held accountable for their actions. For instance, the inhabitants of Sodom and Gomorrah are destroyed on account of their wickedness (Gen. 19.1-29; cf. Gen. 13.13), as Westermann has also pointed out. Another example may be seen in the wife-sister episode in Gen. 12.10-20 which records Abraham's dealings with an Egyptian king. In this story, Pharaoh appears to be judged by YHWH with plagues because he took Sarai (Gen. 12.17). Similarly, YHWH judged Abimelech's household with barrenness on account of Sarah's being taken from Abraham (Gen. 20.18). In both cases, the offenders acted unknowingly (Gen. 12.18-19; 20.3-6). Hamilton rightly observes that, in these two texts, even sins of ignorance are judged.[58] But what is particularly noteworthy is his observation that there is no word of judgment pronounced against Abraham. Pharaoh asked three questions of Abraham: 'What is this you have done to me? Why did you not tell me that she was your wife? Why did you say, "She is my sister", so that I took her for my wife?' (NRSV, Gen. 12.18-19). One observes that there is no protestation

---

53. Hamilton, *Genesis 1–17*, p. 44. Lamech's killing a youth is a possible exception to this, however, since no punishment is mentioned (Gen. 4.23).

54. Westermann, *The Promises to the Fathers*, pp. 44–56 (= *Die Verheißungen an die Väter*, pp. 47–58).

55. Westermann, *The Promises to the Fathers*, p. 50 (= *Die Verheißungen an die Väter*, p. 53)

56. Westermann, *Genesis 1–11*, p. 19 (= *Genesis*, Bd. I, p. 26).

57. C. Westermann, *Genesis 12–36: A Continental Commentary* (trans. J.J. Scullion; Minneapolis: Augsburg Publ. House, 1985), p. 167 (= *Genesis*, Bd. II [BKAT, Neukirchen–Vluyn: Neukirchen–Vluyner Verlag, 1977–79], p. 195).

58. Hamilton, *Genesis 1–17*, p. 45.

of innocence from Abraham. It is clear that he is the guilty party.[59] Westermann notes that Pharaoh's reproach is the final word in the story, showing that the narrator does not approve of Abraham's behaviour.[60] To be sure, Sarah was the daughter of Abraham's father, although she had a different mother (Gen. 20.12).[61] Yet it cannot be denied that Abraham deceived the Egyptian king.[62] Ross notes, in fact, that 'deception is a recurring theme in the book, a theme that will become more and more pronounced in the lives of the patriarchs'.[63] If Abraham is the guilty party, why, then, does God not hold him accountable for his actions? Von Rad rightly observes that when God intervenes in the story, it is 'not to punish Abraham for his lie and betrayal, but to save Sarah'.[64]

Abraham appears to be the guilty party in the second wife-sister episode as well (Gen. 20.1-18).[65] Westermann notes that Abraham responds to Abimelech's accusation by explaining his actions, yet unlike Abimelech, Abraham is not declared guiltless. He suggests that the dialogue deals with the issue of guilt and that in the final analysis, Abimelech is declared guiltless, but Abraham is not.[66] Wenham similarly notes that when Abraham is challenged by Abimelech, 'he resorts to lying, claiming he described Sarah as his sister wherever they went'.[67] He concludes that the incident 'makes us realize that Abraham is not such a saint as we might have concluded from chap. 18'.[68] Robinson comes to a similar conclusion with respect to Abraham's actions regarding his wife (Gen. 12.10-20; 20.1-18): 'the threat to the promise is accordingly very grave, and one can only shake one's head over Abraham. Still, God intervenes to set matters right. The point of both stories seems to be that the accomplishment of the promise is independent of the actions or faithfulness of the recipients of the promise'.[69] In both stories, even though Abraham's actions seem somewhat dubious, God acts in a favourable way towards the patriarch. Robinson concludes that 'if justice is not precisely done, God does protect the genealogical line'.[70] What, then, is the significance of the absence of divine judgment against Abraham? Why is there no word of rebuke from YHWH?

Jacob's behaviour is also questionable. As with other scholars, Cohn observes that in the primaeval history, God intervenes to punish those who are guilty. He notes, however, that in the Abrahamic cycle 'the moral status of human actions is

59. Cassuto, *Genesis*, Vol. 2, pp. 351–52; Nachman, *Genesis*, p. 173; Skinner, *Genesis*, p. 250; von Rad, *Genesis*, p. 168 (= *Das erste Buch Mose*, p. 128); Wenham, *Genesis 1–15*, pp. 290–91.

60. Westermann, *Genesis 12–36*, p. 166 (= *Genesis*, Bd. II, p. 194).

61. This type of relationship is condemned in Israelite law (Lev. 18.9; 20.17; Deut. 27.22).

62. Driver, *Genesis*, p. 149; Kidner, *Genesis*, p. 116; Wenham, *Genesis 16–50*, p. 73; Westermann, *Genesis 12–36*, pp. 166–67 (= *Genesis*, Bd. II, pp. 194–95).

63. Ross, *Creation and Blessing*, p. 272.

64. Von Rad, *Genesis*, p. 168 (= *Das erste Buch Mose*, p. 128).

65. Vawter, *On Genesis*, p. 245; Wenham, *Genesis 16–50*, pp. 72–75.

66. Westermann, *Genesis 12–36*, p. 327 (= *Genesis*, Bd. II, p. 400).

67. Wenham, *Genesis 16–50*, p. 75.

68. Wenham, *Genesis 16–50*, p. 75.

69. Robinson, 'Literary Functions', pp. 595–608 (605 n. 16).

70. Robinson, 'Literary Functions', pp. 595–608 (605).

far more ambiguous'.[71] Cohn observes that, not only are individual actions in the Abrahamic cycle morally questionable, but Jacob's 'entire role as protagonist rests on deceit'.[72] He notes that Jacob receives God's blessing *in spite* of his deceit, concluding that 'conventional morality and custom cannot hold back God's chosen'.[73] It seems to be the case that God is overlooking Jacob's questionable behaviour, thereby underscoring that he has not chosen the patriarchs based on their morality.[74] So what is the significance of this for the realization of the promise of increase to the patriarchs?

c. *God's Faithfulness to His Promise of Increase in spite of the Patriarchs*
It has been argued thus far that in Genesis 1–11 sin and divine judgment can endanger the realization of the primaeval blessing. If the patriarchs are 'possessed of the same frailties as are all other human beings', as Sarna observes, then the possibility remains that the actions of the patriarchs can endanger the realization of their increase. Yet since the primaeval blessing has been changed into a divine *promise*, there is also the suggestion that the behaviour of the patriarchs *cannot* jeopardize its realization. A number of scholars maintain, therefore, that if the actions of the patriarchs are interpreted in light of the divine promises, they show that God will fulfil them 'beyond all human failure'.[75] Hamilton thus suggests that the point of the patriarchal narratives is not that the patriarchs are always morally upright, but that God is faithful to bring about his promises. He concludes that Genesis 12–50 brings together 'the promises of God to the patriarchs and the faithfulness of God in keeping those promises. Even if the bearers of those promises represent the greatest threat to the promises, the individual lives of the promise bearers cannot abort those promises'.[76]

The aforementioned scholars have concluded that God will fulfil his promises in spite of the behaviour of the patriarchs. The implication of this is that God is in some sense withholding his judgment against the patriarchs for the sake of his promise. In other words, God is not counting their sins against them. We have noted that in the primaeval history sin has the potential to endanger the realization of the primaeval blessing. If the divine *promise* of increase given to the patriarchs is read against Genesis 1–11, then God's withholding or restraining his judgment may be implicit in the promise itself since his judgment against sin could jeopardize its fulfilment.[77] This may well be the reason why the crime and

71. Cohn, 'Narrative Structure', pp. 3–16 (7).
72. Cohn, 'Narrative Structure', pp. 3–16 (11).
73. Cohn, 'Narrative Structure', pp. 3–16 (11). Ross makes the same point in reference to Abraham's deception in Gen. 12.10-20, that 'outside the land, God would protect the blessing, in spite of Abraham's deception…' (*Creation and Blessing*, p. 272).
74. Hamilton, *Genesis 1–17*, p. 43; cf. Goldingay, 'The Patriarchs', pp. 11–42 (19); Sarna, *Genesis*, p. 94.
75. Von Rad, *Genesis*, p. 169 (= *Das erste Buch Mose*, p. 129); cf. Cohn, 'Narrative Structure', pp. 3–16 (11, 14); Sailhamer, *The Pentateuch as Narrative*, p. 141; Westermann, *Genesis 12–36*, p. 329 (= *Genesis*, Bd. II, p. 403).
76. Hamilton, *Genesis 1–17*, p. 46.
77. It is interesting to note that in the golden calf incident, Israel's sin, which provokes the divine

punishment schema so dominant in the primaeval history has not been applied to the patriarchs.[78] God is withholding or restraining his punishment in order that his promise be fully realized.[79] We may conclude, therefore, that even though the creation is endangered by human sin and in danger of being destroyed because of God's judgment in the primaeval history,[80] the continuation of creation is guaranteed through the divine promise to the patriarchs. This seems to be the essential difference between the blessing of increase in Gen. 9.1 and the *promise* of increase to the patriarchs: Gen. 9.1 does not guarantee its outcome, but its outcome is guaranteed when it is in the form of a divine promise. But the question still remains how one is to reconcile the absence of judgment against the patriarchs in Genesis 12–50 with the 'crime and punishment' schema in Genesis 1–11.

We noted that the element of grace after the Babel judgment is already present in the Table of Nations in the emergence of Shem's line as the primary line, and that the divine promises to the patriarchs may be seen as a further development of the grace theme. With this background in view, God's withholding or restraining his judgment against the patriarchs may well be interpreted as the outworking of his grace. Divine grace means that God does not treat them as they deserve. Instead of judgment, he shows them mercy. Clines thus argues that the patriarchal narratives function as the 'mitigation' element of the judgment-grace schema.[81] If this is the case, what the patriarchs are receiving is the 'mitigation' element of the divine action. This may well explain why there is no word of judgment pronounced against them. We may conclude, then, that there is divine grace at work after the flood in relation to humanity (Gen. 8.21), yet there is also particular grace at work in relation to the patriarchs. Moreover, since God's intention for his creation is being taken up by Abraham's progeny, the continuation of creation through them underscores the dynamic nature of divine forgiving grace.

5. *God's Intention in Creation Advances through the Divine Promise*

It is important to recall at this point the view commonly held by scholars, that YHWH's scattering the Babelites ensures that the creation mandate of Gen. 9.1 is

---

judgment (Exod. 32.1-9), endangers the realization of the divine promise. YHWH told Moses that he would destroy the Israelites and make him into a great nation instead (Exod. 32.10). It is not insignificant that when Moses petitions YHWH to relent from his judgment, he appeals not only to YHWH's reputation (Exod. 32.12), but also to YHWH's promise of increase and land made to the patriarchs. YHWH's remembering his *promise* resulted in his relenting from his decision to destroy Israel (Gen. 32.12-14).

78. As has been noted, Er and Onan are exceptions (cf. Gen. 38.7, 10).

79. This idea is suggested in Mic. 7.18-19 where God's faithfulness to the patriarchs is associated with his pardoning iniquity: 'Who is a God like you, pardoning iniquity and passing over the transgression of the remnant of your possession? He does not retain his anger forever, because he delights in showing clemency. He will again have compassion on us; he will tread our iniquities under foot. You will cast our sins into the depths of the sea. You will show faithfulness to Jacob and unswerving loyalty to Abraham, as you have sworn to our ancestors from the days of old' (NRSV).

80. Rendtorff, '"Covenant" as a Structuring Concept', pp. 385–93 (393).

81. Clines, *The Theme of the Pentateuch*, p. 78.

carried out. According to this view, scattering is equated with 'filling the earth'. Thus when YHWH scatters the Babelites, the command to 'fill the earth' is being realized – even though humans have been defiantly opposing it. This means that through the dispersion, YHWH continues 'the execution of the creation he began in Genesis 1'.[82] Scholars conclude, therefore, that YHWH's scattering the Babelites restores the 'order intended from the beginning'.[83] Contrary to this view, however, we have argued that God's intention for creation outlined in Gen. 9.1 is not being realized through scattering. We further noted that YHWH's scattering the Babelites may even have an adverse effect on the realization of the primaeval blessing. In short, God's intention for his creation is not being realized through scattering, but through a divine *promise.* Thus Wenham rightly concludes that Genesis 1–11 shows 'how the promises made to the patriarchs fulfill God's original plans for humanity'.[84] God does indeed take action to ensure the fulfilment of the primaeval commands, as scholars have suggested. The action God takes to ensure that Gen. 9.1 is fully realized, however, is not scattering, but his promise of increase to the patriarchs.

We may recall at this point that some scholars maintain that God *compels* obedience to the primaeval commands when he scatters the Babelites.[85] Thus it is argued that God fulfils his intention for creation even if it is against the will of humans. We suggest, however, that God does not compel obedience to the primaeval commands. Rather, he makes promises to the patriarchs concerning their increase that are to be received by faith. The implication is that creation advances not through coercion, but by faith. This is not to deny the importance of obedience (e.g. Gen. 12.4; 22.1-19),[86] but simply to acknowledge that the primaeval blessing is being realized through those who willingly receive the promise by faith. In short, scattering does not restore the 'order intended from the beginning', but the created order is being restored through the divine promise given to Abraham and his seed.[87]

Given that the advancement of the primaeval blessing through Abraham's descendants is to be seen as God's gracious action, then, by implication, the continuation of the created order through Abraham is the result of divine grace. Thus Clines' conclusion about the flood story, that it is 'an affirmation of the story of

---

82. Van Wolde, *Words Become Worlds,* pp. 102–103; cf. Kikawada, 'Genesis 11.1-9', pp. 18–32 (32); Ross, *Creation and Blessing,* p. 247; Turner, *Announcements of Plot,* p. 32.

83. Vawter, *On Genesis,* p. 157; cf. Brueggemann, *Genesis,* pp. 98–99.

84. Wenham, *Genesis 1–15,* p. li; cf. Mathews, *Genesis 1–11.26,* p. 174.

85. Harland, 'The Sin of Babel', pp. 515–33 (531); Kikawada and Quinn, *Before Abraham Was,* p. 71; Mann, ' "All the Families of the Earth" ', pp. 341–53 (347); Turner, *Announcements of Plot,* p. 32.

86. For a helpful discussion of the import of obedience, see Harland, *The Value of Human Life,* pp. 47–48.

87. Steck has observed that when YHWH acts in the primaeval history, he is reacting to humanity's deeds, yet in Gen. 12.1-3 YHWH takes the initiative. Steck suggests, therefore, that this initiative is comparable to the initiative of creation, indicating that Gen. 12.1-3 marks a new beginning of the divine action with humanity. Steck further argues that the promises to the patriarchs restore the quality of life that is diminishing in Genesis 1–11 ('Genesis 12,1-3', pp. 525–54 [550–51]).

creation, and speaks ultimately not of divine punishment but of God's faithfulness to the work of His hands',[88] also applies to the patriarchs. That is, the patriarchal narratives are an affirmation of the creation story and speak ultimately of God's faithfulness to his creation. Given that the promise of increase is a continuation of the primaeval blessing, its realization may be seen as a reaffirmation of the divine intentions for humankind.[89] The patriarchs, therefore, take up the creation story as it is through them that the primaeval blessing is guaranteed and advancing.

6. *Conclusion*

We have argued thus far that the primaeval blessing is being realized in a more general way in the Table of Nations, yet there is also a particular blessing at work in Shem's line (Gen. 10.21-31; 11.10-26). The primaeval blessing is subsequently reaffirmed to Abraham's progeny in the form of a divine promise. The threatening circumstances in the patriarchal narratives underscore that God himself will bring about his promise. Given that sin poses a threat to the realization of the primaeval blessing in Genesis 1–11, the question was raised whether sin could in any way jeopardize the fulfilment of the promise of increase. The stories about the patriarchs demonstrate that the patriarchs are not without sin, yet God continues to fulfil his promise in spite of their behaviour. The implication is that God is in some sense withholding his judgment against the patriarchs in order that his promise be fully realized. We have suggested that this is the essential difference between the more general blessing on the nations (Gen. 9.1) and the particular blessing at work in Israel through Abraham: the announcement in Gen. 9.1 does not guarantee that the blessing will be fully realized, but its outcome is guaranteed when it is in the form of a divine promise. Thus God's intention for creation is advancing in Abraham's progeny who have become 'bearers of the creation theme'.[90] The promise of increase, therefore, contributes significantly to the realization of the primaeval blessing after the flood, since the blessing is not only being taken up by Abraham's progeny, but its outcome is assured by God. If, then, the advancement of the primaeval blessing through Abraham's progeny is divinely guaranteed, we may well ask the question whether there is any indication that the promise of increase given to the patriarchs is *fulfilled* in Genesis. Moreover, given that the promise of increase is a reaffirmation of the creation blessing announced after the flood (Gen. 9.1), it is worth investigating whether Abraham's progeny in any way fulfil the primaeval blessing.

---

88. Clines, 'Noah's Flood', pp. 128–42 (140).

89. Clines, *The Theme of the Pentateuch*, p. 78.

90. We have adopted this expression from Robinson, who has used it with reference to the genealogies in Genesis ('Literary Functions', pp. 595–608 [601]).

Chapter 8

REALIZATION OF THE PRIMAEVAL BLESSING THROUGH ISRAEL

1. *The Twelve Sons of Jacob as Recipients of the Promise of Increase*

The promise of increase given to the patriarchs is primarily realized in the book of Genesis at an individual level as Abraham, Isaac and Jacob 'multiply'. This individual aspect also contributes to the realization of the promise in a more general way, however, since these individuals constitute part of Israel. An important text which testifies to the promise of increase being realized at an individual level, while at the same time contributing to the realization of the promise at the broader level, is Gen. 35.22b-26. The names of Jacob's twelve sons are given at the conclusion of Isaac's Toledot:

> Now the sons of Jacob were twelve. The sons of Leah: Reuben (Jacob's firstborn), Simeon, Levi, Judah, Issachar, and Zebulun. The sons of Rachel: Joseph and Benjamin. The sons of Bilhah, Rachel's maid: Dan and Naphtali. The sons of Zilpah, Leah's maid: Gad and Asher. These were the sons of Jacob who were born to him in Paddan-aram (NRSV, Gen. 35.22b-26).

While the placement of the list at this point in the narrative is rather abrupt, the view of Coats, that this unit is 'totally isolated in context' and that 'no itinerary formula binds it to its surroundings',[1] is somewhat of an overstatement. To begin with, the placement of the list at Gen. 35.22b-26 is not isolated from its context, given that the birth of Benjamin, Jacob's last son, has just been mentioned in the preceding verses (Gen. 35.18). The birth of Benjamin by Rachel brings to completion the twelve sons of Jacob (cf. Gen. 29.32–30.24). The genealogy draws attention to this by noting that 'the sons of Jacob were *twelve*' (ויהיו בני־יעקב שנים עשר, Gen. 35.22b).

Secondly, the list of Jacob's twelve sons is connected geographically to its immediate literary context. The genealogy concludes with the statement that 'these were the sons of Jacob who were born to him *in Paddan-aram*' (Gen. 35.26; cf. Gen. 46.15). The location of Paddan-aram clearly connects the genealogy to the preceding narrative since it was the place to which Jacob had fled (Gen. 28.2, 5). Prior to Jacob's leaving his father, Isaac instructed him to take a wife from the daughters of Laban (Gen. 28.2). He then blessed Jacob, saying, 'May God Almighty bless you and make you fruitful and numerous, that you may become a company of peoples' (NRSV, Gen. 28.3). Jacob left for Paddan-aram with no wife

---

1. Coats, *Genesis*, p. 243.

or children. According to the narrative context, Jacob's returning to his father's house with twelve sons testifies to the realization of Isaac's blessing of increase upon Jacob (Gen. 28.3).

Thirdly, we also read in the immediately preceding context that God had blessed Jacob/Israel saying: 'I am God Almighty: be fruitful and multiply; a nation and a company of nations shall come from you' (NRSV, Gen. 35.11a). If Gen. 35.22b-26 is read against this background, then the genealogy witnesses to the fact that the blessing is in the process of being realized. Weimar has suggested that the placement of the list in Gen. 35.22b-26 indicates that the birth of Jacob's sons is an *anfängliche Erfüllung*, 'initial fulfilment', of the promise of blessing.[2] It is worth noting, however, that while Jacob's 'multiplying' indicates that the blessing is in the process of being realized, the blessing of increase is clearly not *fulfilled* since Jacob himself states that his numbers were *few* (Gen. 34.30).

2. Jacob's Twelve Sons: the Culmination of the Genealogical Schema

That Jacob has *twelve* sons may have further significance. It is common for key figures in Genesis to have two[3] or three[4] sons. In Gen. 35.22b-26 Jacob's twelve sons are listed according to their mothers, Leah (35.23), Rachel (35.24), Bilhah (35.25) and Zilpah (35.26). Jacob's fathering twelve sons distinguishes him, therefore, from the other patriarchs. Yet it has been noted that one son in particular usually takes up the position of the main line and that secondary lines are presented first, whereas the main line is presented last. That Jacob has twelve sons, rather than two or three, and that there is no reversal of primogeniture in the genealogy seems to indicate that Gen. 35.22b-26 marks a new stage in the genealogical schema. The implication appears to be that all twelve sons constitute the main line. The genealogical schema is outlined on page 113, opposite.

It is not insignificant that the chronological schema in 1 Chronicles 1 also changes with the twelve sons of Israel. Williamson has noted, for example, that the reversal of primogeniture seen in the primaeval and patriarchal genealogies in 1 Chronicles 1 changes in 1 Chron. 2.1-2 – a text which may even be derived from Gen. 35.23-26[5] – with the names of Israel's twelve sons. He suggests that the 'elaborate pattern of genealogical arrangement reaches its climax in these

---

2. Weimar, 'Aufbau und Struktur', pp. 174–203 (185); cf. Coats, *Genesis*, p. 244.

3. Eber fathered Peleg and Joktan (Gen. 10.25); Abraham fathered Ishmael and Isaac (Gen. 16.15; 21.2-3; plus another six sons by Keturah, Gen. 25.2); Isaac fathered Jacob and Esau (Gen. 25.24-26); and Joseph fathered Ephraim and Manasseh (Gen. 41.50-52; 46.27; 48.5). Another example may be seen in the birth of the twins, Perez and Zerah, to Judah and Tamar (Gen. 38.27-30).

4. Adam fathered Cain, Abel and Seth (Gen. 4.1-2, 25); Lamech fathered Jabal, Jubal and Tubalcain (Gen. 4.20-22); Noah fathered Shem, Ham and Japheth (Gen. 5.32); and Terah fathered Abram, Nahor and Haran (Gen. 11.26).

5. Williamson, *1 and 2 Chronicles*, p. 45. Williamson notes that the list could have been taken from Exod. 1.2-5, although he concludes that Gen. 35.23-26 is more likely since Joseph has been integrated into the Genesis list (p. 45). The placement of Dan after Zebulun in 1 Chron. 2.1-2 is not found in Gen. 35.23-26 or Exod. 1.2-5.

verses'.[6] The genealogy in Gen. 35.22b-26 might similarly be seen, therefore, as the culmination of the genealogical schema in Genesis. What is the significance of this in terms of the realization of the promise of increase?

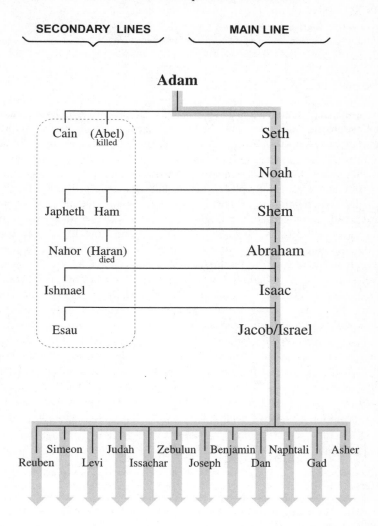

3. *Realization of the Promise of Increase through Jacob's Twelve Sons*

That Jacob has twelve sons and that there is no reversal of primogeniture seems to indicate that the promise of increase will be realized through all twelve sons who now constitute the main line. This is not to deny that there are intimations

6.   Williamson, *1 and 2 Chronicles*, p. 45.

that certain sons will have a position of pre-eminence. Bailey has observed, for example, that Gen. 35.22b-26 is structured in the form of a chiasm.[7]

A   Now the sons of Jacob were twelve (v. 22b).
  B   The sons of Leah: Reuben (Jacob's firstborn), Simeon, Levi, Judah, Issachar, and Zebulun (v. 23).
   C The sons of Rachel: Joseph and Benjamin (v. 24).
   C' The sons of Bilhah, Rachel's maid: Dan and Naphtali (v. 25).
  B'   The sons of Zilphah, Leah's maid: Gad and Asher (v. 26a).
 A'   These were the sons of Jacob who were born to him in Paddan-aram (v. 26b).

Bailey concludes that the chiastic structure focuses attention on Rachel and her sons (Joseph and Benjamin), and the sons of her maid (Dan and Naphtali), by placing them in a position of favour over Leah and her sons (Reuben, Simeon, Levi, Judah, Issachar and Zebulun) and those of her maid. He suggests that focus on Rachel's sons, Joseph and Benjamin, foreshadows events to come. Sasson also observes that the genealogy places Joseph in the seventh position, thus giving him a place of pre-eminence.[8] That Leah's sons do not have the prime position accords with the immediately preceding context which mentions that 'Reuben went and lay with Bilhah, his father's concubine; and Israel heard of it' (NRSV, Gen. 35.22a), and with the later death-bed blessing of Jacob which indicates that Reuben is disqualified from the firstborn position (Gen. 49.3-4). This point is reiterated in 1 Chron. 5.1 which states that Reuben's birthright was given to the sons of Joseph because he had defiled his father's bed. Bailey's observation, therefore, that the chiastic structure of Gen. 35.22b-26 intimates that Joseph rather than Reuben will have a pre-eminent position, accords with the immediate context. Cohn has also observed that special attention has been given to Rachel and her sons, Joseph and Benjamin, in Gen. 46.8-27, thus placing them in a favourable position.[9] This may even foreshadow Joseph's central role in the Toledot of Jacob. Notably, it is Joseph who is especially favoured by his father (Gen. 37.3; cf. Gen. 33.2[10]), and Benjamin by Joseph (Gen. 43.34). It also seems to be the case that in the Joseph narrative, Reuben, Jacob's firstborn,[11] and Judah[12] have an

---

7. Bailey, 'Genealogies in Genesis', pp. 267–82 (270–71).
8. Sasson, 'A Genealogical "Convention"', pp. 171–85 (183).
9. Bailey notes that only Rachel is introduced with an additional statement (Gen. 46.19) and that the syntax of Gen. 46.20, which introduces Joseph's sons, is irregular. Instead of the more common verbless clause, 'these are the sons of…', v. 20 begins with a *wayyiqtol* form, וילד. Bailey thus concludes that special focus has been given to Jacob's 'beloved' wife, Rachel, and her sons ('Genealogies in Genesis', pp. 267–82 [272–73]); cf. Hamilton, *Genesis 18–50*, p. 597.
10. Joseph's favoured position (and Rachel's) is already indicated in Gen. 33.2. When Jacob was about to meet Esau, he placed his maids and their children in the front position, whereas he protected Rachel and Joseph by placing them behind.
11. For example, Reuben was the one who spoke up against his brothers when they plotted to kill Joseph (Gen. 37.21-22; cf. Gen. 42.22). He also negotiated with his father regarding Benjamin, saying that Jacob could put his own two sons to death if he did not return Benjamin alive (Gen. 42.37).
12. For example, Judah spoke out when his brothers plotted to kill Joseph (Gen. 37.26-27); Judah is also featured in Gen. 38; Judah is the one who dialogues with his father regarding Joseph's demand that a brother be brought to him (Gen. 43.3, 8); Judah pleads with Joseph after the cup had been

important role in relation to their father and brothers, although secondary to Joseph.

In sum, while there are intimations already in Gen. 35.22b-26 and 46.8-27 that particular sons of Jacob will be pre-eminent – the significance of which may even be seen in Israel's subsequent history – the absence of any clear reversal of primogeniture in Gen. 35.22b-26 seems to indicate that the promise of increase will be realized through Jacob's twelve sons who now constitute the main line.[13] There seems to be a movement in the narrative, therefore, from individual Israel to corporate Israel. That the blessing will be realized through corporate Israel is confirmed in Gen. 47.27, which states that *Israel* (the people) were 'fruitful and multiplied' (Gen. 47.27), and in Exod. 1.7, which refers to the proliferation of Israel in Egypt. We suggest, therefore, that the genealogy of the twelve sons of Jacob 'specifies through whom the blessing of v. 11, "Be fertile and increase", is to be realized and through whom the people of Israel came into being'.[14] It may even be concluded that Jacob's twelve sons, who are also identified simply as *Israel* in Gen. 47.27, have assumed the position of the main son through whom the blessing will be realized.

4. *The Primaeval Blessing and Israel*

The genealogy in Gen. 35.22b-26 may have further significance for the narrative. Some scholars suggest that Gen. 35.22b-26 marks the first stage of the transition from the patriarchs to the people of Israel. Weimar maintains, for example, that Gen. 35.22b-26 signifies the beginning of Israel as a people.[15] Westermann similarly suggests that according to P, Jacob and his twelve sons (35.22b-26) represent the people of Israel.[16] He further notes that the promises of increase and land made to Jacob, whose name has been changed to Israel, are determinative for the people of Israel.[17] It may well be the case that, while the blessing is given to Jacob in Gen. 35.11, the fact that it is pronounced to Jacob *after* his name had been changed to *Israel* anticipates that the blessing will be realized through Israel as a people. Accordingly, the placement of the genealogy of Jacob's twelve sons in Gen. 35.22b-26 indicates that the blessing will be realized through them. Jacob similarly notes that although the primaeval blessing is given to Noah and his sons in Gen. 9.1, Noah himself does not further multiply. Rather, the blessing will be realized through his *sons*. He suggests that there is a parallel between Noah and

---

found with Benjamin (Gen. 44.16-34); and Judah was sent by his father to lead the way to Egypt (Gen. 46.28).

13. Westermann draws the same conclusion from the list of Jacob's descendants in Gen. 47.8-27. See C. Westermann, *Genesis 37–50: A Continental Commentary* (trans. J.J. Scullion; Minneapolis: Augsburg Publ. House, 1986), p. 158 (= *Genesis*, Bd. III [BKAT; Neukirchen–Vluyn: Neukirchener Verlag, 1980–82], p. 174).

14. Sarna, *Genesis*, p. 245.

15. Weimar, 'Aufbau und Struktur', pp. 174–203 (185).

16. Westermann, *Genesis 12–36*, p. 552 (= *Genesis*, Bd. III, p. 673).

17. Westermann, *Genesis 12–36*, p. 557 (= *Genesis*, Bd. III, p. 679).

Jacob, since the blessing announced to Jacob will similarly be realized through his *sons* (cf. Gen. 35.11).[18] This would also account for the fact that the divine promises given to Abraham, Isaac and Jacob are not reaffirmed to Jacob's twelve sons,[19] since they are already in view in Gen. 35.11.

That corporate Israel is in view in Gen. 35.11 is further intimated by the death notice of Jacob's beloved wife, Rachel, in Gen. 35.19. Prior to Rachel's death, her giving birth to Benjamin brings to completion the twelve sons of Jacob. Her death at this important juncture is suggestive that Jacob himself will not further 'multiply', but that the blessing of increase in Gen. 35.11 will be realized through his descendants who are identified as 'Israel'. Fretheim maintains, in fact, that there is a merging of individual Israel with corporate Israel in the patriarchal narratives: 'Jacob is Israel; this claim informs and animates these chapters. Jacob remains a person in his own right, but over the course of the story he becomes Israel, so that finally he is more than an individual'.[20]

Westermann has noted the same feature in Gen. 46.4a where God says to Jacob, 'I myself will go down with you to Egypt, and I will also bring you up again'. He notes that the second statement, 'I will bring you up again', looks forward to the Exodus and that there is a change in the object of the sentence: in the first sentence Jacob is in view; however, in the second sentence it is Jacob, the people, who are in view.[21] Thus there is a merging of individual Jacob with corporate Jacob. Hamilton also comments that 'here is an intriguing illustration of the oscillation between the individual and the collective, a well-known feature of Old Testament thought. There is no problem here at all of passing from the individual to the community and back to the individual without any awareness of the transitions'.[22] It could thus be argued that when we read that *Israel* 'were fruitful and multiplied' (Gen. 47.27), this could be construed as being an initial realization of the blessing of increase given to individual Israel in Gen. 35.11. It is important to note, however, that the blessing of increase given to Israel in Gen. 35.11 does not simply recall God's promises to Abraham and Isaac. It is, in fact, reminiscent of the primaeval blessing found in Gen. 1.28 and 9.1.

a. *Reaffirmation of the Primaeval Commands to Israel in Genesis 35.11*
It is not insignificant that Gen. 35.11 marks the only text where the qal imperatives, 'Be fruitful and multiply', occur together outside the primaeval history.[23] As has been noted, the promise of increase to the patriarchs usually occurs in the hiphil form. Why, then, are imperatives *reissued* to Israel? Do they have any theological significance? Brueggemann has rightly noted that the formula in Gen. 35.11

18. Jacob, *Das erste Buch der Tora*, p. 241.
19. This point has been noted by Gilbert, although he suggests that Jacob's sons do not receive the blessing of increase because twelve sons would guarantee the future ('"Soyez féconds et multipliez"', pp. 729–42 [732]).
20. Fretheim, *The Pentateuch*, p. 86.
21. Westermann, *Genesis 37–50*, p. 156 (= *Genesis*, Bd. III, p. 172).
22. Hamilton, *Genesis 18–50*, p. 592.
23. The qal imperatives of רפה and רבה occur together only in Gen. 1.28; 9.1 and 35.11.

is derived from Gen. 1.28, although he does not discuss why imperatives appear in this new context.[24] Von Rad observes that the blessing to Jacob is a word for word parallel to the blessing given to Abraham in Genesis 17 and that the promises given to Abraham are fully renewed to Jacob. He further notes that the blessing is expanded by the creative command, 'Be fruitful and multiply', yet he does not discuss *why* the creative command is used in 35.11. He simply states that, according to P, the command was obeyed.[25] The presence of qal imperatives in Gen. 35.11 is particularly noticeable in light of the parallel text in Gen. 17.1-8.[26] If a comparison is being made between God's promises to Abraham and his promises to Jacob, then one might expect that the hiphil forms of פרה and רבה would be employed in Gen. 35.11, as they are in Gen. 17.2 (רבה) and 17.6 (פרה). Why, then, are qal imperatives used in Gen. 35.11, rather than the hiphil verbal form? It seems likely that the commands in Gen. 35.11 are intended to recall the primaeval blessing. We may now return to the question posed earlier – whether the presence of 'primaeval' commands in Gen. 35.11 has theological significance.

Weimar has compared the list of Jacob's sons in Gen. 35.22b-26 with the list of Noah's sons in Gen. 10.1-32. He observes that both are preceded by 'primaeval' commands (Gen. 9.1, 7; 35.11) and suggests that the two lists show the immediate fulfilment of the blessing. Weimar concludes, therefore, that the commands are employed in Gen. 35.11 because the blessing has become effective immediately as in Gen. 10.1-32.[27] Weimar has rightly drawn attention to the import of the 'primaeval' commands that are given to Jacob. His explanation for their occurrence in Gen. 35.11, however, is problematic for two reasons.

First, his argument that the commands are present in Gen. 9.1 and 35.11 because they are immediately effective in the following genealogies needs closer examination. In the case of Gen. 9.1, the commands are given to Noah and his sons. The ensuing genealogy clearly shows that Shem, Ham and Japheth 'increased' significantly (Gen. 10.1-32). In Gen. 35.11, however, according to the narrative context, Jacob has already fathered eleven sons (Gen. 29.32–30.24). Thus Gen. 35.11 does not demonstrate that the blessing has become immediately effective in the same way that Gen. 10.1-32 does. As has been noted, Jacob's

24. Brueggemann, 'The Kerygma of the Priestly Writers', pp. 397–414 (404–405). Gilbert also notes that imperatives occur in Gen. 35.11; however, he maintains they have the sense of promise. He then suggests that the commands in Gen. 1.28 and 9.1 are to be understood in a similar way (' "Soyez féconds et multipliez" ', pp. 729–42 [732]). Gilbert's view is problematic, however, since he does not explain *why* qal imperatives occur only in these few texts. According to our interpretation, the presence of commands in Gen. 35.11 has theological significance.

25. Von Rad, *Genesis*, p. 339 (= *Das erste Buch Mose*, p. 276).

26. Sarna notes that both texts have a number of common features which include: (a) reference to El Shaddai (Gen. 17.1; 35.11); (b) change of name (Gen. 17.5; 35.10); (c) promise of a great nation and kings (Gen. 17.4-6; 35.11) and (d) the promise of land (Gen. 17.8; 35.12). Sarna also notes that Jacob's travelling from Shechem (Gen. 33.18-19) to Bethel (Gen. 35.1, 6) and building altars at both places (Gen. 33.20; 35.1, 7) parallels Abraham's itinerary (Gen. 12.6-8). He suggests that Jacob's journey has a symbolic meaning and that Abraham is a prototype (*Genesis*, p. 241).

27. Weimar, 'Aufbau und Struktur', pp. 174–203 (185 n. 48); cf. von Rad (*Genesis*, p. 339 [= *Das erste Buch Mose*, p. 276]).

wife, Rachel, gives birth to Benjamin (Gen. 35.18) and then she dies. Thus the blessing is effective only in the birth of one son, Benjamin. This is in contrast to Shem, Ham and Japheth who father *seventy* sons (Gen. 10.1-32). Furthermore, after Jacob had fathered eleven sons, he himself states that he was few in number (Gen. 34.30). We may assume that the birth of Benjamin would not change this significantly. Thus it could be concluded that the blessing of increase is only *beginning* to be realized. Accordingly, Gen. 35.22b-26 does not testify to the *fulfilment* of the blessing, as Weimar proposes.

Secondly, Weimar has not given adequate attention to the relationship of Gen. 9.1 to 1.28 and to the reason why the primaeval commands are reissued to Noah and his sons after the flood. Anderson, on the other hand, has drawn attention to the similarities between Gen. 1.26-28 and 9.1-7 and concludes that 'the Priestly tradents clearly intend that the two should be read together'.[28] If the two texts are read together, the repetition of the commands to 'be fruitful and multiply, and fill the earth' in Gen. 9.1, which are identical to those given in Gen. 1.28, indicates that the primaeval blessing has been renewed after the flood. This view is held by a number of scholars.[29] Cassuto notes, for example, that the blessing given to the first man (Gen. 1.28) is confirmed and renewed in identical terms in Gen. 9.1, indicating that the blessing will be realized through Noah and his sons.[30] Clines also writes that 'the "uncreation" which God has worked with the Flood is not final; creation has not been permanently undone. Old unities of the natural world are restored (8.22), and the old ordinances of creation are renewed (9.1-7)'.[31]

Genesis 9.1-7 may be seen, therefore, as the renewal of the order of creation, albeit with some modifications.[32] Relevant to the present discussion is the fact that the primaeval commands do not occur in Gen. 9.1 simply because they are effective immediately in Gen. 10.1-32. Rather, their reappearance in Gen. 9.1 indicates that the primaeval blessing, which is renewed after the flood, will be realized through Noah and his sons. Weimar has not considered the import of Gen. 9.1 in relation to Gen. 1.28. Instead, he simply compares Gen. 9.1 with 35.11.

28. B.W. Anderson, 'Creation and the Noachic Covenant', in P.N. Joranson and K. Butigan (eds.), *Cry of the Environment: Rebuilding the Christian Tradition* (Santa Fe: Bear & Co., 1984), pp. 45–61 (47).

29. Cassuto, *Genesis*, Vol. 2, p. 124; Gunkel, *Genesis*, p. 148; Mathews, *Genesis 1–11.26*, p. 397; von Rad, *Genesis*, p. 131 (= *Das erste Buch Mose*, p. 98); Westermann, *Genesis 1–11*, p. 461 (= *Genesis*, Bd. I, p. 617).

30. Cassuto, *Genesis*, Vol. 2, p. 124.

31. Clines, 'Noah's Flood', pp. 128–42 (138).

32. For a discussion of the modifications made after the flood, see Hamilton, *Genesis 1–17*, pp. 312–15; Mathews, *Genesis 1–11.26*, pp. 400–406.

b. *Reissuing of the Primaeval Commands to Noah (Genesis 9.1) and Israel (Genesis 35.11)*

If Gen. 9.1 is read in connection with 1.28, however, the reiteration of the commands after the flood indicates that the primaeval blessing will be realized through Noah and his sons. We suggest that the repetition of the 'primaeval' commands in Gen. 35.11 has a similar function. It indicates that the primaeval blessing, which is renewed to Israel (Gen. 35.11), will be realized through his sons (Gen. 35.22b-26), who are also identified as Israel (Gen. 47.27).

Given that the primaeval blessing is advancing in Abraham's progeny in particular, it is not surprising to find that the 'primaeval' commands are reissued to Jacob. It seems to be the case that God's purposes for creation – first given to humankind in Gen. 1.28 and then renewed to Noah and his sons in Gen. 9.1 – continue through Israel. Realization of the primaeval blessing thus progresses from Noah to Israel. The implication is that the story of creation, which began in Genesis 1, is being taken up by Israel in particular. This point is underscored by the presence of the two linear genealogies in the primaeval history (Gen. 5.1-32; 11.10-26), which establish a connection between Adam and Abraham. Robinson has argued that the Genesis 5 genealogy is intended to take up the creation story.[33] The reiteration of the primaeval blessing at the outset of Seth's genealogy (Gen. 5.1-2) highlights the close connection between creation and the linear genealogical line, which reaches its climax with Israel. The genealogies in Genesis not only establish a relationship between creation and Israel (Gen. 5.1-32; 11.10-26; cf. 1 Chron. 1.1–2.1), but the reissuing of the 'primaeval' commands to Israel further suggests that the creation story is being taken up by them and that God's purpose for humankind is being fulfilled through them. It could even be argued that corporate Israel have assumed the position of the 'main' son through whom the creation blessing advances.[34] In Gen. 46.8-27 the *descendants* of Jacob's twelve sons are given. The question may be raised whether this list contributes to the multiplication theme. Does it indicate that the promise of increase has been *fulfilled* in any way?

5. *The Seventy Descendants of Israel (Genesis 46.8-27) and the Promise of Increase*

Genesis 46.8-27 is preceded by a brief narrative (Gen. 46.1-7) which states at its outset that God would make Jacob a great nation in *Egypt* (Gen. 46.1-4). Already in the introductory verses there are allusions to the exodus (Gen. 46.4a).[35] According to the literary context, the function of the genealogy is to list the number of Jacob's descendants who went with Jacob to Egypt. Particular attention is given

33. Robinson, 'Literary Functions', pp. 595–608 (600).
34. Is this the background to Exod. 4.22-23 where corporate *Israel* are identified as God's first-born son?
35. Hamilton, *Genesis 18–50*, p. 592; Wenham, *Genesis 16–50*, p. 442; Westermann, *Genesis 37–50*, p. 156 (= *Genesis*, Bd. III, p. 172).

to how many children (and grandchildren) were born to each mother: thirty-three to Leah (46.8-15); sixteen to Zilpah (46.16-18); fourteen to Rachel (46.19-22); and seven to Bilhah (46.23-25).[36] The list of names is then followed by a summary statement:

> All the persons belonging to Jacob who came into Egypt, who were his own offspring, not including the wives of his sons, were sixty-six persons in all. The children of Joseph, who were born to him in Egypt, were two; all the persons of the house of Jacob who came into Egypt were seventy (NRSV; Gen. 46.26-27).

While there is some question regarding how the total number is reckoned,[37] there does seem to be an established tradition that Jacob's descendants numbered seventy when they arrived in Egypt (Gen. 46.27; Exod. 1.5; Deut. 10.22). This number may convey the idea of totality, which would underscore that Jacob's family in their entirety went to Egypt.[38] Scholars have further noted that the descendants of Noah in Gen. 10.1-32, who are similarly listed in the form of a segmented genealogy, also number seventy.[39] Some scholars have suggested, therefore, that Noah's descendants in the Table of Nations prefigure the descendants of Jacob in Gen. 46.8-27. Sarna comments, for example, that the number seventy in Gen. 10.1-32 may function to

---

36. See Hamilton for a discussion of the differences between the names appearing in Gen. 46.8-27, Num. 26.12-14 and 1 Chronicles 2–8 (*Genesis 18–50*, pp. 593–96, 599). Wenham and Westermann suggest that the list of names in Gen. 46.8-27 is early because of the presence of El rather than YHWH in the theophoric names, and because names occurring in Gen. 46.8-27 are similar to names found in the book of Judges (Wenham, *Genesis 16–50*, pp. xxxi–xxxiii, 442; Westermann, *Genesis 37–50*, p. 161 [= *Genesis*, Bd. III, pp. 178–79]). It may well be the case that the genealogy reflects an early tradition and that it was inserted into its narrative context at a later date (see the discussion of Westermann, *Genesis 37–50*, pp. 157–61 [= *Genesis*, Bd. III, pp. 174–78]).

37. The sixty-six descendants in v. 26 probably exclude Er and Onan who died in Canaan (Gen. 46.12; cf. Gen. 38.7, 10), and Joseph and his two sons since they were already in Egypt (Gen. 46.20); thus leaving sixty-five sons. If Dinah is included in the count (Gen. 46.15), the number of those who went to Egypt would be sixty-six (Gen. 46.26). The final reckoning of seventy persons in v. 27 probably includes Jacob as well as Joseph and his two sons. Scholars have noted, however, that the number seventy is not always used in a precise way. Gideon's sons are a case in point. Gideon had seventy sons (Judg. 8.30; 9.2) who were all killed except for Jotham (Judg. 9.5). Even though one son remained alive, the narrator states that Gideon's *seventy* sons were killed (Judg. 9.5). Scholars thus conclude that the number seventy is a round number (Cassuto, *Genesis*, Vol. 2, pp. 176–77; Th. C. Vriezen, 'Exodusstudien Exodus I', *VT* 17 [1967], pp. 334–53 [351]). The LXX reckons the total number of Jacob's descendants at seventy-five persons (Gen. 46.27; cf. Exod. 1.5) by excluding Jacob and Joseph from the number and by including seven additional sons of Joseph so that there are nine in total (Gen. 46.27). The tradition of seventy persons is maintained in the LXX in Deut. 10.22, however.

38. Cassuto, *Genesis*, Vol. 2, pp. 175–80; Sarna, *Genesis*, p. 317; Wenham, *Genesis 16–50*, p. 444.

39. The number seventy is reckoned in the Table by excluding Nimrod (Sarna, *Genesis*, p. 69). Scholars have further noted that the number seven (or multiples of seven) is prominent in both texts. In Gen. 10.1-32, for example, Japheth (Gen. 10.2) and Mizraim (Gen. 10.13-14) have seven sons each, and Japheth has seven grandsons (Gen. 10.3-4). For a detailed discussion of the numbers seven and twelve in the Table, see Cassuto, *Genesis*, Vol. 2, p. 179. Multiples of seven are also prominent in Gen. 46.8-27 (Hamilton, *Genesis 18–50*, pp. 598–99; Sasson, 'A Genealogical "Convention"', pp. 171–85 [181]).

intensify the general prefiguring thrust of the Table. The number seventy resonates with the composition of the offspring of Jacob who went down to Egypt. The special significance this assumes is demonstrated not only by its emphasis in Gen. 46.27 but also by its reiteration twice more, in Exodus 1.5 and Deuteronomy 10.22. It is as though the totality of the nations and the totality of the Israelites who migrate to Egypt are intertwined.[40]

Given that the primaeval blessing has been reissued both to Noah (Gen. 9.1) and Israel (Gen. 35.11), it is not surprising to find that Noah's descendants prefigure the descendants of Israel. Moreover, we have argued so far that the primaeval blessing is in the process of being realized in Gen. 10.1-32, but is not fulfilled there. It was suggested that vast numbers of people would be required for Noah's descendants to 'fill the earth' and that their numbering seventy does not meet this requirement. Accordingly, we noted that there is no statement that Noah's descendants *'filled* the earth' (cf. Gen. 9.1). Analogously, the seventy descendants of Israel in Gen. 46.8-27 indicate that the primaeval blessing reissued to Israel is also in the process of being realized. As with Noah's descendants in Gen. 10.1-32, the blessing given to Israel has not yet been fulfilled in Gen. 46.8-27. Jacob's seventy children can hardly encompass the multitude envisaged by the promise that Abraham's seed would be like the 'dust of the earth' which cannot be numbered (e.g. Gen. 13.16). That they *can* be numbered suggests that the blessing has not yet been realized. Accordingly, in Deut. 26.5 we read that Jacob, the wandering Aramean, went down to Egypt *'few in number*, and there he became a great nation' (cf. Deut. 10.22). The following diagram compares the descendants of Noah with the descendants of Jacob:

Primaeval commands reissued to Noah and his sons (Gen. 9.1): ↓	*Primaeval commands reissued to Israel* (Gen. 35.11): ↓
Realization through Noah's three sons (Gen. 9.1). ↓	Realization through Jacob's twelve sons (Gen. 35.22-26). ↓
The blessing is in the *process* of being realized through Noah's seventy descendants (Gen. 10.1-32), but is *not yet fulfilled.*	The blessing is in the *process* of being realized through Jacob's seventy descendants (Gen. 46.8-27), but is *not yet fulfilled.*

In short, the blessing given to Israel is in the *process* of being realized in Gen. 46.8-27, but is not fulfilled at this point. It seems to be the case, therefore, that the primaeval blessing is being realized in two concentric circles[41] – one with humankind as a whole and the other with Israel in particular. The seventy descendants of Israel in Gen. 46.8-27 could, therefore, be understood as a small-scale world comparable to the macrocosmic world. The following diagram illustrates these two concentric circles:

40. Sarna, *Genesis*, p. 69.
41. We have adopted these terms which have been used by Harland (*The Value of Human Life*, p. 148).

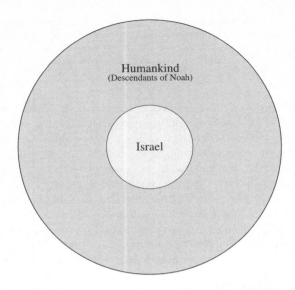

We suggest, in fact, that fulfilment of the primaeval blessing will *first* occur in the small-scale world of Israel.

6. *Initial Fulfilment of the Blessing to Israel in Genesis 47.27*

A summary statement about what transpired after Jacob's descendants had settled in Egypt occurs in Gen. 47.27: 'Thus Israel settled in the land of Egypt, in the region of Goshen; and they gained possessions in it, and were fruitful and multiplied exceedingly' (NRSV). This is the first occasion where the verbs פרה and רבה, which are usually used in Genesis to speak of a future action (whether a command or a promise), describe what has already happened.[42] This text, therefore, seems to mark the initial fulfilment of the promise of increase to the patriarchs and the commands to Israel. Jacob's descendants, who are simply identified as Israel, have not only multiplied, but they have been fruitful and multiplied *exceedingly* (ויפרו וירבו מאד).

That the primaeval commands, 'Be fruitful and multiply' (Gen. 35.11), reissued to Israel, are being realized in Gen. 47.27 accords with the view noted by several scholars, that throughout the priestly material there is a command-execution sequence.[43] That is, the priestly writer is concerned to show the execution of a command given by God.[44] Genesis 47.27 may be seen, therefore, as the first

42. Brueggemann, 'The Kerygma of the Priestly Writers', pp. 397–414 (405); Gilbert, ' "Soyez féconds et multipliez" ', pp. 729–42 (732).

43. B.W. Anderson, 'A Stylistic Study of the Priestly Creation Story', in G.W. Coats and B.W. Long (eds.), *Canon and Authority* (Philadelphia: Fortress Press, 1977), pp. 148–62 (151–52); J. Blenkinsopp, 'The Structure of P', *CBQ* 38 (1976), pp. 275–92 (275–83).

44. E.g. Gen. 7.5; 17.23; 21.4; Exod. 7.10, 20; 12.28; 16.34. For a comprehensive list, see Blenkinsopp, 'The Structure of P', pp. 275–92 (276–77).

explicit statement that the primaeval commands to 'be fruitful and multiply' (Gen. 1.28; 9.1; cf. Gen. 35.11) have been executed. Thus we may conclude that Gen. 47.27 marks the initial fulfilment of the promise of increase *and* of the primaeval commands, yet nowhere do we read that the descendants of Israel have become as 'the stars of the heaven' (e.g. Gen. 15.5; 22.17; 26.4) or as the 'sand of the seashore' (e.g. Gen. 22.17; 32.12). Thus the promise of many descendants is still a *future* reality. Clines has rightly observed, therefore, that although the promise of descendants has begun to take effect in Genesis, the book concludes with the promise largely unrealized.[45] Accordingly, while Israel have been 'fruitful and multiplied' (Gen. 47.27), nowhere is it stated in Genesis that they have '*filled* the *land*' (cf. Gen. 1.28; 9.1). The implication is that the primaeval commands have not been *fully* executed in the book of Genesis.

7. *Conclusion*

The linear genealogical line that begins with Adam (Gen. 5.1-32; 11.10-26; cf. 1 Chron. 1.1-27), culminates in Gen. 35.22b-26 with the *twelve* sons of Jacob. The absence of any reversal of primogeniture suggests that the 'primaeval' blessing reissued to Jacob (Gen. 35.11) will be realized through all *twelve* sons, who are identified simply as 'Israel' (Gen. 47.27). It would appear, therefore, that corporate Israel have assumed the position of the main son through whom the promise of increase will be realized. It was suggested that the renewal of the 'primaeval' commands to Jacob, when his name was changed to Israel, indicates that God's creational purposes will be taken up by Israel as a people. Given that Jacob's descendants number seventy (Gen. 46.27), there is the intimation that they are a small-scale world comparable to the large-scale world of humanity (cf. Gen. 10.1-32). The first indication in the Genesis narrative that the promise of increase has been realized is in Gen. 47.27, yet there is no suggestion that it has been fulfilled at this stage in the narrative. The opening verses of Exodus, however, resume the theme of Israel's multiplication.

---

45. Clines, *The Theme of the Pentateuch*, pp. 45–46.

Chapter 9

FULFILMENT OF THE PRIMAEVAL BLESSING
IN EGYPT (EXODUS 1.1-7)

1. *The Book of Exodus as the Continuation of Genesis*

The book of Exodus begins by reiterating the names of the sons of Israel who went to Egypt with Jacob. Scholars have observed that the introductory verses indicate that the book of Exodus is being presented as the continuation of Genesis.[1] First, it is noted that the MT of Exod. 1.1 begins with a conjunctive ו: ואלה שמות בני-ישראל, '*And* these are the names of the sons of Israel'. G.I. Davies has examined the textual history of the ו in Exod. 1.1. He suggests that, while the LXX omits it in the rendering ΤΑΥΤΑ τὰ ὀνόματα, as does the Vulgate, the MT is to be preferred.[2] He concludes that the presence of the conjunctive ו in the MT means that the commentator is obliged to consider Genesis when studying the opening verses of Exodus.

This view was espoused by the medieval scholar, Nachmanides, who has commented on the conjunctive ו in Exod. 1.1. He notes that Exod. 1.1 resumes Gen. 46.8 and concludes, therefore, that although Genesis and Exodus comprise

---

1. Cassuto, *Exodus*, p. 7; G.F. Davies, *Israel in Egypt: Reading Exodus 1–2* (JSOTSup, 135; Sheffield: Sheffield Academic Press, 1992), p. 35; J.I. Durham, *Exodus* (WBC; Waco, TX: Word Books, 1987), p. 3; J.P. Fokkelman, 'Exodus', in *The Literary Guide to the Bible*, pp. 56–65 (59); Mathews, *Genesis 1–11.26*, p. 45; S. Talmon, 'The Presentation of Synchroneity and Simultaneity in Biblical Hebrew', in J. Heinemann and S. Werses (eds.), *Studies in Hebrew Narrative Art throughout the Ages* (Scripta Hierosolymitana, 27; Jerusalem: Magnes Press, 1978), pp. 9–26 (16).

2. G.I. Davies, ' "And" – The First Word of the Book of Exodus'. Professor Davies presented this lecture at the Old Testament Seminar, University of Cambridge, England, 1999. I am grateful to him for providing me a transcript of his lecture. Davies discusses the textual history of the ו in Exod. 1.1 in detail and maintains that the LXX and Vulgate may reflect the translators' own rendering, particularly after the establishment of the Pentateuch into separate 'books'. Davies notes that, while the division of Genesis and Exodus is reflected in Qumran manuscripts, there are two manuscripts which include both Genesis and Exodus on the one scroll (4QGen-Exod[a]; 4QpalGen-Exod[1]; cf. E. Tov, *Textual Criticism of the Hebrew Bible* [Minneapolis: Fortress Press, 1992], p. 104) as well as two additional manuscripts where this may have been the case (4QExod[b]; Mur1). Davies observes that only 4QpalGen-Exod[1] includes Exod. 1.1. He notes that even though Exod. 1.1 begins with אלה, the editors of 4QpalGen-Exod[1] (Ulrich and Sanderson) acknowledge that a scribe may have written a large isolated ו as the first letter of Exod. 1.1 in the otherwise blank line 4, which would signal the beginning of Exodus. Davies concludes that, even if the reading without the ו goes back to Hebrew manuscripts, the more difficult reading with the ו is to be preferred.

two books, Exodus is a continuation of the book of Genesis.[3] More recent scholars have similarly concluded that the ו in Exod. 1.1 underscores the continuity between Genesis and Exodus.[4] Durham, for instance, is of the opinion that the conjunctive ו is 'an indication of an all-important continuity obscured already both by the growth of the closing part of the Book of Genesis and by the division of the text into "books"... The connection of the text of Exodus with what has preceded must be emphasized, not further obscured'.[5] It seems to be the case, therefore, that the book of Exodus is being presented as the continuation of Genesis.

Secondly, it is observed that the opening verses of Exodus recall Gen. 46.8-27, which records Jacob's entry into Egypt with his family.[6]

> These are the names of the sons of Israel who came to Egypt with Jacob, each with his household: Reuben, Simeon, Levi, and Judah, Issachar, Zebulun, and Benjamin, Dan and Naphtali, Gad and Asher. The total number of people born to Jacob was seventy. Joseph was already in Egypt (NRSV, Exod. 1.1-5).

The first six words of Exod. 1.1 are identical to the first six words of Gen. 46.8. The two texts read as follows:

Gen. 46.8	Exod. 1.1
ואלה שמות בני־ישראל הבאים מצרימה	ואלה שמות בני־ישראל הבאים מצרימה
יעקב ובניו	את יעקב איש וביתו באו

While there are differences between Gen. 46.8 and Exod. 1.1,[7] the repetition of the first six words from Gen. 46.8 gives a 'clear rhetorical indication of the continuity intended not only in the narrative, but in the underlying theological assertion'.[8] This connection between Genesis and Exodus is seen also in Exod. 1.5, which recalls the statement found at the conclusion of the genealogy. A comparison between Gen. 46.26-27 and Exod. 1.5 is outlined as follows:

---

3. Nachman, *Genesis*, pp. 6–7. For a discussion of Nachmanides and other medieval scholars who discuss resumptive repetition, see Talmon, 'Synchroneity and Simultaneity', pp. 9–26 (14–16).

4. Cassuto, *Exodus*, p. 7; Davies, *Israel in Egypt*, p. 32; Talmon, 'Synchroneity and Simultaneity', pp. 9–26 (16); Weimar, 'Aufbau und Struktur', pp. 174–203 (198 n. 105).

5. Durham, *Exodus*, pp. 3–4.

6. The relationship of Exod. 1.1-5 to Gen. 35.22b-26 and 46.8-27 is disputed. Some scholars argue that Exod. 1.1-5 is the primary P text and that Gen. 35.22b-26 and 46.8-27 are secondary expansions by a later editor (Davies, '"And" – The First Word in the Book of Exodus'; von Rad, *Genesis*, pp. 402–403 [= *Das erste Buch Mose*, pp. 330–31]; P. Weimar, *Untersuchungen zur priesterschriftlichen Exodusgeschichte* [Würzburg: Echter Verlag, 1973], pp. 15–25). Vriezen argues that the genealogy in Exod. 1.2-4 is the original P text, which has been expanded and inserted into both Gen. 46.8-27 and Exod. 1.1-7 by a later editor ('Exodusstudien Exodus 1', pp. 334–53 [347–53]). It is not within the scope of the present study to discuss the origin of these texts. As has been noted, our focus has been on interpreting the text according to its final form. For further discussion of this topic, see Driver, *Genesis*, p. 365; Hamilton, *Genesis 18–50*, pp. 593–99; Vriezen, 'Exodusstudien Exodus 1', pp. 334–53 (344–51); Weimar, *Exodusgeschichte*, pp. 15–25.

7. In Gen. 46.8 Jacob is included in the designation בני ישראל, whereas in Exod. 1.1 we are told that בני ישראל went *with* Jacob. Thus בני ישראל in Exod. 1.1 refers to Jacob's *sons*. In Exod. 1.7, however, בני ישראל refers to Israel as a people.

8. Durham, *Exodus*, p. 3.

Gen. 46.26-27	*Exod. 1.5*

Gen. 46.26-27 column (RTL):

כל־הנפש הבאה ליעקב מצרימה יצאי ירכו
מלבד נשי בני־יעקב כל־נפש ששים ושש
כל־הנפש לבית־יעקב הבאה מצרימה שבעים

Exod. 1.5 column (RTL):

ויהי כל־נפש יצאי ירך־יעקב שבעים נפש
ויוסף היה במצרים

The reference to those 'who went forth from the loin of Jacob' (יצאי ירך־יעקב)
in Exod. 1.5 reflects Gen. 46.26 where Jacob's descendants are referred to as
those who 'went forth from his loin' (יצאי ירכו). In Gen. 46.26, however, Jacob's
descendants (who are from his loin) number sixty-six, whereas in Exod. 1.5 they
number seventy. The number seventy, therefore, does not recall v. 26, but v. 27.
Exod. 1.5 thus seems to be a brief summary of vv. 26 and 27.[9] We may conclude,
therefore, that Exod. 1.1 recalls the introduction to the list of Jacob's descendants
who went to Egypt (Gen. 46.8), and Exod. 1.5 recalls its conclusion (Gen. 46.26-
27). The context of Gen. 46.8-27 has clearly been brought to the foreground of
the Exodus narrative. Vriezen rightly concludes that, in the final redaction, a
strong connection has been made between the story of the patriarchs and the
exodus narrative.[10]

Thirdly, the list of Jacob's sons in Exod 1.2-4 (not including Joseph who was
already in Egypt) reflects the order of sons found in Gen. 35.23-26 (rather than
Gen. 46.8-27).[11] The order of Jacob's sons in Gen. 35.23-26, Gen. 48.8-25 and
Exod. 1.2-4 is outlined as follows (in an abbreviated form, listing only the twelve
sons):

> Gen. 35.23-26 Reuben, Simeon, Levi, Judah, Issachar, Zebulun, Joseph, Benjamin,
>   Dan, Naphtali, Gad and Asher.
> Gen. 46.8-25   Reuben, Simeon, Levi, Judah, Issachar, Zebulun, Gad, Asher, Joseph,
>   Benjamin, Dan and Naphtali.
> Exod. 1.2-4   Reuben, Simeon, Levi, Judah, Issachar, Zebulun, Benjamin, Dan,
>   Naphtali, Gad and Asher.

The order of the first six sons is the same in all three lists. However, the order of
the last six sons is different. The list in Gen. 46.8-25 presents the sons according
to their mothers: Leah and her maid Zilpah, followed by Rachel and her maid
Bilhah. The lists in Gen. 35.23-26 and Exod. 1.2-4 are identical (with the exception
that Joseph is missing from Exod. 1.2-4), presenting the sons according to their
mothers Leah, Rachel, Bilhah (Rachel's maid) and Zilpah (Leah's maid). We
noted earlier that the placement of Gen. 35.23-26 indicates that the 'primaeval'
blessing reissued to Jacob/Israel (Gen. 35.11) will be realized through his twelve
sons. The book of Exodus thus begins by listing the twelve sons of Israel through
whom the blessing will be realized. That the genealogy from Gen. 35.23-26 is
recalled in Exod. 1.2-5 further indicates that the book of Exodus is being
presented as the continuation of the Genesis narrative.

9.   According to those scholars who argue that Gen. 46.8-27 is dependent on Exod. 1.1-5, Gen.
46.26-27 would be seen as an *expansion* of Exod. 1.5.

10.   Vriezen, 'Exodusstudien Exodus 1', pp. 334–53.

11.   Weimar maintains that Gen. 35.22b-26 is a secondary expansion of Exod. 1.2-4 (*Exodusgeschichte*, pp. 36–38) whereas Vriezen argues that Gen. 35.22b-26 and Exod. 1.2-4 are parallel texts,
but one is not dependent on the other ('Exodusstudien Exodus 1', pp. 334–53 [347 n. 1]).

Fourthly, reference to the death of Joseph in Exod. 1.6 also recalls Genesis where his death has already been mentioned (Gen. 50.26).[12] The statement in v. 6b, however, that Joseph's brothers and that generation died, advances the story-line beyond Genesis – which concludes with Joseph's brothers still living (Gen. 50.24-26). Exodus 1.6 may be identified, therefore, as the sequel to the book of Genesis since v. 6b looks beyond Genesis to events that transpire after the death of Joseph and his generation.

Fifthly, scholars have rightly noted that Israel's fecundity in Egypt (Exod. 1.7) clearly recalls the primaeval blessing (Gen. 9.1, 7; cf. Gen. 35.11) and the divine promise of increase (e.g. Gen. 17.2, 6; 26.4). It is thus concluded that Israel's increase, which appears to have taken place during their long stay in Egypt (Exod. 12.40; cf. Gen. 15.13), signals the fulfilment of God's promise to the patriarchs. We shall return to the import of Exod. 1.7 in the following discussion. It is sufficient to note at this point that the theme of multiplication in v. 7 recalls the book of Genesis; thus it provides further support that the book of Exodus is being presented as a continuation of the Genesis narrative.

Lastly, G.F. Davies has observed that the story of Genesis is essential for the plot of Exod. 1.1-7. He suggests that Exod. 1.1-7 has two plots: 'danger-escape from danger' and 'promise-fulfilment'. Davies notes that no information has been given in Exod. 1.1-7 that would indicate why the children of Israel were even in Egypt or why they had multiplied to such an extent. He concludes, therefore, that the reader is required to supply data from Genesis, remembering the story of Israel and God's promise to increase Abraham's descendants.[13] Davies has demonstrated that Exod. 1.1-7 can only be properly understood against the background of the Genesis narrative. Before considering the import of the book of Genesis for Exod. 1.1-7, it is necessary, however, to discuss briefly whether Exod. 1.1-7 is a literary unit or not.

2. Does Exodus 1.7 Introduce a New Section or
Does It Belong to Exodus 1.1-6?

According to the final form of the text, the story-line advances in Exod. 1.7 beyond the book of Genesis with the comment

ובני ישראל פרו וישרצו וירבו ויעצמו במאד מאד ותמלא הארץ אתם

That the subject בני ישראל precedes the verb may indicate that a new episode begins in v. 7.[14] Reference to Joseph's death in v. 6 would support this view, since his death concludes the book of Genesis (Gen. 50.26). It is also common

---

12. G.I. Davies suggests that Gen. 50.22-26 reflects multiple authorship, comprising two accounts (Gen. 50.22-24; 50.25-26). He maintains that the death of Joseph in Exod. 1.6 concludes the J account in Gen. 50.22-24 which does not mention his death ('"And" – The First Word of the Book of Exodus'). Other scholars attribute v. 6 to the priestly writer (G.W. Coats, 'A Structural Transition in Exodus', *VT* 22 [1972], pp. 129–42 [133]; Durham, *Exodus*, p. 3).

13. Davies, *Israel in Egypt*, p. 28.

14. Cf. Joüon, §155*nd*.

for the death of a key figure to conclude a Toledot (e.g. Gen. 9.29; 25.7-11; 35.28-29). It could be argued, therefore, that Joseph's death in v. 6 concludes the first section and that Israel's increase in v. 7 (cf. Exod. 1.9, 10, 20) begins a new section. Accordingly, Coats suggests that Exod. 1.1-14 has a two-part structure: the first element comprises a name list which concludes with the death of Joseph (vv. 1-6) and the second element introduces the Exodus tradition (vv. 8-14).[15] His view is somewhat inconsistent, however, since he argues that, according to structural analysis of the text in its final form, the principal break comes between vv. 7 and 8.

Vriezen maintains that, according to the final form, the new narrative cycle begins in v. 8 with the rise of the new king. He suggests that the 'death' (מות) of a key figure (cf. Exod. 1.6) and the 'rising' (קום) of a new leader (cf. Exod. 1.8) is a traditional formula that marks the transition from one cycle of tradition to the next (e.g. Judg. 2.8, 10).[16] Vriezen maintains that, while Exod. 1.7 originally followed the P genealogy (Exod. 1.2-4), it is now to be considered part of the textual unit of vv. 1-6.[17] Thus vv. 1-7 are a unit, with the new narrative cycle beginning in v. 8. Verse 8 is especially marked, not only by the presence of a new Pharaoh, but by the fact that he *did not know Joseph*. Israel's favourable position in Egypt was clearly due to Joseph's prominent position (Gen. 45.17-20; 47.5-6). Thus v. 8 has ominous overtones, foreshadowing that Israel's favourable position is under threat. We suggest, therefore, that while Israel's increase provides the background to the ensuing story (Exod. 1.9, 10, 20), it is the rise of the new king that actually marks the beginning of the new episode.[18] This view is reflected in the Masoretic open paragraph marker (פ) at the end of v. 7, indicating that v. 8 begins a new paragraph on a new line. Several English translations also begin a new paragraph in v. 8: '*Now* a new king arose…' (NRSV, NASB).

If v. 8 begins a new section, the subject בני ישראל may well precede the verb (i.e. ובני ישראל פרו) in order to establish a contrast.[19] The point seems to be that, even though the children of Israel numbered only seventy when they arrived in Egypt (v. 5) and Joseph's generation had died (v. 6), this is not the conclusion to the story. Rather, the children of Israel increased exceedingly. The contrast between Israel's numbering seventy and their subsequent proliferation in Egypt is underscored in Deut. 10.22, 'Your ancestors went down to Egypt seventy persons; and now the LORD your God has made you as numerous as the stars' (cf. Deut. 26.5). Thus the NRSV begins v. 7a with the translation: '*But* the Israelites were fruitful and prolific…' (cf. NIV, NASB). In sum, according to the final form of the text, Exod. 1.1-7 seems to be a textual unit which concludes with the statement about Israel's increase in Egypt. The descendants of Israel, who numbered seventy

---

15. Coats, 'A Structural Transition', pp. 129–42 (132–34).

16. For examples of this idiom (e.g. Josh. 1.1-2) and other texts where a similar *idea* is present (even if the identical verbs are not used), see Vriezen, 'Exodusstudien Exodus 1', pp. 334–53 (334–42).

17. Vriezen, 'Exodusstudien Exodus 1', pp. 334–53 (346).

18. Davies, *Israel in Egypt*, p. 25; Sailhamer, *The Pentateuch as Narrative*, p. 244.

19. An example of this syntax may be seen in Exod. 14.29, which has בני ישראל as the subject (Joüon §155*nb*).

when they arrived in Egypt (Exod. 1.5), have multiplied exceedingly to such a degree that the land was filled with them. Exodus 1.7 also sets the scene for the ensuing story, since Israel's increase threatens the new Egyptian king.

3. *Exodus 1.7 and the Promise of Increase to the Patriarchs*

The statement in Exod. 1.7 provides an important transition from the patriarchal narratives to the exodus tradition, but also concludes the book of Genesis by picking up the reproductive aspect of the promises given to the patriarchs.[20] As has been noted, the first indication of an *initial* fulfilment of the blessing to Israel occurs in Gen. 47.27 where it is said of Israel, when they were in Egypt: ויפרו וירבו מאד. This theme of increase is resumed in Exod. 1.7 with the reiteration of the verbs פרה and רבה and the adverb מאד:

ובני ישראל פרו וישרצו וירבו ויעצמו במאד מאד ותמלא הארץ אתם

Since the verbs פרה and רבה occur on several occasions in both the primaeval blessing (Gen. 1.28; 9.1, 7) and the promises of increase to the patriarchs (e.g. Gen. 17.2), the background to Exod. 1.7 could be either of these contexts or both. The verb עצם, 'be powerful, numerous', however, is not used in any of the Abrahamic promises, although it does occur in the statement by Abimelech, when he said that Isaac had become 'too powerful' for him (Gen. 26.16). The adjectival form of עצם is also used in YHWH's statement to Abraham, that he would become a 'great and *mighty* nation' (Gen. 18.18). It is difficult to determine, however, whether עצם means 'grow strong' (NRSV) or 'be numerous' (NIV) in Exod. 1.7, since either meaning is suitable in the context.[21] In either case, it is evident that the children of Israel are multiplying significantly and thus they are becoming powerful.

Israel's increase is further underscored by the repetition of the adverb מאד in v. 7.[22] The expression במאד מאד (Exod. 1.7) occurs in Genesis 17 with the verbs רבה (Gen. 17.2) and פרה (Gen. 17.6; cf. Gen. 17.20). God had promised Abraham that he would make him 'exceedingly numerous' (וארבה אותך במאד מאד, Gen. 17.2) and 'exceedingly fruitful' (והפרתי אתך במאד מאד, Gen. 17.6). Israel's extraordinary increase in Egypt might be seen, therefore, as the fulfilment of God's promise of increase to Abraham. Ironically, Egypt had been a threat to the multiplication of Abraham's seed (Gen. 12.10-20); now Israel's multiplication is a threat to Egypt (Exod. 1.9).

---

20. Weimar argues that Exod. 1.1-4, 5b-7 originally concluded the Jacob cycle (*Exodusgeschichte*, pp. 15, 21).

21. The meaning 'grow strong' (cf. LXX, καὶ κατίσχυον σφόδρα σφόδρα) accords with Gen. 26.16 and Exod 1.20. However, the meaning 'be countless' suggested by Koehler-Baumgartner for עצם in Exod. 1.7 (KB³, Vol. 2, p. 868; cf. NIV, 'be numerous') is congruent with the idea of increase in Exod. 1.7. The idea of being numerous also accords with other texts where עצם is used in parallel with רבב, 'multiply' (e.g. Pss. 38.19 [20]; 69.4 [5]). For a detailed discussion of עצם as a 'superiority formula', see Weimar, *Exodusgeschichte*, pp. 30–33.

22. GKC, §133*k*.

Given that the book of Exodus continues the Genesis narrative and that the promise of many descendants is largely unrealized in Genesis, scholars have rightly concluded that Exod. 1.7 marks the fulfilment of the promise of increase given to the patriarchs.[23] Cross has noted, however, that it is a *preliminary* fulfilment, since Israel's increase is still considered a future reality (cf. Deut. 1.10), for they have not yet multiplied in the land promised to them.[24]

It is important to note, however, that the language used in Exod. 1.7 not only recalls the promise of increase to the patriarchs, but also the primaeval blessing. The verb שׁרץ, 'breed abundantly', for example, is reminiscent of the primaeval command given to Noah and his sons after the flood: שׁרצו בארץ, 'breed abundantly on the earth' (Gen. 9.7). The connection between Gen. 9.7 and Exod. 1.7 is underscored by the fact that שׁרץ does *not* occur in the promise of increase to the patriarchs. Similarly, the verb ארץ + מלא in the statement, ותמלא הארץ אתם, 'and the land was filled with them' (Exod. 1.7) recalls the primaeval blessing, ומלאו את־הארץ, 'and fill the earth', given to humankind (Gen. 1.28) and Noah and his sons (Gen. 9.1). It is not insignificant that מלא + ארץ (with humans as the subject) is absent from Genesis 12-50. Given that שׁרץ and ארץ + מלא recall the *primaeval* blessing rather than the promise of increase to the patriarchs, we may enquire whether the presence of 'creation' language in Exod. 1.7 has any theological significance.

4. *The Import of Creation Language in Exodus 1.7*

A number of scholars acknowledge that Exod. 1.7 recalls the primaeval blessing. Childs writes, for instance, that the 'vocabulary of v. 7 reflects the promise of blessing to Adam (Gen. 1.28; 9.1) as well as the promise to Abraham (12.1ff.)'. He concludes, however, that 'God, the creator, has fulfilled his promise to the fathers' and that v. 7 'serves as a fulfillment of the patriarchal promise of the past' while also providing the background for the exodus.[25] Other scholars similarly acknowledge that language from the primaeval blessing appears in Exod. 1.7,[26] yet they conclude that the promise to the *patriarchs* is fulfilled in v. 7. They do

23. B.S. Childs, *The Book of Exodus: A Critical, Theological Commentary* (Philadelphia: Westminster Press, 1974), pp. 2–3; Coats, 'A Structural Transition', pp. 129–42 (136); G.H. Davies, *Exodus* (Torch Bible Commentary; London: SCM Press, 1967), p. 59; Davies, *Israel in Egypt*, p. 28; Durham, *Exodus*, p. 3; W.H. Gispen, *Exodus* (Bible Student's Commentary; Grand Rapids: Zondervan, 1982), p. 31; N.M. Sarna, *Exploring Exodus: The Heritage of Biblical Israel* (New York: Schocken Books, 1983), p. 15; Weimar, 'Die Toledot-Formel', pp. 65–93 (90).

24. Cross refers to Israel's time in Egypt in terms of a 'preliminary' fulfilment of the blessing (*Canaanite Myth*, p. 296). He argues that the primary use of the formula is related to the land of Canaan and Israel's multiplying there (Lev. 26.9).

25. Childs, *Exodus*, pp. 2–3.

26. For example, Durham notes that שׁרץ has been taken from Gen. 9.7. However, he concludes that the verb is simply being used to highlight Israel's extraordinary increase. Similarly, he suggests that the statement, 'and the land was filled with them', is being used to dramatize Israel's increase (*Exodus*, pp. 4–5).

not discuss why *creation* language has been used in this context and whether it has any theological significance.[27]

Coats has also observed that the language used in Exod. 1.7 recalls P's creation terminology as well as Gen. 47.27. Coats then argues, however, that v. 7 (and vv. 13-14) must be understood primarily in light of God's promise to Abraham, and concludes that 'for both J and P the promise to Abraham is fulfilled *at just this point*'.[28] Given that Exod. 1.7 clearly recalls the primaeval blessing, why, then, must it be read *primarily* in relation to God's promises to the patriarchs?[29] Similarly, if Gen. 1.28 is central to the plot of Genesis,[30] is it possible that it is also central to the plot of Exod. 1.1-7? Yet Davies maintains that Exod. 1.1-7 marks the fulfilment of God's promise to multiply the patriarchal family.[31] Why has priority been given to the *Abrahamic* promises? If the reader is required to supply data from Genesis – from 'the story of Israel and his sons and the promise that God made to propagate Abraham's descendants'[32] as Davies proposes – then does not the presence of creation language in Exod. 1.7[33] mean that the reader is also required to supply data from the *primaeval* history?

The commonly held view that the primaeval blessing is fulfilled in the Table of Nations may have prevented these scholars from giving adequate attention to creation language in Exod. 1.7, since this view implies that the blessing has already been realized in the primaeval history. In Exod. 1.7, however, *four* verbs from the primaeval blessing are used (פרה, רבה, שרץ and מלא + ארץ), yet the question has not been considered whether the primaeval blessing is being fulfilled in any way in Exod. 1.7. We have argued so far that Genesis 1–11 concludes with the primaeval blessing being largely *unrealized*. According to our view, therefore, there is the expectation of a *forthcoming* fulfilment of the creation blessing.

5. *Exodus 1.7 and the Primaeval Blessing*

Some scholars have concluded, however, that the creation language used in Exod. 1.7 is theologically significant. Fretheim maintains, for example, that Israel's 'filling the land' is an explicit reference to Gen. 1.28 and 9.1. He notes that the connection between Exod. 1.7 and the primaeval blessing is underscored by the absence of a reference to the *specific* location of Egypt or Goshen, which would

27. Gilbert, ' "Soyez féconds et multipliez" ', pp. 729–42; G. Larsson, *Bound for Freedom: The Book of Exodus in Jewish and Christian Traditions* (Peabody, MA: Hendrickson, 1999), p. 6; Sarna, *Exploring Exodus*, p. 15.

28. Coats, 'A Structural Transition', pp. 129–42 (136).

29. Cf. Gispen, *Exodus*, pp. 31–32.

30. Clines, *What Does Eve Do to Help?*, p. 51; Turner, *Genesis*, p. 24.

31. Davies, *Israel in Egypt*, p. 28.

32. Davies, *Israeli in Egypt*, p. 28.

33. J.S. Ackerman has also noted that there are a number of allusions to the primaeval history in Exodus 1–2 ('The Literary Context of the Moses Birth Story [Exodus 1–2]', in Kenneth R.R. Gros Louis, *et al.* [eds.], *Literary Interpretations of Biblical Narratives*, Vol. 1 [Nashville: Abingdon Press, 1974], pp. 74–119).

have blurred the relationship.[34] He concludes, therefore, that Israel's fruitfulness in Egypt is a fulfilment of the *creational* word of God.[35] Weimar also maintains that the promise of blessing to Noah and Abraham is being fulfilled in Exod. 1.7[36] and that the blessing of creation has thus been renewed.[37] Other scholars have also concluded that Israel's increase in Egypt is being presented as the fulfilment of the primaeval commands.[38]

The point of Exod. 1.7 seems to be that Israel have multiplied to such an extent, ותמלא הארץ אתם, 'so that the land was *filled* with them' (NRSV, NIV, NASB). This is precisely what God intended for humankind (Gen. 1.28; 9.1, 7). We have argued that the primaeval blessing, which is not fulfilled in Gen. 10.1-32, is advancing in Shem's line in particular. It was noted that in the patriarchal narratives, the blessing of fecundity is changed into a divine *promise* given to Abraham and his seed. The reissuing of the 'primaeval' commands to Jacob/Israel in Gen. 35.11 shows that God's intention for creation will be realized through Israel (cf. Gen. 35.22b-26). Since the promise of increase to the patriarchs is a reaffirmation of the *primaeval* blessing, it is not surprising to find that the fulfilment of the promise to Israel is couched in creation language. In other words, Israel's proliferation in Egypt marks not only the fulfilment of the promise of increase to the patriarchs, but also indicates that the primaeval blessing is being fulfilled. Ackerman thus concludes that in Exod. 1.7 'the narrator is clearly saying that the destiny of man, as announced at the Creation and after the Flood, is in the process of being fulfilled by the descendants of Israel'.[39] Exodus 1.7, therefore, brings to conclusion this central theme of the primaeval history (Gen. 1.28; 9.1) by presenting Israel's multiplication in Egypt as the fulfilment of all *three* commands, 'Be fruitful and multiply, *and* fill the earth'. Realization of the primaeval blessing after the flood, therefore, advances from Noah to Israel.

6. *Exodus 1.7: Fulfilment of the Primaeval Blessing* in Microcosm

It is important to observe, however, that fulfilment of the primaeval commands through Israel is not identical to what is envisaged in Gen. 9.1. Instead of Noah's descendants filling the earth (9.1), it is only *Israel* who fill the land. Moreover, הארץ in Exod. 1.7 is the land of *Egypt*, whereas הארץ in Gen. 1.28 and 9.1 refers to the *earth,* that is, to the entire habitable world. Given that the land of Israel had

---

34. T.E. Fretheim, 'The Plagues as Ecological Signs of Historical Disaster', *JBL* 110 (1991), pp. 385–96 (385 n. 3).

35. T.E. Fretheim, 'The Reclamation of Creation: Redemption and Law in Leviticus', *Int* 45 (1991), pp. 354–65 (356).

36. Weimar, *Exodusgeschichte*, pp. 30-34. A similar view is espoused by Davies, '"And" – The Relationship of Exod. 1.1-7 to the Book of Genesis', Old Testament Seminar.

37. Weimar, *Exodusgeschichte*, p. 36.

38. R.J. Burns, *Exodus, Leviticus, Numbers* (OTM; Wilmington: Michael Glazier, Inc., 1983), pp. 27–28; B. Jacob, *The Second Book of the Bible: Exodus* (trans. W. Jacob; Hoboken: Ktav Publ. House Inc., 1992), p. 9; J.G. Janzen, *Exodus* (Louisville: Westminster John Knox Press, 1997), pp. 15–16; Keil and Delitzsch, *The Pentateuch*, Vol. 1, p. 419; Mathews, *Genesis 1–11.26*, p. 174.

39. Ackerman, 'The Moses Birth Story', p. 77.

been promised to Abraham's progeny, it seems somewhat unusual that 'fulfil-ment' language is being used with regard to *Egypt*. Does this foresee that God's purposes for Abraham and his seed will reach beyond the borders of Israel? In any case, since the Israelites are filling the land of Egypt rather than the entire earth as in 1.28, it seems to be the case that Exod. 1.7 marks the fulfilment of the primaeval blessing *in microcosm*.[40] Fretheim thus concludes that 'in some sense Israel is represented as having fulfilled the creational command, and hence Israel is a microcosmic fulfillment of God's intentions for creation'.[41] Some scholars have suggested that already in Gen. 46.8-27 there is the intimation that the seventy descendants of Israel are a small-scale world comparable to the macro-cosmic world represented by the seventy descendants of Noah (Gen. 10.1-32).[42] It may not be so surprising, therefore, that Israel's increase is being presented as the fulfilment of the primaeval blessing in microcosm. The point seems to be that God's creational purposes intended for the macrocosmic world (Gen. 1.28; 9.1, 7) are being fulfilled in the small-scale world of Israel (Exod. 1.7).

7. *One or Two Fulfilments of the Primaeval Blessing?*

We may recall at this point the view commonly held by scholars, that the primae-val blessing is fulfilled in the *Table of Nations*. Brueggemann argues, for example, that the spreading out of Noah's progeny (Gen. 10.32) was 'part of God's plan for creation and the fulfillment of the mandate of 1.28'.[43] He also maintains that the intent of creation finally comes to fulfilment in the spreading out of the Canaan-ites (Gen. 10.18). It is important to note his comments on Exod. 1.7 as well. Brueggemann maintains that the theme of Israel's multiplication in Exod. 1.7 'stretches from creation to liberation, from the blessing announced to its realiza-tion – which is the perennial story in Israel and the stress which P wishes to make. God does keep his promise… They are not yet in the land, but signs of the realization of Yahweh's promise are already apparent'.[44] Brueggemann seems to conclude that there are *two* fulfilments of the primaeval blessing – one in the Table of Nations and the other in Exod. 1.7. Cassuto espouses a similar view. He suggests that the primaeval blessing is fulfilled in Gen. 9.19 and 10.1-32,[45] while also concluding that *Israel* fulfil the primaeval blessing in microcosm in Exod. 1.7.[46] As with Brueggemann, Cassuto sees two fulfilments of the primaeval blessing.

40. Cf. Cassuto, *Exodus*, p. 9; Fretheim, 'The Plagues', pp. 385–96 (385 n. 3).

41. Fretheim, 'The Plagues', pp. 385–96 (385 n. 3).

42. Ackerman, 'The Moses Birth Story', p. 78; Blenkinsopp, *The Pentateuch*, pp. 88, 144; Cassuto, *Genesis*, Vol. 2, p. 180; Mathews, *Genesis 1–11.26*, p. 437; Ross, *Creation and Blessing*, p. 680; Waltke, *Genesis*, p. 577; Wenham, *Genesis 1–15*, p. 214; *idem*, *Genesis 16–50*, p. 442.

43. Brueggemann, *Genesis*, p. 98.

44. Brueggemann, 'The Kerygma of the Priestly Writers', pp. 397–414 (406).

45. Cassuto, *Genesis*, Vol. 2, pp. 148–49, 188, 225.

46. Cassuto, *Exodus*, p. 9.

We have argued so far, however, that the primaeval blessing announced after the flood is *not* fulfilled in Gen. 10.1-32, but is in the process of being realized. We further suggested that the reversal of primogeniture in the Table indicates that the blessing is being taken up in Shem's genealogy (Gen. 10.21-31; 11.10-26). The creation blessing is then reaffirmed to Abraham's progeny in the form of a divine promise and renewed to Israel in the form of 'primaeval' commands (Gen. 35.11). We observed that the book of Genesis concludes with the promise of increase being largely *unrealized.* Similarly, the primaeval commands have been partially executed in Genesis, but not fully since nowhere is it stated that people 'swarmed' and 'filled the earth'.[47] Since the opening verses of Exodus are being presented as the continuation of the book of Genesis, however, we suggest that Exod. 1.7 is the *first* indication in the Genesis narrative that the primaeval blessing has been fulfilled. In other words, there are not *two* fulfilments of the primaeval blessing, but *one.* The implication of this is that God's creative purposes are not being fulfilled first in the Table of Nations (10.1-32), then Israel. On the contrary, according to our interpretation, the primaeval blessing is being fulfilled *first* in the small-scale world of Israel (Exod. 1.7). Realization of the primaeval blessing, therefore, progresses not from Noah to the nations, but from Noah to Israel. The blessing is then intended to extend to the nations *through* Israel (Gen. 12.3). Since the primaeval blessing is being realized in the small-scale world of Israel, the question may be raised whether this has any bearing on how one interprets the Genesis 1 creation story.

8. *Execution of the Primaeval Commands –*
through Scattering or a Promise?

We noted earlier that scholars have observed that there is a 'command-execution' sequence in the Genesis 1 creation account.[48] That is, God gives commands and then executes them. In some cases, the execution of the commands is immediate. For example, in Gen. 1.3 we read that God said, '"Let there be light"; and there was light'. In other instances, a command is followed by a further action of God. For example, in Gen. 1.24 God says, 'Let the earth bring forth living creatures of every kind...', then in v. 25 we are told that God *made* the living creatures. Anderson rightly comments that 'in the creation story God is the one who both announces and fulfills his word'.[49] Yet when the primaeval commands are issued to humankind in Gen. 1.28, there is no immediate fulfilment of the commands. Given that *Israel's* increase marks the fulfilment of the primaeval commands and that God is the one who brings it to pass, it may even be the case that God's causing Israel to increase is to be identified as the *execution* of his creational

47. Accordingly, Weimar notes that Gen. 9.7 finds fulfilment only in Exod. 1.7. He suggests that the clear reference back to Gen. 9.7 is intended to confirm that the creation blessing is being fulfilled in Exod. 1.7 (*Exodusgeschichte*, p. 30).

48. Anderson, 'The Priestly Creation Story', pp. 151–52; Blenkinsopp, 'The Structure of P', pp. 275–92 (275–83); Westermann, *Genesis 1–11*, pp. 84–85 (= *Genesis*, Bd. I, pp. 117–18).

49. Anderson, 'The Priestly Creation Story', p. 152.

word. That is, God gives the commands, 'Be fruitful and multiply, and fill the earth', to humankind (Gen. 1.28; cf. Gen. 9.1), and God himself then fulfils them through Israel. He does not, however, execute the primaeval commands by scattering people. We may recall the view of van Wolde at this point, who argues that YHWH's scattering the Babelites 'continues the execution of the creation he began in Genesis 1'.[50] Brueggemann similarly maintains that the intent of creation finally comes to fulfilment through scattering.[51] Contrary to this view, however, we have argued that the divine promise to the patriarchs, not the dispersion, restores the created order.[52] Israel's multiplication in Egypt could thus be understood as the execution of the primaeval commands which God both announces (Gen. 1.28; 9.1) *and* fulfils (Exod. 1.7). It seems to be the case, therefore, that the divine promise of increase is the *means* by which the primaeval commands are being executed.[53] To be sure, the execution of the commands through Israel is not as immediate as the command-execution sequence of creation in Genesis 1 and as Psalm 33.9 suggests ('For he spoke, and it came to be; he commanded, and it stood firm', NRSV). Nevertheless, Exod. 1.1-7 indicates that the primaeval commands, 'Be fruitful and multiply, and fill the earth', first announced to humankind in Gen. 1.28 and then renewed to Noah (9.1) and to Israel (35.11), have been executed in Exod. 1.7, albeit in microcosm. The creation story is being fulfilled, therefore, through Israel. In light of our conclusion, we may recall the view of Porten and Rappaport, that Exod. 1.7 is the structural parallel to Gen. 1.28 since they both have a sequence of five non-identical verbs.[54] They conclude, in fact, that Exod. 1.7 is the *climax* of Genesis 1.[55] This is in accordance with our view that Exod. 1.7 marks the fulfilment of the primaeval commands outlined in Gen. 1.28 and 9.1.

Given that the *execution* of the commands in Genesis 1 is an act of creation itself, this has implications for how one understands the emergence of Israel. If Israel's increase in Egypt is seen as the 'execution' of the primaeval commands by God, then the forming of Israel as a people is God's 'creative' act. It may be not so surprising, therefore, to find that the formation of Israel is couched in

50. Van Wolde, *Words Become Worlds*, pp. 102–103.

51. Brueggemann, *Genesis*, p. 98; cf. Vawter, *On Genesis*, p. 157.

52. As has been noted, Steck maintains that God's initiative with Abraham is comparable to God's initiative in creation; it marks a new beginning of the divine action with humanity ('Genesis 12,1-3', pp. 525–54 [550–51]).

53. One notes that hiphil verbal forms appear on several occasions Genesis 1 with reference to the creation. For example, we are told that God *separated* the light from the darkness (בדל, Gen. 1.4; cf. hiphil forms in Gen. 1.6, 7, 11, 12, 14, 15, 17, 18). Is it possible that the hiphil form of פרה and רבה in the promise of increase to the patriarchs is similar in function to the *execution* formula in Genesis 1 in that God gives commands (Gen. 1.28) and then causes their fruition?

54. Porten and Rappaport, 'Poetic Structure in Genesis IX 7', pp. 363–69 (369). The verbal sequence that occurs in Gen. 1.28 is פרה←רבה←מלא←כבש←רדה. Porten and Rappaport have observed that five non-identical verbs are also employed in Exod. 1.7: פרה←שרץ←רבה←עצם←מלא. Ackerman has also observed that the three verbs from Gen. 1.28 have been arranged in Exod. 1.7 in a 1-3-5 sequence, with two additional verbs being placed in the 2-4 positions ('The Moses Birth Story', p. 77).

55. Porten and Rappaport, 'Poetic Structure in Genesis IX 7', pp. 363–69 (368).

creation language.[56] This view of God's creativity activity in relation to Israel is already implicit in Exod. 1.7 if this text is read in light of the Genesis narrative.

Our conclusions about Exod. 1.7 may also shed light on how Genesis 1–11 is related thematically to Genesis 12–50. Scholars are in agreement that God's promises to the patriarchs are central to the patriarchal narratives. If God's promise to 'make fruitful and multiply' Abraham's progeny is fulfilling the creation mandate given in Gen. 1.28, then the patriarchal narratives do not simply concern God's redemptive plan. To be sure, this is central. But when interpreted against the background of Genesis 1–11, the patriarchal narratives explain *how* God is fulfilling his creation mandate given to humankind. Thus the theme of creation, which is explicit in the primaeval history, forms the background for the patriarchal narratives.

9. *Redemption Ensures that God's Creational Work Will Advance*

If God's *creational* purposes are being worked out through the small-scale world of Israel, and being fulfilled in Exod. 1.7, then Pharaoh's actions and God's deliverance of Israel may have further theological significance. Pharaoh's attempt to thwart Israel's increase by enslaving the Israelites (Exod. 1.10-13) and by planning to kill their sons (Exod. 1.16, 22) would have consequences for the *creation*. That is, Pharaoh's actions have the potential to subvert God's creational work.[57] Fretheim has suggested, in fact, that the exodus redemption is the defeat of anti-creational forces which threaten to undo creation. He notes that the exodus is being portrayed as a cosmic battle in which Pharaoh, who is elsewhere identified with the chaos monster, is defeated.[58] In short, when the exodus redemption is interpreted against the background of Genesis,[59] it is not simply deliverance from slavery. To be sure, deliverance from slavery is a major theme, but the exodus is more. It is God's victory over Pharaoh who is seeking to thwart God's creational work. The deliverance from Egypt, therefore, 'frees the creation *to become* what God intended'.[60] The implication is that the goal of the redemption is not simply freedom from slavery, but establishment of God's *creational* purposes. God's defeat of Pharaoh means that his intention for creation, being worked out in the small-scale world of Israel, will continue to advance. It is important to note,

56. Deut. 32.18; Isa. 43.1, 5-7, 15; 44.2, 24; 45.9-10.
57. For a thought-provoking discussion of this topic, see Fretheim, 'Reclamation of Creation', pp. 354–65 (354–60).
58. For example, in Isa. 51.9 the defeat of Pharaoh is described as God's cutting Rahab in pieces (cf. Ps. 87.4; Isa. 30.7). Hans-Joachim Kraus suggests that Egypt's being identified with Rahab means that Egypt is the epitome of a chaotic primaeval power (*Psalms 60–150: A Commentary* [trans. H.C. Oswald; Minneapolis: Augsburg Fortress, 1989], p. 188). Fretheim also notes that Pharaoh/Egypt is identified as the sea monster in other texts such as Ezek. 29.3-5 and 32.2 ('Reclamation of Creation', pp. 354–65 [357]).
59. For a discussion of the importance of interpreting Exodus in light of Genesis, and redemption in light of creation, see Fretheim, 'Reclamation of Creation', pp. 354–65 (354–56).
60. Fretheim, 'Reclamation of Creation', pp. 354–65 (359).

however, that the advancement of God's creational work through Israel has implications for the macrocosmic world.

10. *Blessing to the Macrocosmic World through Israel*

It is not insignificant that when YHWH promises to bless Abraham (Gen. 12.1-3), there is also a promise of blessing for the macrocosmic world, that in Abraham 'all the families of the earth shall be blessed' (NRSV, Gen. 12.3).[61] Regardless of how the niphal form of ברך in Gen. 12.3 is translated,[62] it is evident that YHWH's blessing to Israel through Abraham is intended to extend to the macrocosmic world.[63] Thus it is a reaffirmation of the primaeval intentions for humanity.[64] Wolff has suggested that, according to the *Yahwistic* primaeval history, the five-fold occurrence of ברך in Gen. 12.1-3 is the counterpart to the five-fold occurrence of ארר in Genesis 1–11, observing that the word of blessing is precisely what humankind need.[65] If Genesis 1–11 is read according to its final form, however, then the word of blessing *is* present in the primaeval history since humankind are under the general blessing of Gen. 9.1. Yet we have also observed that there is a particular blessing at work in Shem's line which leads to Abraham. We suggest that what is envisaged in Gen. 12.3 is not an extension of the more general blessing, since the nations are already under this blessing. Rather, Gen. 12.3 concerns the extension of the *particular* blessing to the nations. Since the blessing to Abraham and his descendants means that they receive divine grace rather than judgment, Gen. 12.3 sets forth the possibility that the nations can also be partakers of divine grace.

11. *Conclusion*

We have argued that Exod. 1.1-7 is being presented as the continuation of the Genesis story and that Israel's proliferation in Egypt marks not only the fulfilment of the promise of increase to the patriarchs, but also the fulfilment of the primaeval blessing (Gen. 1.28; 9.1). Since the Israelites are filling the land of Egypt, it was suggested that the blessing is being fulfilled in microcosm. Thus we concluded that God's intention for his creation is being fulfilled in the small-

61. The 'families of the earth' (משפחת האדמה) in Gen. 12.3 (cf. Gen. 28.14) are identified elsewhere as גויי הארץ (e.g. Gen. 18.18; 22.18; 26.4). The term משפחה, however, connects Gen. 12.3 with the Table of Nations (Gen. 10.5, 18, 20, 31, 32).

62. For an extensive discussion of this verb, see O.T. Allis, 'The Blessing of Abraham', *PTR* 25 (1927), pp. 263–98.

63. Clines, *The Theme of the Pentateuch*, pp. 78–79; Muilenburg, 'Abraham and the Nations', pp. 393–96. For a discussion of how the blessing extends to the nations in Genesis and other biblical texts, see Wolff, 'The Kerygma of the Yahwist', pp. 131–58 (147–58) (= 'Das Kerygma des Jahwisten', pp. 73–98 [88–98]).

64. Clines, *The Theme of the Pentateuch*, p. 29.

65. Wolff, 'The Kerygma of Yahwist', pp. 131–58 (145) (= 'Das Kerygma des Jahwisten', pp. 73–98 [86]). For an insightful discussion of how God's blessing to Israel counters the diminishing life of Genesis 1–11, see Steck, 'Genesis 12,1-3', pp. 525–54 (540–53).

scale world of Israel. Since God's blessing on Israel through Abraham has as its goal the extension of the blessing to the nations, the book of Genesis points forward with the expectation that there will be a *future* fulfilment of the blessing in the macrocosmic world. God's particular blessing to Israel is thus the means through which the divine intention for creation will be restored to the world.

CONCLUSION

1. *Summary of Argument*

We have been engaged in the study of how the primaeval blessing renewed to Noah and his sons in Gen. 9.1 is being realized after the flood. There has been widespread scholarly consensus that the creation blessing is fulfilled in the Table of Nations. Scholars maintain that Noah's descendants are not only multiplying, but also filling the earth in accordance with 9.1. Since the dispersion is introduced in Gen. 9.19, this verse is understood to contribute positively to the multiplication theme. Scholars further argue that YHWH's scattering the Babelites brings about the dispersion, thus YHWH himself is ensuring that his creational commands are fulfilled.

A cursory examination of the language used in Genesis 9–11 raised an initial question, however, whether these chapters do, indeed, indicate that the blessing is fulfilled immediately after the flood. It became apparent that there were inconsistencies in translations of key verbs in these texts. Furthermore, the internal structure within the Table of Nations did not appear to have been considered in sufficient detail. It was also observed that minimal attention had been given to the function of the linear Shemite genealogy in Gen. 11.10-26 and to the promise of increase given to the patriarchs in relation to the primaeval blessing. It thus became apparent that the prevailing view regarding how the primaeval blessing is being realized after the flood was in need of re-examination.

The question was raised in Chapter 1 whether the statement in Gen. 9.19b, 'and from these the whole earth was peopled' (NRSV), is as positive as scholars assume. An examination of the verb נפץ shows that it means 'scatter, disperse' and that it introduces the scattering motif which is reiterated in the following chapters (פוץ: Gen. 10.18; 11.4, 8, 9). Scholars acknowledge that נפץ means, literally, 'scatter, disperse', but they translate the verb by 'people' or 'populate' in accordance with either the NRSV ('was peopled') or NASB ('was populated'). It was shown that early translations of נפץ do not support these English translations and that the verb 'populate' did not appear until 1952 when the RSV was published. The possibility was thus raised whether the more recent translations of נפץ have been influenced by the prevailing view that the primaeval blessing is being realized in Gen. 9.19. We concluded that it is preferable to translate נפץ by 'scatter' (cf. NIV) as this reflects more accurately the meaning of the Hebrew verb and underscores the connection between 9.19 and the scattering motif present in the Hebrew text (cf. 10.18; 11.4, 8, 9). If נפץ means 'scatter', rather than 'people' or 'populate', it is not so evident that the primaeval blessing is fulfilled in v. 19

since God did not command Noah and his sons to scatter, but to *fill* the earth. Moreover, given that scattering seems to be negative in the Babel story, it is unlikely that Gen. 9.19 would be as positive as scholars suppose. The presence of the scattering motif in close proximity to Gen. 9.1 raised the question, however, whether 'scattering' is in any way related to the realization of the primaeval blessing after the flood.

We considered in Chapter 2 whether the statement made by the Babelites, 'otherwise we shall be scattered abroad' (Gen. 11.4), means that they do not want to fill the earth. We observed that the conjunction פֶּן, 'lest, so as not' (Gen. 11.4), indicates that Noah's descendants are not simply disobeying the primaeval command, but are fearful of it. Yet since 'filling the earth' constitutes the divine *blessing*, it seemed unlikely that Noah's descendants would be fearful of it. Moreover, since פוץ does not occur in Gen. 9.1 or 9.7, the question was raised whether scattering is, indeed, in accordance with the primaeval blessing. We noted that פוץ is commonly associated with judgment; thus it seemed unlikely that the primaeval blessing would include the notion of scattering. We concluded that the 'scattering' of the Babelites is not to be equated with 'filling the earth'. Accordingly, it was suggested that Noah's descendants are not rejecting the command to 'fill the earth', but are fearful of being scattered. Even though our preliminary conclusions saw a distinction between 'scattering' and 'filling', the question whether YHWH's scattering the Babelites fulfils the blessing in any way was in need of further consideration.

In Chapter 3 we examined the commonly held view that the primaeval blessing is fulfilled through YHWH's *scattering* Noah's descendants. A detailed examination of פוץ showed that the verb is often associated with judgment and is used to represent one of the curses of the Mosaic covenant. It was noted that some scholars, who argue that YHWH's scattering the Babelites is not to be understood as divine judgment, give no attention to the meaning of פוץ or the context in which it occurs. Other scholars, who acknowledge that פוץ *can* have negative connotations, argue that the *context* supports a positive view of scattering. Four verses are cited by scholars to support this view: Gen. 9.19 (נפץ); 10.5 (פרד); 10.18 (פוץ) and 10.32 (פרד). With regard to Gen. 9.19 and 10.18, we noted that although *English* translations of נפץ in Gen. 9.19 ('was populated', 'was peopled') and פוץ in 10.18 ('spread abroad') affirm a positive context, it is not so apparent in the Hebrew text. We suggested that נפץ could be identified as a *Leitwort* and that it foreshadows the Babel judgment. With regard to Gen. 10.18, we noted that most English translations are inconsistent since they commonly translate פוץ by 'spread abroad' in 10.18, but by 'scatter, scatter abroad' in the Babel story. Since פוץ is used with reference to the Canaanites, it is possible that 10.18 has negative connotations. It was suggested, therefore, that there was no conclusive evidence that 'scattering' is positive in Gen. 9.19 and 10.18. Since 'scattering' is often associated with judgment and is frequently used with reference to the divine judgment of exile, the scattering motif in Gen. 9.19 and 10.18 may even have ominous overtones. We further concluded that YHWH's scattering Noah's descendants does not restore the created order intended from the beginning, since God did not command Noah and his sons to *scatter*. On the contrary, 'scattering' could even have an adverse effect on the realization of the primaeval blessing after the flood. We suggested, therefore, that נפץ and פוץ be translated by 'scatter' rather than 'disperse' (cf. ESV), since the language of 'scattering' has negative connotations associated with divine judgment.

Scholars have argued, however, that the primaeval blessing is fulfilled in Gen. 10.1-32 through the 'spreading out' of Noah's descendants in Gen. 10.5 (פרד) and 10.32 (פרד). The question was thus considered in Chapter 4 whether the blessing announced to Noah and his sons in Gen. 9.1 is in any sense *fulfilled* in the Table of Nations. It was noted at the outset that language reminiscent of the primaeval blessing is not present in Gen. 10.1-32. The verb פרד, which *is* employed in Gen. 10.5 and 10.32, commonly means 'divide, separate'. It was observed that the LXX, Vulgate, and Targums Onqelos and Pseudo-Jonathan reflect this meaning. A summary of English translations further showed that פרד in Gen. 10.5 and 10.32 was commonly translated by 'divide' (e.g. KJV, AV, ASV) until 1952 when the RSV translation, 'spread, spread abroad', appeared. A few years prior to the RSV, Moffatt had translated פרד by 'spread abroad' in his new translation of the Bible (1924). Since Moffatt served on the committee preparing the RSV translation, it was suggested that he may have influenced it. Moffatt's translation, 'spread abroad', was accepted by H.C. Leupold, whose commentary published in 1942 brought together this new translation alongside the view that Noah's descendants were required to spread abroad in accordance with the primaeval commands. Ten years after the publication of Leupold's commentary, the RSV followed the new translation first espoused by Moffatt. The question was raised, however, whether פרד does, indeed, mean 'spread abroad'. Our examination of the verb showed that it commonly means 'divide, separate'. Thus it was suggested that Gen. 10.5 and 10.32 may well refer to the division or separation of Noah's descendants, as indicated in Deut. 32.8. We concluded, therefore, that while the primaeval blessing is clearly in the *process* of being realized in the Table, there is no conclusive evidence to indicate that the blessing is *fulfilled* in Gen. 10.1-32.

This view was confirmed in Chapter 5 by considering the placement of the genealogies *within* the Table of Nations. We observed that the reversal of primogeniture of Noah's three sons presents Shem's line last, thereby focusing attention on his line. The reversal in the Table was compared with the Toledot structure in the patriarchal narratives, which presents the main line last. It was thus suggested that Japheth and Ham are secondary lines and that Shem's line is the main line. This view was confirmed by examining the 'primaeval' genealogies in the first chapter of Chronicles where the reversal of primogeniture is also present. We further noted that, in the patriarchal narratives, the Abrahamic blessing is taken up in the main line, and suggested, therefore, that the presentation of Shem's genealogy last in the Table intimates that the primaeval blessing will advance in his line in particular. This interpretation was supported by considering the function of the *linear* Shemite genealogy in Gen. 11.10-26. We concluded that just as the primaeval blessing is advancing in the Sethite genealogy before the flood (Gen. 5.1-32), it is being taken up in the parallel Shemite genealogy after the flood. We maintain, therefore, that while the primaeval blessing is in the *process* of being realized in Gen. 10.1-32, it is not fulfilled in the Table. Rather, the blessing is being taken up in Shem's line (Gen. 10.21-31; 11.10-26). Accordingly, the blessing announced to Noah and his sons looks forward to a *future* fulfilment beyond the primaeval history.

Observations made about the function of the Shemite genealogy were seen to have implications for how one understands the conclusion to the primaeval history. Von Rad's view, that God's gracious action is missing after the Babel judgment, was re-examined in Chapter 6 in light of the reversal of primogeniture present in the Table. Given that Gen. 10.1-32 describes what took place *after* the Babel judgment, the question was raised whether the 'missing' element of grace is in any way present in the Table. We suggested that the emergence of Shem's line as the primary line intimates that divine grace has not been fully exhausted after the Babel judgment. Rather, it is effective in the Shemite genealogy (Gen. 10.21-31; 11.10-26). Since the primaeval blessing seems to be advancing in Shem's line in particular, the genealogy indicates that God's intention for creation will not be thwarted. The placement of Shem's genealogy both before (Gen. 10.21-31) and after (11.10-26) the Babel judgment underscores that divine grace is effective both before and after the judgment. Since the *linear* Shemite genealogy leads to Abraham, the question was raised whether the primaeval blessing is being realized in any way through Abraham and his descendants.

We observed in Chapter 7 that the primaeval blessing is reaffirmed to Abraham's progeny in the form of a divine promise. Yet it was noted that the nations still remain under the more general blessing of Gen. 9.1. The question was raised, therefore, why a *promise* of increase was even necessary, when fecundity is already assumed in Gen. 9.1. It was observed that in the primaeval history, sin and divine judgment can threaten the realization of the more general blessing. We thus concluded that the essential difference between the blessing on the nations (Gen. 9.1) and the particular outworking of the blessing to Israel through Abraham is that sin has the potential to endanger the realization of the more general blessing, whereas the multiplication of the patriarchs is guaranteed because it has been promised by God. Inherent in the promise, therefore, is the notion that God will withhold his judgment against the patriarchs. Accordingly, the patriarchal narratives show that God's promises to the patriarchs will be realized in spite of threatening circumstances and, indeed, in spite of the patriarchs themselves. Since the primaeval blessing is being taken up by Abraham's progeny, we concluded that God's intention for his creation is not being accomplished through scattering, but through a divine promise. The patriarchs are, therefore, bearers of the creation theme.

We noted in Chapter 8 that the promise of increase to the patriarchs is being realized through Jacob's *twelve* sons (Gen. 35.22b-26). Since there is no reversal of primogeniture in the genealogy, we concluded that all twelve sons have assumed the position of the main son through whom the promise will be realized. It was observed that the 'primaeval' commands are reissued to Jacob when his name was changed to Israel (Gen. 35.11). This affirms that God's creational purposes will be realized through Jacob and his twelve sons (Gen. 35.22b-26), who are identified simply as 'Israel' (Gen. 47.27). It was further suggested that Jacob's descendants, who number 'seventy' (Gen. 46.27), are being depicted as a small-scale world comparable to the large-scale world represented by Noah's descendants (10.1-32). Even though Jacob's descendants have evidently increased to 'seventy' (Gen. 46.27), the promise of increase is not yet fulfilled at this point in the narrative. It was suggested that the first indication that the promise of increase to the patriarchs is being realized is in Gen. 47.27 where it is stated that Israel 'were fruitful and multiplied exceedingly'. We thus concluded that while this marks an *initial* fulfilment of the promise of increase and the 'primaeval' commands given to Israel (Gen. 35.11), the blessing is largely unrealized in the book of Genesis. This theme is resumed, however, in the opening verses of Exodus.

We noted in Chapter 9 that Exod. 1.1-7 is being presented as the continuation of the Genesis narrative. The sequel to the story is taken up in Exod. 1.6b, with the statement that Joseph's generation had died, and in Exod. 1.7, with the remark that the Israelites greatly multiplied in Egypt. We observed that Israel's multiplication is couched in creation language. It was suggested, therefore, that Israel's proliferation in Egypt marks both the fulfilment of the promise of increase to the patriarchs *and* the primaeval blessing since Israel have not only multiplied, but have also 'swarmed' and 'filled the earth' in accordance with Gen. 9.1 and 9.7. According to our analysis, there are not *two* fulfilments of the blessing – one in the Table of Nations and the other in Exod. 1.7. Neither is the primaeval blessing *first* fulfilled through the nations (Gen. 10.1-32), *then* through Israel (Exod. 1.7). On the contrary, we concluded that the creation blessing is *first* being fulfilled through Israel in Exod. 1.7. The multiplication of Israel in Egypt may be understood, therefore, as the successful execution of the primaeval commands, albeit in microcosm. Thus the creation story is being taken up by Israel. We noted, however, that God's blessing upon Israel through Abraham is not for their sake alone, but for the sake of the macrocosmic world (Gen. 12.3). Israel are, therefore, bearers of the creation theme to the world since God's intention for the macrocosmic world, which is largely unrealized in Gen. 10.1-32, will be fulfilled through them. Realization of the primaeval blessing after the flood, therefore, progresses from Noah to Israel, but *fulfilment* of the blessing begins with Israel (Exod. 1.7).

2. *Implications for Further Study in Genesis*

The present discussion raises additional questions which are in need of further examination. First, we have focused on the realization of the first *three* imperatives, 'Be fruitful and multiply, and fill the earth'. While a few scholars have discussed how the last two imperatives – humankind's subjugation of the earth and dominion over the created order – are being realized in Genesis[1] and the

---

1. Clines, *What Does Eve Do to Help?*, pp. 53–55; Turner, *Announcements of Plot*, pp. 33–47.

Pentateuch,[2] there is need for an in-depth exegetical analysis of these commands in light of the present study. Turner maintains that the curse against the ground means that the subjugation of the earth is an impossible task. He further suggests that humankind's dominion over the created order after the flood has become a despotic rule, while also noting that, in an ironic way, animals (through the serpent) have an ongoing dominion over humans.[3] In our study we have shown that realization of the first three commands, which can be thwarted by sin and divine judgment in the primaeval history, is taking place amidst threatening circumstances in the patriarchal narratives, as God himself brings the commands to fruition. The question may well be raised, therefore, whether sin and divine judgment announced in the primaeval history continue to have a negative effect on the realization of the last two commands or whether there is any indication that God himself will bring them about *in spite* of human sin. Can we assume, for example, that if the curse against the ground were to be reversed in some way by God,[4] then the subjugation of the earth would be attainable? With regard to humankind's rule over the created order, it is worth considering whether this command relates in any way to the multiplication theme[5] and to the royal motif in the patriarchal narratives (Gen. 17.6; 35.11; cf. Gen. 49.10). Since the created order outlined in Gen. 1.28 is being accomplished through a divine promise, we may further enquire whether God's promises to the patriarchs restore God's intention for creation expressed in the last two commands as well.

Secondly, we have suggested that inherent in God's promise of increase to the patriarchs is his withholding judgment so that the divine promise be fully realized. If Gen. 12.3 envisages that the *particular* blessing to Abraham will extend to the nations, we may expect, then, that when individuals or nations are blessed through Israel, they will also receive mercy instead of judgment. Wolff suggests that one way the blessing is extended to the nations is through intercessory activity for those who are perishing. He cites Genesis 18 as an example, noting that the narrative is introduced with a reiteration of God's intention to bless the nations through Abraham (Gen. 18.18). Wolff maintains that the divine blessing will be extended to the nations through divine forgiveness of guilt and the cancelling of the decision to destroy.[6] Given that God's blessing upon Israel means that he will withhold his judgment, it is worth investigating whether this theme of mitigation reappears when the blessing is extended to the nations.

2.   Brueggemann, 'The Kerygma of the Priestly Writers', pp. 397–414 (407–13). Brueggemann sees a close connection between the subjugation of the earth and Israel's conquest of the land.

3.   Turner, *Announcements of Plot,* pp. 41, 48.

4.   Steck has made an interesting observation. He argues that the curse of Gen. 3.17 is becoming ineffective through the divine promises given to Abraham (Gen. 12.1-3). He maintains that the reversal of the curse does not take effect in Gen. 8.21, as Rendtorff proposes, but in God's blessing on the patriarch. That is, the curse is countered by God's blessing on the patriarch, which effects a blessing on his land, causing it to be productive (Steck, 'Genesis 12,1-3', pp. 525–54 [540–41]).

5.   Several texts suggest that there is a close relationship between multiplying and dominion (e.g. Gen. 22.17; 24.60; cf. Exod. 1.7-10; Ps. 105.23-24).

6.   Wolff, 'The Kerygma of the Yahwist', pp. 131–58 (148) (= 'Das Kerygma des Jahwisten', pp. 73–98 [88–89]).

Thirdly, we have suggested that the linear genealogical line culminates with the twelve sons of Jacob, who constitute the main line (Gen. 35.22b-26), and that the blessing is being realized through them, that is, through Israel (e.g. Gen. 47.27; Exod. 1.1-7). In our study, we have simply identified the main line and secondary lines; however, we have not discussed how the notion of firstborn relates to these lines. This is worth further consideration. Moreover, towards the end of Genesis we read of Jacob's death-bed blessing on his sons, indicating that Reuben has forfeited his firstborn status, and that Simeon and Levi are under judgment. Thus Judah seems to have assumed a position of honour above his brothers. While the primaeval blessing is being realized through all twelve sons (Gen. 47.27; Exod. 1.7), the pre-eminence of Judah does raise the question whether there will be a further narrowing down of the genealogical line. One may well enquire, therefore, whether God's intention for creation will be realized through Jacob's twelve sons or whether it will be taken up in one line in particular.

Our study raises a further question regarding the relationship between creation and election. We have shown that the promise of increase given to Abraham and his progeny is to be interpreted against the background of the creation story: it shows that God's intention for his creation, which is largely unrealized in the primaeval history, is being taken up by Israel. The book of Genesis thus establishes an intrinsic connection between the creation story and salvation history. Von Rad has discussed this relationship in detail, observing that creation does not stand alone, but is incorporated into the realm of history that leads to Israel. He then draws the conclusion that the doctrine of creation is subordinate to the doctrine of redemption[7] and that creation serves the purposes of redemption.[8] Our study raises questions, however, about the correctness of this view. Is it possible that redemption actually serves the purposes of creation?[9] We have argued that the divine promise of increase given to the patriarchs is the means by which God's intention for his creation is being realized after the flood. In other words, salvation history is the continuation of the *creation* story. Our study thus suggests that the doctrine of creation is the theological basis for the doctrine of redemption.

In conclusion, it has been our hope that this investigation of how the primaeval blessing is being realized after the flood would shed light on the theology of the final author of Genesis. Reflection on the theology of Genesis shows that salvation history is grounded in God's intention for his creation. The primaeval history not only looks back to the creation story, but also points forward to a future fulfilment of God's creative purposes through Israel. If the primaeval

---

7.   G. von Rad, 'The Theological Problem of the Old Testament Doctrine of Creation', in *The Problem of the Hexateuch and Other Essays* (trans. E.W. Trueman Dicken; Edinburgh and London: Oliver & Boyd, 1966), pp. 131–43.

8.   Von Rad, 'The Theological Problem', pp. 131–43 (134). Von Rad notes, for example, that according to Deutero-Isaiah, the 'creation of the world and the redemption of Israel both exemplify the same divine dispensation' and then concludes that 'both result from one and the same divine purpose of redemption' (pp. 131–43 [135]). Is it equally possible, however, that both result from the same divine purpose of creation?

9.   Cf. Fretheim, 'The Reclamation of Creation', pp. 354–65.

blessing is interpreted in its narrative context, then it shows that God's particular blessing to Israel is the means through which his intention for creation – thwarted by sin and divine judgment in the primaeval history, but preserved by grace – will be restored to the world. When the blessing to the nations is fully carried out, then they, like Abraham's progeny, will receive divine grace instead of judgment. The particular blessing progresses by means of a divine promise, from Noah to Israel, but it is not for Israel's sake alone, but for the sake of the world. Israel are, therefore, bearers of the creation story, but they are more. They are to be bearers of the creation story to the world.

BIBLIOGRAPHY AND FURTHER READING

Ackerman, J.S., 'The Literary Context of the Moses Birth Story [Exodus 1–2]', in Kenneth R.R. Gros Louis, *et al.* (eds), *Literary Interpretations of Biblical Narratives*, Vol. 1 (Abingdon Press, 1974), pp. 74–119.

Alford, H., *The Book of Genesis and Part of the Book of Exodus* (London: Strathan & Co., 1872).

Allis, O.T., 'Dr. Moffatt's "New Translation" of the Old Testament', *PTR* 23 (1925), pp. 267–317.

—'The Blessing of Abraham', *PTR* 25 (1927), pp. 263–98.

—'An "American" Translation of the Old Testament', *PTR* 26 (1928), pp. 109–41.

Alter, R., *The Art of Biblical Narrative* (New York: Basic Books, 1981).

—*Genesis: Translation and Commentary* (New York: W.W. Norton & Co., 1996).

Andersen, F.I., *The Sentence in Biblical Hebrew* (The Hague: Mouton & Co., 1974).

Andersen, T.D., 'Genealogical Prominence and the Structure of Genesis', in R.D. Bergen (ed.), *Biblical Hebrew and Discourse Linguistics* (SIL; Winona Lake: Summer Institute of Linguistics, 1994), pp. 242–63.

Anderson, B.W., 'A Stylistic Study of the Priestly Creation Story', in G.W. Coats and B.W. Long (eds), *Canon and Authority* (Philadelphia: Fortress Press, 1977), pp. 148–62.

—'From Analysis to Synthesis: The Interpretation of Genesis 1–11', *JBL* 97 (1978), pp. 23–39.

—'The Tower of Babel: Unity and Diversity in God's Creation', *Currents in Theology and Mission* 5 (1978), pp. 69–81; revised and reprinted in *From Creation to New Creation* (Overtures to Biblical Theology; Minneapolis: Fortress Press, 1994), pp. 165–78.

—'Creation and the Noachic Covenant', in P.N. Joranson and K. Butigan (eds), *Cry of the Environment: Rebuilding the Christian Creation Tradition* (Santa Fe: Bear & Co., 1984), pp. 45–61.

Atkinson, D., *The Message of Genesis 1–11* (The Bible Speaks Today; Leicester: InterVarsity Press, 1990).

Bacon, B.J., *Genesis of Genesis* (Hartford: Student Publ. Co., 1893).

Bailey, N.A., 'Some Literary and Grammatical Aspects of Genealogies in Genesis', in R.D. Bergen (ed.), *Biblical Hebrew and Discourse Linguistics* (SIL; Winona Lake: Eisenbrauns, 1994), pp. 267–82.

Blenkinsopp, J., 'The Structure of P', *CBQ* 38 (1976), pp. 275–92.

—*The Pentateuch* (New York: Doubleday, 1992).

Braun, R., *1 Chronicles* (WBC; Waco, TX: Word Books, 1986).

Brook, A.E. and N. McLean, *The Old Testament in Greek*, Vol. 1, Part 1 (London: Cambridge University Press, 1906).

Brueggemann, W., 'The Kerygma of the "Priestly Writers"', *ZAW* 84 (1972), pp. 397–414.

—*Genesis: A Bible Commentary for Teaching and Preaching* (IBC; Atlanta: John Knox Press, 1982).

—*Theology of the Old Testament: Testimony, Dispute, Advocacy* (Minneapolis: Fortress Press, 1997).

Buber, M., 'Leitwort Style in Pentateuch Narrative', in M. Buber and F. Rosenzweig (eds), *Scripture and Translation* (trans. L. Rosenwald and E. Fox; Bloomington and Indianapolis: Indiana University Press, 1994), pp. 114–28.

Burns, R.J., *Exodus, Leviticus, Numbers* (OTM; Wilmington: Michael Glazier, Inc., 1983).

Calvin, J., *A Commentary on Genesis* (trans. J. King; Edinburgh: Banner of Truth, 1965 [1578]).

Cassuto, U., *A Commentary on the Book of Genesis*, Vol. 1 (trans. I. Abrahams; Jerusalem: Magnes Press, 1961).

—*A Commentary on the Book of Genesis*, Vol. 2 (trans. I. Abrahams; Jerusalem: Magnes Press, 1964).

—*A Commentary on the Book of Exodus* (trans. I. Abrahams; Jerusalem: Magnes Press, 1967).

Childs, B.S., *The Book of Exodus: A Critical, Theological Commentary* (Philadelphia: Westminster Press, 1974).

—*Introduction to the Old Testament as Scripture* (Philadelphia: Fortress Press, 1979).

Clines, D.J.A., 'Noah's Flood: The Theology of the Flood Narrative', *Faith and Thought* 100 (1972–73), pp. 128–42.

—'Theme in Genesis 1–11', *CBQ* 38 (1976), pp. 483–507.

—'The Significance of the "Sons of God" Episode (Genesis 6.1-4) in the Context of the Primeval History (Genesis 1–11)', *JSOT* 13 (1979), pp. 33–46.

—*The Theme of the Pentateuch* (JSOTSup, 10; Sheffield: JSOT Press, 1979).

—*What Does Eve Do to Help? and Other Readerly Questions to the Old Testament* (JSOTSup, 94; Sheffield: JSOT Press, 1990).

Coats, G.W., 'A Structural Transition in Exodus', *VT* 22 (1972), pp. 129–42.

—'The Curse in God's Blessing: Gen. 12,1-4a in the Structure and Theology of the Yahwist' in J. Jeremais and L. Perlitt (eds.), *Die Botschaft und die Boten* (Neukirchen–Vluyn: Neukirchener Verlag, 1981), pp. 31–41.

—*Genesis, with an Introduction to Narrative Literature* (Forms of the Old Testament Literature, Vol. 1; Grand Rapids: Eerdmans, 1983).

Cohen, J., *'Be Fertile and Increase, Fill the Earth and Master It': The Ancient and Medieval Career of a Biblical Text* (Ithaca, NY: Cornell University Press, 1989).

Cohn, R.L., 'Narrative Structure and Canonical Perspective in Genesis', *JSOT* 25 (1983), pp. 3–16.

Cross, F.M., *Canaanite Myth and Hebrew Epic: Essays in the History of the Religion of Israel* (Cambridge, MA: Harvard University Press, 1973).

Davies, G.F., *Israel in Egypt: Reading Exodus 1–2* (JSOTSup, 135; Sheffield: Sheffield Academic Press, 1992).

Davies, G.H., *Exodus* (Torch Bible Commentary; London: SCM Press, 1967).

Davies, G.I., '"And" – The First Word of the Book of Exodus' (Old Testament Seminar, University of Cambridge, England, 1999).

Díez Macho, A., *et al.* (eds.), *Biblia Polyglotta Matritensia IV: Targum Palaestinense in Pentateuchum*, L. 1: *Genesis* (Madrid: Consejo Superior de Investigaciones Científicas, 1988).

Dillmann, A., *Genesis: Critically and Exegetically Expounded*, Vol. 1 (trans. WM.B. Stevenson; Edinburgh: T&T Clark, 1897 [1892]).

—*Genesis: Critically and Exegetically Expounded*, Vol. 2 (trans. WM.B. Stevenson; Edinburgh: T&T Clark, 1897 [1892]).

Driver, S.R., *Deuteronomy* (ICC; Edinburgh: T&T Clark, 1896).

—*The Book of Genesis* (London: Methuen, 14th edn, 1943 [1904]).

Dumbrell, W.J., *Covenant and Creation* (Grand Rapids: Baker Book House, 1984).

Durham, J.I., *Exodus* (WBC; Waco, TX: Word Books, 1987).

Evans, W., *The Books of the Pentateuch* (New York: Revell, 1916).

Farmer, K.A., 'What Is "This" They Begin to Do?', in F.C. Homgren and H.E. Schaalman (eds.), *Preaching Biblical Texts: Expositions by Jewish and Christian Scholars* (Grand Rapids: Eerdmans, 1995), pp. 17–28.

Fokkelman, J.P., *Narrative Art in Genesis: Specimens of Stylistic and Structural Analysis* (Assen: Van Gorcum, 1975).

—'Exodus', in R. Alter and F. Kermode (eds.), *The Literary Guide to the Bible* (Cambridge, MA: Harvard University Press, 1987), pp. 56–65.

—'Genesis', in R. Alter and F. Kermode (eds.), *The Literary Guide to the Bible* (Cambridge, MA: Harvard University Press, 1987), pp. 36–55.

Fretheim, T.E., *Creation, Fall and Flood: Studies in Genesis 1–11* (Minneapolis: Augsburg, 1969).

—'The Plagues as Ecological Signs of Historical Disaster', *JBL* 110 (1991), pp. 385–96.

—'The Reclamation of Creation: Redemption and Law in Leviticus', *Int* 45 (1991), pp. 354–65.

—*The Pentateuch* (Nashville: Abingdon Press, 1996).

Gall, A.F. von, *Der Hebräische Pentateuch der Samaritaner* (Berlin: Alfred Töpelmann, 1966 [1918]).

Garrett, D., *Rethinking Genesis: The Sources and Authorship of the First Book of the Pentateuch* (Grand Rapids: Baker Book House, 1991).

Gilbert, M., ' "Soyez féconds et multipliez" (Gen. 1, 28)', *NRT* 96 (1974), pp. 729–42.

Gispen, W.H., *Exodus* (Bible Student's Commentary; Grand Rapids: Zondervan, 1982).

Goldingay, J., 'The Patriarchs in Scripture and History', in A.R. Millard and D.J. Wiseman (eds.), *Essays on the Patriarchal Narratives* (Leicester: InterVarsity Press, 1980), pp. 11–42.

Greenwood, G.G., *The Book of Genesis Treated as an Authentic Record,* Vol. 1, Part 1 (London: The Church Printing Co., 2nd edn, 1904).

Gunkel, H., *Genesis* (from the 9th German Impression, 1977 = 3rd edn, 1910; trans. M.E. Biddle; Macon, GA: Mercer University Press, 1997).

Haag, H., 'חמם', *TDOT,* Vol. 4, pp. 478–87.

Hamilton, V.P., *The Book of Genesis: Chapters 1–17* (NICOT; Grand Rapids: Eerdmans, 1990).

—*The Book of Genesis: Chapters 18–50* (NICOT; Grand Rapids: Eerdmans, 1995).

Harland, P.J., *The Value of Human Life: A Study of the Story of the Flood (Genesis 6–9)* (VTSup, 64; Leiden: E.J. Brill, 1996).

—'Vertical or Horizontal: The Sin of Babel', *VT* 48 (1998), pp. 515–33.

Hartley, J.E., *Genesis* (NIBC; Peabody, MA: Hendrickson, 2000).

Hartman, T.C., 'Some Thoughts on the Sumerian King List and Genesis 5 and 11B', *JBL* 91 (1972), pp. 25–32.

Head, P.M., 'The Curse of Covenant Reversal: Deuteronomy 28.58-68 and Israel's Exile', *Churchman* 111 (1997), pp. 218–26.

Helyer, L.R., 'The Separation of Abram and Lot: Its Significance in the Patriarchal Narratives', *JSOT* 26 (1983), pp. 77–88.

Hendel, R.S., *The Text of Genesis 1–11: Textual Studies and Critical Edition* (Oxford: Oxford University Press, 1998).

Hess, R.S., 'The Genealogies of Genesis 1–11 and Comparative Literature', *Bib* 70 (1989), pp. 241–54.

Holzinger, H., *Genesis* (Freiburg: J.C.B. Mohr [Paul Siebeck], 1898).

Jacob, B., *The First Book of the Bible: Genesis* (ed. and trans. E.I. Jacob and W. Jacob; New York: Ktav Publ. House, Inc., 1974) = *Das erste Buch der Tora: Genesis* (Berlin: Schocken Verlag, 1934).

—*The Second Book of the Bible: Exodus* (trans. W. Jacob; Hoboken: Ktav, 1992).

Janzen, J.G., *Exodus* (Louisville, KY: Westminster John Knox Press, 1997).

Japhet, S., *I & II Chronicles* (OTL; Westminster: John Knox Press, 1993).

Jastrow, M., *A Dictionary of the Targumim, the Talmud Babli and Yerushalmi, and the Midrashic Literature*, Vol. 1 (New York: Pardes, 1950 [1886]).

Jenkins, A.K., 'A Great Name: Genesis 12.2 and the Editing of the Pentateuch', *JSOT* 10 (1978), pp. 41–57.

Johnson, M.D., *The Purpose of the Biblical Genealogies* (SNTS, 8; Cambridge, England: Cambridge University Press, 1969).

F. Josephus, *The Jewish Antiquities* (trans. H.St.J. Thackeray, *et al.*; LCL; Cambridge, MA: Harvard University Press, 1930–1965).

Keil, C.F. and F. Delitzsch, *Commentary on the Old Testament: The Pentateuch*, Vol. 1 (trans. J. Martin; repr.; Grand Rapids: Eerdmans, n.d. [1866]).

Kidner, D., *Genesis* (TC; Chicago: InterVarsity Press, 1967).

Kikawada, I.M., 'The Shape of Genesis 11.1-9', in J.J. Jackson and M. Kessler (eds.), *Rhetorical Criticism: Essays in Honor of J. Muilenburg* (Pittsburg: Pickwick Press, 1974), pp. 18–32.

Kikawada, I.M. and A. Quinn, *Before Abraham Was: The Unity of Genesis 1–11* (Nashville: Abingdon Press, 1985).

Koehler, L. and W. Baumgartner, W., *Lexicon in Veteris Testamenti libros*, Vol. 2 (Leiden: E.J. Brill, 1953).

—*Hebräisches und Aramäisches Lexicon zum Alten Testament*, Bd. III (revised by W. Baumgartner and J.K. Stamm; Leiden: E.J. Brill, 1983).

König, E., *Die Genesis eingeleitet, übersetzt, erklärt* (Gütersloh: Bertelsman, 1919).

Kraus, Hans-Joachim, *Psalms 60–150: A Commentary* (trans. H.C. Oswald; Minneapolis: Augsburg Fortress, 1989).

Lange, J.P., *A Commentary on the Holy Scriptures: Genesis* (trans. P. Schaff; Grand Rapids: Zondervan, 1864).

Larsson, G., 'Chronological Parallels between the Creation and the Flood', *VT* 27 (1977), pp. 490–92.

—'The Chronology of the Pentateuch: A Comparison of the MT and the LXX', *JBL* 102 (1983), pp. 401–409.

—*Bound for Freedom: The Book of Exodus in Jewish and Christian Traditions* (Peabody, MA: Hendrickson, 1999).

Lenormant, F., *The Book of Genesis* (London: Longmans, Green & Co., 1886).

Leupold, H.C., *Exposition of Genesis*, Vol. 1 (Grand Rapids: Baker Book House, 1949 [1942]).

—*Exposition of Genesis*, Vol. 2 (Grand Rapids: Baker Book House, 1953).

Lewis, C. and C. Short, *A Latin Dictionary* (Oxford: Clarendon Press, 1975).

Lewis, J.P., 'English Versions', *ABD*, Vol. 6, pp. 816–34.

Lohfink, N., ' "Seid fruchtbar und füllt die Erde an!": Zwingt die priesterschriftliche Schöpfungsdarstellung in Gen 1 die Christen zum Wachstumsmythos?', *BK* 30 (1975), pp. 77–82.

Long, B.O., 'Framing Repetitions in Biblical Historiography', *JBL* 10 (1987), pp. 385–99.

Luther, M., *Luther's Commentary on Genesis*, Vol. 1 (trans. J.T. Mueller; Grand Rapids: Zondervan, 1958).

Luyten, J., 'Primeval and Eschatological Overtones in the Song of Moses (DT 32,1-43)', in N. Lohfink (ed.), *Das Deuteronomium* (Leuven: Leuven University Press, 1985), pp. 341–47.

Mann, T.W., ' "All the Families of the Earth": The Theological Unity of Genesis', *Int* 45 (1991), pp. 341–53.

Martin, W.J., ' "Dischronologized" Narrative in the Old Testament', in *Congress Volume, Rome 1968* (VTSup, 17; Leiden: E.J. Brill, 1969), pp. 179–86.

Mathews, K.A., *Genesis 1–11.26* (NAC; Nashville: Broadman & Holman, 1996).

McConville, J.G., *I & II Chronicles* (Philadelphia: Westminster Press, 1984).

Merrill, E.H., *Deuteronomy* (NAC; Nashville: Broadman & Holman, 1994).

Miller, P.D., 'The Blessing of God', *Int* 29 (1975), pp. 240–51.

Mitchell, H.G., *The World Before Abraham* (Cambridge, MA: Houghton, Mifflin and Co., 1901).

Moffatt, J., *The Old Testament: A New Translation by James Moffatt*, Vol. 1 (New York: George H. Doran Co., 1924).

Muilenburg, J., 'Abraham and the Nations', *Int* 19 (1965), pp. 387–98.

Nachman, Rabbi Moshe ben, *Ramban (Nachmanides): Commentary on the Torah, Genesis* (trans. Rabbi C.B. Chavel; New York: Shilo Publishing House, Inc., 1971).

Nacpil, E.P., 'Between Promise and Fulfilment', *SEAsiaJT* 10 (1968), pp. 166–81.

Noth, M., *A History of Pentateuchal Traditions* (trans. B.W. Anderson; Atlanta: Scholars Press, 1981).

Och, B., 'The Garden of Eden: From Re-Creation to Reconciliation', *Judaism* 37 (1988), pp. 340–51.

Paul, W., *The Hebrew Text of the Book of Genesis* (Edinburgh: W. Blackwood & Sons, 1852).

Porten, P. and U. Rappaport, 'Poetic Structure in Genesis IX 7', *VT* 21 (1971), pp. 363–69.

Powis Smith, J.M., *The Old Testament: An American Translation* (trans. A.R. Gordon, T.J. Meek, J.M. Powis Smith and L. Waterman; ed. J.M. Powis Smith; Chicago: The University of Chicago Press, 1939).

Procksch, O., *Die Genesis übersetzt und erklärt* (Leipzig: Deicherische Verlagsbuchhandlung, 2nd edn, 1924).

Rad, G. von, *Old Testament Theology: The Theology of Israel's Historical Traditions*, Vol. 1 (trans. D.M. Stalker; New York: Harper & Brothers, 1962) = *Theologie des Alten Testaments*, Bd. I: *Die Theologie der geschichtlichen Überlieferungen Israels* (Munich: Chr. Kaiser Verlag, 1957).

—*Genesis: A Commentary* (trans. J.H. Marks; OTL; Philadelphia: Westminster Press, rev. edn, 1973) = *Das erste Buch Mose: Genesis* (Göttingen: Vandenhoeck & Ruprecht, 9th edn, 1972 [1958]).

—*Old Testament Theology: The Theology of Israel's Prophetic Traditions*, Vol. 2 (trans. D.M.G. Stalker; Edinburgh and London: Oliver and Boyd, 1965) = *Theologie des Alten Testaments*, Bd. II: *Die Theologie der prophetischen Überlieferungen Israels* (Munich: Chr. Kaiser Verlag, 1960).

—'The Theological Problem of the Old Testament Doctrine of Creation', in *The Problem of the Hexateuch and Other Essays* (trans. E.W. Trueman Dicken; Edinburgh and London: Oliver & Boyd, 1966), pp. 131–43.

Rahlfs, A. (ed.), *Septuaginta*, Vol. 1 (Stuttgart: Deutsche Bibelgesellschaft, 1935).

Rendsburg, G.A., *The Redaction of Genesis* (Winona Lake: Eisenbrauns, 1986).

Rendtorff, R., 'Gen 8.21 und die Urgeschichte des Jahwisten', *KD* 7 (1961), pp. 69–78.

—' "Covenant" as a Structuring Concept in Genesis and Exodus', *JBL* 108 (1989), pp. 385–93.

Robinson, R.B., 'Literary Functions of the Genealogies of Genesis', *CBQ* 48 (1986), pp. 595–608.

Rogerson, J., *Genesis 1–11* (Old Testament Guides; Sheffield: JSOT Press, 1991).

Ross, A.P., 'The Table of Nations in Genesis 10 – Its Structure', *BSac* 137 (1980), pp. 340–53.

—'The Dispersion of the Nations in Genesis 11.1-9', *BSac* 138 (1981), pp. 119–38.

—'The Table of Nations in Genesis 10 – Its Content', *BSac* 138 (1981), pp. 22–34.

—*Creation and Blessing: A Guide to the Study and Exposition of Genesis* (Grand Rapids: Baker Books, 1988).

Ruppert, W., ' "Machen wir uns einen Namen…" (Gen 11,4): Zur Anthropologie der vorpriesterschriftlichen Urgeschichte', in R. Mosis and L. Ruppert (eds.), *Der Weg zum Menschen: zur philosophischen und theologischen Anthropologie: für Alfons Deissler* (Freiburg: Herder, 1989), pp. 28–45.

Sailhamer, J., *The Pentateuch as Narrative* (Library of Biblical Interpretation; Grand Rapids: Zondervan, 1992).

—*Genesis Unbound* (Sisters: Multnomah Books, 1996).

Sanders, H.A. and C. Schmidt, *The Minor Prophets in the Freer Collection and the Berlin Fragment of Genesis* (New York: Macmillan, 1927).

Sanders, P., *The Provenance of Deuteronomy 32* (Leiden: E.J. Brill, 1996).

Sarna, N.M., *Genesis* (JPS Torah Commentary; New York: Schocken Books, 1970).

—*Exploring Exodus: The Heritage of Biblical Israel* (New York: Schocken Books, 1983).

Sasson, J.M., 'A Genealogical "Convention" in Biblical Chronography?', *ZAW* 90 (1978), pp. 171–85.

—' "The Tower of Babel" as a Clue to the Redactional Structuring of the Primeval History (Gen. 1–11.9)', in G. Rendsburg, *et al.* (eds.), *The Bible Word: Essays in Honor of Cyrus H. Gordon* (New York: Ktav and the Institute of Hebrew Culture and Education of New York University, 1980), pp. 211–19.

Scanlin, H.P., 'Bible Translation by American Individuals', in E.S. Frerichs (ed.), *The Bible and Bibles in America* (Atlanta: Scholars Press, 1988), pp. 43–82.

Scharbert, J., 'Der Sinn der Toledot-Formel in der Priesterschrift', in H. J. Stoebe (ed.), *Wort-Gebot-Glaube: Beiträge zur Theologie des Alten Testaments: W. Eichrodt FS* (Zurich: Zwingli Verlag, 1970), pp. 45–56.

—'ברך', *TDOT*, Vol. 2, pp. 279–308.

Seybold, K., 'Der Turmbau zu Babel: Zur Entstehung von Genesis XI 1-9', *VT* 26 (1976), pp. 453–79.

Skinner, J., *A Critical and Exegetical Commentary on Genesis* (ICC; Edinburgh: T&T Clark, 2nd edn, 1930).

Smith, G.V., 'Structure and Purpose in Genesis 1–11', *JETS* 20 (1977), pp. 307–19.

Snijders, L.A., 'מלא', *TDOT,* Vol. 8, pp. 297–307.

Speiser, E.A., *Genesis* (AB; New York: Doubleday, 1969).

Sperber, A., *The Bible in Aramaic*, Vol. 1: *The Pentateuch according to Targum Onkelos* (Leiden: E.J. Brill, 1959).

Steck, H., 'Genesis 12,1-3 und die Urgeschichte des Jahwisten', in H.W. Wolff (ed.), *Probleme biblischer Theologie: G. von Rad FS* (Munich: Chr. Kaiser Verlag, 1971), pp. 525–54.

Steinberg, N., 'The Genealogical Framework of the Family Stories in Genesis', *Semeia* 46 (1989), pp. 41–50.

Talmon, S., 'The Presentation of Synchroneity and Simultaneity in Biblical Hebrew', in J. Heinemann and S. Werses (eds.), *Studies in Hebrew Narrative Art throughout the Ages* (Scripta Hierosolymitana, 27; Jerusalem: Magnes Press, 1978), pp. 9–26.

Tengström, S., *Die Toledotformel und die literarische Struktur der priesterlichen Erweiterungs-schicht im Pentateuch* (Lund: Gleerup, 1981).

Thomas, W.H. Griffith, *Genesis: A Devotional Commentary* (Grand Rapids: Eerdmans, 1946 [1907–1908]).

Thompson, J.A., *Deuteronomy* (TC; Leicester: InterVarsity Press, 1974).

—*1 Chronicles* (NAC; Nashville: Broadman and Holman, 1994).

Tov, E., *Textual Criticism of the Hebrew Bible* (Minneapolis: Fortress Press, 1992).

Tsumura, D., *The Earth and the Waters in Genesis 1 and 2: A Linguistic Investigation* (JSOTSup, 83; Sheffield: Sheffield Academic Press, 1989).

Turner, L.A., *Announcements of Plot in Genesis* (JSOTSup, 96; Sheffield: JSOT Press, 1990).

—*Genesis* (Readings: A New Biblical Commentary; Sheffield: Sheffield Academic Press, 2000).

Vawter, B., *On Genesis: A New Reading* (Garden City, NY: Doubleday, 1977).

Vriezen, Th.C., 'Exodusstudien Exodus I', *VT* 17 (1967), pp. 334–53.

Waltke, B.K., *Genesis: A Commentary* (Grand Rapids: Zondervan, 2001).

Waltke, B.K. and M. O'Connor, *An Introduction to Biblical Hebrew Syntax* (Winona Lake: Eisenbrauns, 1990).

Wegner, P.D., *The Journey from Texts to Translations: The Origin and Development of the Bible* (Michigan: Baker Books, 1999).

Weigle, L.A. (ed.), *The Genesis Octapla* (New York: Thomas Nelson & Sons, 1965).

Weimar, P., *Untersuchungen zur priesterschriftlichen Exodusgeschichte* (Würzburg: Echter Verlag, 1973).

—'Aufbau und Struktur der priesterschriftlichen Jakobsgeschichte', *ZAW* 86 (1974), pp. 174–203.

—'Die Toledot-Formel in der priesterschriftlichen Geschichtsdarstellung', *BZ* 18 (1974), pp. 65–93.

Wenham, G.J., *Genesis 1–15* (WBC; Waco: Word Books, 1987).

—*Genesis 16–50* (WBC; Dallas: Word Books, 1994).

—'The Priority of P', *VT* 49 (1999), pp. 240–58.

—*Story as Torah: Reading the Old Testament Ethically* (Grand Rapids: Baker Academic, 2004).

Westermann, C., *Genesis 1–11: A Continental Commentary* (trans. J.J. Scullion; Minneapolis: Fortress Press, 1994) = *Genesis*, Bd. I (BKAT; Neukirchen–Vluyn: Neukirchener Verlag, 1974).

—*The Promises to the Fathers: Studies on the Patriarchal Narratives* (trans. D.E. Green; Philadelphia: Fortress Press, 1980) = *Die Verheißungen an die Väter: Studien zur Vätergeschichte* (Göttingen: Vandenhoeck & Ruprecht, 1976).

—*Genesis 12–36: A Continental Commentary* (trans. J.J. Scullion; Minneapolis: Augsburg Publ. House, 1985) = *Genesis*, Bd. II–III (BKAT; Neukirchen–Vluyn: Neukirchener Verlag, 1977–82).

—*Genesis 37–50: A Continental Commentary* (trans. J.J. Scullion; Minneapolis: Augsburg Publ. House, 1986) = *Genesis*, Bd. III (BKAT; Neukirchen–Vluyn: Neukirchener Verlag, 1980–82).

Williamson, H.G.M., *Israel in the Books of Chronicles* (Cambridge, England: Cambridge University Press, 1977).

—*1 and 2 Chronicles* (NCBC; London: Marshall Morgan & Scott, 1982).

Wilson, R.R., 'The Old Testament Genealogies in Recent Research', *JBL* 94 (1975), pp. 169–89.

—*Genealogy and History in the Biblical World* (YNER, 7; New Haven: Yale University Press: 1977).

Wolde, E. van, *Words Become Worlds: Semantic Studies of Genesis 1–11* (Biblical Interpretation Series, 6; Leiden: E.J. Brill, 1994).

—*Stories of the Beginning. Genesis 1–11 and Other Creation Stories* (trans. J. Bowden; London: SCM Press, 1996).

—'Facing the Earth: Primaeval History in a New Perspective', in P.R. Davies and D.J.A. Clines (eds.), *The World of Genesis: Persons, Places, Perspectives* (JSOTSup, 257; Sheffield: Sheffield Academic Press, 1998), pp. 22–47.

Wolf, H.M., 'The Transcendent Nature of Covenant Reversals', in A. Gileadi (ed.), *Israel's Apostasy and Restoration: Essays in Honor of Roland K. Harrison* (Michigan: Baker Book House, 1988), pp. 319–25.

Wolff, H.W., 'The Kerygma of the Yahwist', *Int* 20 (1966), pp. 131–58 (= 'Das Kerygma des Jahwisten', *Evangelische Theologie* 24 [1964], pp. 73–98).

Yarchin, W., 'Imperative and Promise in Genesis 12.1–3', *Studia Biblica et Theologica* 10 (1980), pp. 164–78.

INDEXES

INDEX OF REFERENCES

BIBLE

INDEX OF AUTHORS